GWYNEDD - MERCY COLLEGE
GWYNEDD VALLEY, PA.
Library

D1413654

Kenneth Macgowan's experience in the theater has been as extensive as it has been varied.

As director of the Provincetown Playhouse, he was associated with Eugene O'Neill and Robert Edmond Jones. He also directed the Greenwich Village Theater and the Actors Theater in New York, and for several years he was an independent producer on Broadway.

Mr. Macgowan began his work as a critic of the theater while still an undergraduate at Harvard. He was assistant dramatic editor for the *Boston Transcript*. In later years he wrote theater criticism for such publications as the *Philadelphia Evening Ledger*, the *New York Globe*, and *Vogue* magazine. He was also an editor of *Theater Arts* for six years.

The impressive list of books he has written includes *The Theater of Tomorrow*, *Continental Stagecraft* (with Robert Edmond Jones), *Masks and Demons* (with Herman Rosse), *Footlights Across America*, and *A Primer of Playwriting*.

2524

William Melnitz studied the theater arts at the Universities of Cologne and Berlin under two of the greatest authorities in the field, Professors Max Herrmann and Carl Niessen. He worked as a stage director and producer in Frankfurt, Bremen, Vienna, and Switzerland. There he was in close contact with the prominent authors, actors, designers, and directors of that period—one of the most active periods in European theater and the most influential in the development of stagecraft in the entire history of the theater.

Articles by Dr. Melnitz that deal with various aspects of theater history have appeared in all of the pertinent journals—*Educational Theater Journal*, *Western Speech*, *Modern Language Forum*, and *Theater Annual*, to name a few.

In collaboration with Kenneth Macgowan he wrote *The Living Stage*. He has also written *A Five Year Bibliography of Theater Materials*, *Theater of the Weimar Republic*, and *Theater Pictorial*.

Dr. Melnitz is now Professor of Theater Arts at the University of California at Los Angeles.

A SPECTRUM BOOK

PRENTICE-HALL, INC.

792.01
Macgowan

Golden Ages
Of The Theater

GWYNEDD - MERCY COLLEGE
GWYNEDD VALLEY, PA.
Library

KENNETH MACGOWAN

PROFESSOR EMERITUS
UNIVERSITY OF CALIFORNIA,
  LOS ANGELES

1997

WILLIAM MELNITZ

PROFESSOR OF THEATER ARTS
UNIVERSITY OF CALIFORNIA,
  LOS ANGELES

GWYNEDD - MERCY COLLEGE
GWYNEDD VALLEY, PA.
Library

Title-page illustration:
PIERROT. The Italian character of
Pedrolino developed in France into the
familiar Pierrot. Maurice Sand, the son
of George Sand the novelist, identified
him as Pagliacco of the early seventeenth century. (*From Sand,* Masques
et bouffons.)

Third printing .... February, 1962

GOLDEN AGES OF THE THEATER

1997 *2*

© 1959, by PRENTICE-HALL, Inc.
Englewood Cliffs, New Jersey

ALL RIGHTS RESERVED. NO PART OF THIS BOOK MAY BE
REPRODUCED IN ANY FORM, BY MIMEOGRAPH OR ANY OTHER MEANS,
WITHOUT PERMISSION IN WRITING FROM THE PUBLISHERS.

Library of Congress Catalog Card Number: 59-15685

PRINTED IN THE UNITED STATES OF AMERICA
35783-C

preface

THE THEATER AND ITS PLAYS ARE ALWAYS THE REFLECTION OF A CULTURE. This greatest of the popular arts is a synthesis that brings together expressions of other arts—painting, sculpture, and architecture, music, dance, and song. Since some or all of these are united in the service of the word—which is dramatic literature—the theater can be an ideal point of departure for an excursion into the culture of a period.

The age of Pericles in ancient Greece, the centuries of the Renaissance in Italy, Spain, and Elizabethan England, of the Baroque in France, and of the great industrial revolution in all of Europe have also been the periods of truly great theater. In any time-span, both playhouse and play are products of the social conditions and the aesthetic aspects of their age.

In this volume, based on our more comprehensive history of the world theater, *The Living Stage* (fifth printing 1959), we deal only with the main currents of 2,500 years of playgoing, play acting, and play reading. Naturally, so brief an outline cannot cover every topic to the satisfaction of even a single reader. We have therefore included a selective bibliography; it lists the titles of other "paperbacks" that are more specialized but as easily accessible. These books will serve the reader who discovers a particular interest in such topics as the Globe playhouse, the Renaissance stage and its machinery, the ideas of Adolphe Appia, or the theater in the round.

There are a score of "time charts" that visualize the life-span of the chief playwrights. By this means we have been able to cut down greatly the number of dates—hard to remember and confusing to follow—that usually fill any history book. We believe with Goethe that "A teacher who can arouse a feeling for one worthy deed, for a single good poem, accomplishes more

v

than a teacher who fills our memory with rows on rows of natural things classified by name and form."

We have also presented a number of illustrations which will be of interest to the reader, dealing with each of the major types of theater described in this book. Some of these illustrations—the interior of the Hotel de Bourgogne as that theater appeared in 1645 and the maps showing the location of almost two hundred Hellenistic and Roman theaters—have not appeared before in general histories of the theater except in our own THE LIVING STAGE.

The theater in every period has worked within certain conventions, and its audience has readily accepted all of them. We feel that the theater—in both its imaginative and its realistic phases—should not be taken out of its historical setting, but rather that the meaning of the specific form of theater to the audience of its time should be stressed. There is still truth in Hamlet's assertion that players "are the abstract and brief chronicles of the time."

KENNETH MACGOWAN

WILLIAM MELNITZ

contents

Golden Ages
Of
The Theater

The GREAT GREEKS
And The MUCH LESSER LATINS

WHEN WE WATCH THE DANCES OF PRIMITIVE MAN IN A MOTION PICTURE AND study myths and rituals, we see theater come to life. But we don't see *the* theater. We don't see a functioning playhouse and all it has come to mean in terms of plays as well as players.

When we do find the theater, when at last we discover a complete organism, we run up against a very curious and baffling fact. Though this theater is made by civilized men—*highly* civilized men—though it exists in a time when writing has become an art, this theater has practically no history. Except for what we know of rituals and myths, which we have discussed in *The Living Stage*, the first true theater has no really definite past and, except for the extant plays, hardly any present. Unless time has destroyed some pertinent Greek manuscript, no writer of the fifth century B.C., which was the great period of Athens, seems to have taken the trouble to tell us exactly how its theater looked and how it evolved, or to describe its earlier plays.

THE MYSTERY OF THE CLASSIC THEATER

The Greek drama springs at us full-armed like Athene from the head of Zeus. Suddenly it exists—glorious and complete—in the great tragedies of Aeschylus, Sophocles, and Euripides, which were produced, appropriately enough, in the city over which Pallas Athene watched. Yet we have no record

—written or archaeological—of just what the playhouse of the great and classic fifth century looked like. We know that its plays were given in the open air. We know there was a chorus that chanted and danced about an altar. We know that there were only three speaking actors and that they wore masks and "doubled" their roles as required. We know the kind of clothes and shoes they wore. But except for this we have almost no concrete knowledge about the classic Greek theater and how it functioned. There are literally no ruins of fifth-century theaters.

Nevertheless, we have taken it for granted that the chief playing space was circular and that the audience sat in rising rows that curved a little more than half around it. This concept has been based upon the oldest existing play-house, but this structure at Epidarus dates from about 365 B.C., a hundred years after the plays of Aeschylus were acted in Athens. Now, however, come hints of a differently shaped theater in archaic Greece and perhaps in Athens. At Knossos and Phaetos on the island of Crete, we can see what archaeologists call "theatral areas," dating from 2,000 to 1,600 B.C. In each a long straight row of steps join a shorter one at right angles; these faced a paved area used, perhaps, for ritual dances and ceremonies. An Italian archaeologist has found evidence in a few Greek theaters that leads him to believe they were quadrangular instead of semicircular at an early period.

The only important documents we have today are play manuscripts—and only forty-four out of how many lost hundreds? But, of course, if we had to choose between knowing all about the theater of Aeschylus, and having the seven manuscripts we now possess out of his ninety plays, we would decide that we are better off as we stand today.

Except for the few manuscripts of plays, what we know about the Greek theater in its great days comes from scenes painted on vases, a few thousand words of literary criticism written by Aristotle more than a hundred years later, and some astute guesses made by modern archaeologists who have dug up and worked over and reconstructed the Hellenistic theaters built one to three centuries after the death of Euripides. Perhaps we ought to add to this list the writings of Vitruvius, a Roman architect in Caesar's times, and of Pollux, a Greek dictionary-maker about two centuries later. But the two books in which they comment all-too-briefly on stages, scenery, and machines leave us wondering how much of what they describe is classic Greek, how much is imperial Roman, and how much belongs to the Hellenistic period that lay between. Writing within seventy-five years of the death of the last great dramatist, Euripides, Aristotle was so absorbed in the aesthetics of the trage-dies that he tells us almost nothing of the theater that gave them birth.

THE CONTRIBUTION OF ATHENS

The Greece that knew neither Alexander the Great nor the Roman con-querors was a curious civilization. Athens invented the word democracy but did not live completely by it. The slaves and the peasantry, commerce and gold mines, enabled the free Athenians to live in the mind and the arts. Its philosophers were original and apperceptive, its sculptors and architects superb. To science the Greeks contributed inductive reasoning and the basic concept of Copernicus. Yet they did not apply to useful ends the steam engine that they invented, Anaxagoras thought the sun about as large as the Peloponnesus, and Aristotle believed that bees carried stones as ballast in a high wind. Athens and much of Greece was a community that loved talk and thought and writing, as well as art and athletics, and reached at one bound the first pinnacle of dramatic expression. Yet from Plato and Herodotus to Plutarch, no Greek aesthetician or historian except Aristotle bothered to write fully about the supreme accomplishment of their drama—let alone the physical theater—unless, of course, some manuscript has gone the way of lost plays and the missing passages of Plato and Aristotle.

Structurally the Western playhouse has altered greatly since the days of Aeschylus. Acting is vastly different. The stage has changed beyond recognition. Our plays are not the stories of mythical heroes told in verse and accompanied by a chanting and dancing chorus. Yet we can trace a clear path of evolution from the Greek theater to the theater of today. Even in the technique of playwriting we can often see a kinship. Plotwise, the structure of Sophocles' *Oedipus Rex* is the structure of Ibsen's *A Doll's House;* each play starts just before its great crisis and unfolds, in exposition, the past that conditions and dominates its dramatic development.

THREE KINDS OF PLAY FOR ONE GOD

The Greek theater presented three kinds of plays: tragedies, which dealt with heroic legends and often used gods for convenient endings; satyr plays, which burlesqued such legends and indulged in bawdy mimicry set off by a chorus of satyrs; and comedies, which dealt in a broadly farcical way with current life. All three were performed at fixed ceremonies of a religious and civic nature. All three employed a chorus in interludes between scenes of action and often within those scenes. All three were written in verse. All three used masks. And all three seem related in one way or another to what might be called fertility-ideas.

It is quite as easy to believe that the three forms had a common basis as to believe in any of the separate origins that some authorities have proposed. There are those who claim that tragedy grew out of the celebration and worship of Dionysus, who was a nature-god of fertility quite as much as the god of wine. There are those who say that Greek tragedy was rooted in ceremonial rites at the graves of culture-heroes and demigods. But the fact remains that tragedies, satyr plays, and comedies were produced as part of the regular annual ceremonies in honor of Dionysus, his figure was carried in the preliminary procession, and his altar stood in the center of the playing floor. Furthermore, the story of Dionysus was the story of fertile nature dying each year and being reborn, the story of eternal fecundity, and fecundity was reflected in the phallic symbols worn by the actors in early comedy. Aristotle says that comedy grew out of phallic songs, which were ribald hymns in honor of Phales, a god of fertility and a companion of Dionysus. Bacchus—another name for Dionysus among both the late Greeks and the Romans—had as his companions a troupe of satyrs, half-men, half-animals, with the horns, the tail, and the hoofs of goats. And in the satyr plays, these woodland creatures wore the phallus. In the worship of Dionysus, satyrs put on the skins of goats that had been sacrificed to the god. All this emphasis on capricorn as a Dionysiac accessory should prepare you for the discovery that the word "tragedy" comes from the Greek words *tragos*, or goat, and *ode*, or song. At any rate, Greek tragedy, the satyr play, and comedy seem so involved with the attributes of the god of wine and fertility that some see their common origin in the worship of Dionysus.

DRAMATIC ORIGINS

Certain authorities are in refreshing agreement among themselves and with Aristotle on the theory that tragedy grew out of the dithyramb, or choral hymn, sung to Dionysus. They presume that, originally, the dithyramb told the story of this deity who began as the child of Zeus and a mortal, who taught man to grow the grape and other fruits and foodstuffs, and who was destroyed and reborn into godhead. But by the time tragedy was ready to appear, the legends of Dionysus had been supplanted in the dithyrambs by the adventures of culture-heroes. From then on, though Greek tragedy ignored almost completely the personal exploits of its favorite god, yet plays became the most important and spectacular feature of his worship.

The question of just where and just when someone made over the dithyramb or mimetic hero-ritual into the beginnings of a drama is rather uncertain. About 600 B.C. a poet and musician, Arion, from the island of Lesbos, is reputed to have written the first formal lyrics that replaced the improvised words of the dithyramb, but he did this over in the Pelponnesian peninsula at the city of Corinth. Most authorities think that Thespis, who lived in Attica, took the next step by introducing an actor to talk to the chorus, provide narration, and even act out dramatic episodes. One ancient authority puts him second to someone named Epigenes, who lived near Corinth; another makes Thespis sixteenth on the list of originators. Aristotle says that the Dorians of the Peloponnesus claimed the discovery of both comedy and tragedy.

It seems fairly certain, however, that the change from dithyramb to drama came in the middle of the sixth century, and, if the innovator was not Thespis, he did pretty much what Thespis is supposed to have done. Certainly the man who stepped out of the chorus became at that moment the first dramatist as well as the first actor. Tradition says that Thespis also became the first "trouper" when he put his company on a cart and gave per-

GREAT GREEKS—LESSER LATINS 5

formances in other cities. Since he won, in 534 B.C., the first Athenian prize
for tragedy, we may take it that he drove his cart to that ever-receptive city,
and made it his permanent headquarters. Perhaps his wagon had the form of
the ship in which Dionysus was supposed to have first visited Attica, and perhaps it became the boat-on-wheels—recorded on vase paintings—in which the
priest of Dionysus, with his flute-playing satyrs, was driven into the theater
at the beginning of the Dionysiac festivals.

For three centuries after the time of Thespis, Athens was the theatrical
capital of the Grecian world. For the playwright there was only one theater.
It was the theater of Dionysus at the foot of the Acropolis. The three great
writers of tragedy, Aeschylus, Sophocles, and Euripides, and their peer in
comedy, Aristophanes, were Athenian citizens. So was the lesser man, Menander, who wrote domestic farce and lived almost a hundred years after Aristophanes and two hundred after Thespis. If other playwrights of this era
were not born in the shadow of the Parthenon, they came to Athens from the
cities and the islands and the colonies that spread Grecian culture from Sicily
and Italy to Asia Minor, and they competed for the honor of seeing their
plays acted in the city that Milton called "the eye of Greece, the mother of
arts and eloquence." The more important plays were first produced there,
then repeated in the provinces, and, even after centuries, revived in distant
lands. When Rome, triumphant over Carthage, turned to the making of
plays as well as empire, her dramatists did hardly more than translate or
adapt the works of Greece.

THE DIONYSIAC FESTIVALS OF ATHENS

The theater was of vital importance to the Athenian because it was the
climax of a religious and civic ritual. Playgoing was not an everyday habit;
it was confined to certain fixed days out of every year. The festivals dedicated
to Dionysus occurred in late January and early February, and in late March
through the beginning of April. The first of these, which was called the
Lenaea, was the older, and, as time went on, it was mainly reserved for
comedies. The second and the far more important festival was the Great, or
City, Dionysia. Then it was that tragedy dominated, and Aeschylus and his
successors competed for prizes. The splendor and pre-eminence of the City
Dionysia attracted visitors from all over the Grecian world. It was a week
of holiday; all trade was suspended, and government offices—even the courts
of law—were closed. At first, admission to the theater was free; later, when
there was a small charge, tickets were given to those who could not afford to
buy them. The state paid the actors, but the cost of the physical production
of each play was met by a rich citizen, whom we would now call an "angel,"
but who was then honored with the title of *choregus*.

The festivities of the City Dionysia lasted five or six days. The first day
was given up to a great procession led by the priest of Dionysus on his ship-

like float, and to sports, games, and general merrymaking. On the second and sometimes the third day came dithyrambic contests. The last three days were devoted to the plays that competed for the annual prizes.

On each of these three days during the fifth century a different playwright presented three tragedies and a satyr play. When these plays all dealt with a single myth or a single group of related characters, they were called a tetralogy. A good example of the tetralogy is *Oresteia* of Aeschylus, produced in 458 B.C., which included *Agamemnon, The Libation Pourers, The Eumenides,* all three still in existence, and the lost *Proteus,* a satyr play; all dealt with the tragedy of the House of Atreus. When the satyr play was sometimes dropped, the related plays were called a trilogy. Each year Aeschylus generally confined his competing tragedies to a single subject, but Sophocles did this seldom, if ever, and Euripides apparently never.

Greek playwrights were enormously prolific. Aeschylus is said to have written ninety plays, and to have won thirteen first prizes. Sophocles wrote over a hundred, winning eighteen contests. Euripides is supposed to have written ninety-two, but, perhaps because of his unconventional attitude toward the gods and toward the almost sacred characters that he dealt with, he won only five victories. Of the nearly three hundred plays written by the three dramatists, the manuscripts of all but thirty-three have been lost; we have seven from Aeschylus, eight from Sophocles, and, interestingly enough, eighteen from Euripides.

The competing playwrights were selected by an official called an *archon.* After the three days of competition there was a time for severe criticism and the awarding of the annual prize by a small jury drawn by lot.

Half a century after Athens instituted the first contests in tragedy, the city added a competition for comedies. At first a single day was given up to five comic plays by different playwrights. Later there was a comedy each afternoon, following the day's tragedies.

Besides the two dramatic festivals in Athens there was a third type, the Rural Dionysia, which was held in the provincial towns of Attica in December. Here the prize-winning plays from Athens were presented, and new and untried playwrights had a chance at what we would call a "try-out."

ROME'S DEBASED DRAMA

Rome, too, had its dramatic festivals. They were called *ludi,* or games, because they were devoted at first entirely to sports and amusements, such as boxing and rope dancing. Farcical performances from the provinces crept in, and in 240 B.C. a Latin writer introduced a Greek tragedy in translation. At first the *ludi* were given in April, July, September, and November, but later upon any convenient occasion—a military triumph or the funeral of an important citizen. In the year before the death of Sulla in 78 B.C., *ludi* were given on forty-eight days; Roscius, a very popular actor of that day, is said to have played one hundred and twenty-eight times in twelve months. The fondness of the Romans for the combination of plays, games, and violent spectacle was so great that at times performances were staged at night with the aid of torches. The motive behind the *ludi*—which were always free— was akin to that of the "bread and circuses" with which the ruling class diverted and placated the proletariat.

If the Roman theater ever had the religious and civic significance of the Greek, it rapidly lost this and became merely "show business." The commercial manager appeared. The magistrates whose duty it was to supply games for the multitude turned to professionals for both plays and performances. The actor-manager had his troupe of slaves, freedmen, and foreigners. He bought a play outright from its author or adapter, paid for costumes and properties, and assumed all the risks of production and presentation. If the play proved popular, he was given money in proportion to its success, and sometimes a prize of palm leaves or a crown of silver or gold. An inevitable result was the organization of claques to applaud certain actors and shout down others. The games and spectacles that were given in the same theaters as the plays—and often at the same performances—grew bloodier and more violent. The plays themselves became more licentious or were replaced by pantomimes, tableaux, and lewd dances.

PANTOMIMES INSTEAD OF PLAYS

Under the Empire, the most popular dramatic entertainments were pantomimes that used music and dance, costumes and settings to retell Greek myths. In *The Golden Ass,* written about 150 A.D., Apuleius describes one of these shows, which presented the judgment of Paris. In front of the curtain, "by way of prelude a number of beautiful boys and girls were moving with dignity through the graceful mazes of the Greek Pyrrhic dance. . . . Presently the trumpet blew the Retreat . . . and the backdrops were removed [the curtain fell into a slot in the floor] to disclose a far more elaborate performance."

The scene was an artificial wooden mountain, supposed to represent Homer's famous Mount Ida, an imposing piece of stage-architecture, quite high, turfed all over and planted with scores of trees. The designer had contrived that a stream should break out at the top of the mountain and tumble down the side. A herd of she-goats were cropping the grass, and a young man strolled about, supposedly in charge of them, dressed in flowing Asiatic robes with a gold tiara on his head. He represented Paris the Phrygian shepherd. Then a handsome boy came forward . . . the God Mercury.

He came dancing towards Paris and after presenting him with a golden apple explained Jupiter's orders in sign language. . . . The next character to appear was Juno, played by a girl with very fine features. . . . Then Minerva came running in. . . . She was followed by another girl of extraordinary beauty . . . Venus— Venus before marriage. To show her perfect figure to fullest advantage she wore nothing at all except a thin gauze apron.

Juno was accompanied by Castor and Pollux, Minerva by two young men representing Terror and Fear, and Venus by "a whole school of happy little boys crowding around her, so chubby and white-skinned that you might have taken them to be real cupids flown down from heaven. . . . Juno advanced calmly," and Minerva with "quick, excited writhings." To sentimental Lydian airs, "Venus began dancing to the music with slow, lingering steps and gentle swaying of her hips and head. . . . Her eyelids fluttered luxuriously or opened wide to let fly passionate glances, so that at times she seemed dancing with her eyes alone." She promised "with tense gestures . . . that she would marry him [Paris] to the most beautiful woman in the world, her own human counterpart. Young Paris gladly handed her the golden apple in token of her victory. . . ."

Then a fountain of wine, mixed with saffron, broke out from a concealed pipe at the mountain top and its many jets sprinkled the pasturing goats with a scented shower, so that their white hair was stained the rich yellow traditionally associated with the flocks that feed on Mount Ida. The scent filled the whole amphitheatre; and then the stage machinery was set in motion, the earth seemed to gape and the mountain disappeared from view.

THE GREEK CHORUS AND ACTORS

A unique and curious feature of the Greek theater was the chorus that held over from the days of the ancient dithyramb. Thespis is supposed to have had a chorus of fifty. After Aeschylus produced *The Suppliants,* he reduced the chorus to twelve, while Sophocles increased it to fifteen. These men—who often appeared in women's costumes—chanted and moved in rhythmic patterns. They sometimes spoke through their leader or lamented and argued with one another.

When Aeschylus added another actor to the one that Thespis had introduced, and thus made dialog possible, the role of the chorus shrank in importance. In Sophocles' plays the chorus still played a part in the plot, but a smaller part, and the choral ode became almost a lyric interlude between dramatic scenes. Euripides reduced still further the significance of the chorus. The comedy of Aristophanes, which was far stricter and more complicated in form, employed a chorus of twenty-four, but split it in two for scenes of disputation.

There is a rather dubious theory that Sophocles introduced a fourth actor in *Oedipus at Colonus,* a play that he wrote when he was about ninety years old. This seems hardly plausible, because a fourth actor was unnecessary. Through the use of masks and by doubling roles (which was the common practice) Aeschylus could have six characters in *Agamemnon,* and Euripides could have eleven in *The Phoenician Women.*

The Greek actor had to be a highly skilled and very versatile artist. (Imagine the difficulty of playing women like Electra!) While most of his speeches were solemnly declaimed, there was often a great deal of violent action and emotional expression, and certain lyrical passages had to be sung to the accompaniment of a flute player. Greek audiences were highly critical as to the enunciation of the actors and the treatment of the text. When, in the fourth century, actors began to take certain liberties with their lines in a theater where a prompter could not be concealed, Lycurgus prepared authentic texts, and saw that the actors followed them religiously. Taking the opposite attitude from the Romans, who looked down upon actors as little better than the "vagabonds and knaves" of Elizabethan times, the Greeks venerated them as servants of Dionysus, exempted them from military duty, and sometimes entrusted them with diplomatic and political missions.

Though the Romans followed the Greek fashion of not permitting actresses in tragedies or classic comedies, they used as many as six actors in one production. In farces and especially in the pantomimes and tableaux that became more and more popular as the Roman stage decayed, women often took leading roles.

MASKS AND COSTUMES

Like the chorus, the mask is another feature of Greek drama that is alien to our ideas of dramatic production and, like the chorus, it was rooted in religious ritual. The mask was used all over the world long before Thespis smeared his face with purslane or white lead and red cinnabar, or wore a false face of linen, and the mask continued to be worn in the New Comedy of the Greek Menander and in the Roman plays of Plautus and Terence after the chorus had disappeared. Sophocles improved on the linen masks of Thespis by making false faces of carved and painted wood. Cork was also used, and in Rome, terra cotta, or baked clay. Masks were worn by the chorus as well as the actors.

Though the origin of the mask was religious, its use served some very practical purposes. Without differently designed masks it would have been difficult for one actor to play two roles. Further, since the mask fitted over the actor's head like a helmet, it was larger than his natural face, and its features, which were exaggerated and emphasized in shape and color, could be seen more plainly across the vast distances of theaters seating very often as many as 15,000 spectators. The wide-open mouth may have served as a sort of megaphone.

A disadvantage of the mask was, of course, the immobility of its expression. The audience had to use its imagination as lines of dialog indicated a change of mood in a character; yet it was possible for the actor who left the stage wearing a happy visage to return with a sorrowful countenance fitted to the calamity that had happened off stage. A Roman writer of the first Christian century describes a mask, one side of which had a cheerful aspect and the other a serious one, enabling the actor to vary the expression of his face by showing one side or the other to the audience.

The mask indicated the age, sex, mood, and even the station of a charac-

ter. Tragic masks were usually rather serene and beautiful, but the terrifying features of the Furies in *The Eumenides* are said to have created a
panic at the premier of Aeschylus' tragedy. In some of Aristophanes' comedies the chorus wore the masks of birds, bees, or frogs. The realism of the
masks of contemporary persons must have been most faithful, for at the
performance of *The Clouds,* when a character representing Socrates made his
entrance, the philosopher arose from his seat so that the audience might see
the resemblance.

Though the tragedies dealt mainly with people out of Homeric times,
the costumes worn by actors and chorus were a happy compromise between
historical accuracy—which was impossible to them—and the clothes of the
day. The *chiton,* or long garment reaching from neck to ankles, had a grave
aspect that must have helped the actor to feel and convey the solemn mood
of the heroic characters. Yet the *chiton* and the shorter mantle that might be
worn over it were vivid in color—a reminder to us that the statues of
Phidias and other Greek sculptors were not the cold, white marble that we
now associate with classic art, but were gaily painted in realistic colors. Costumes for comedy were in the current style except when gods or mythological
figures appeared.

To set the principals off from the chorus, and to comport with the over-
size masks, the tragic actor wore an exaggerated headdress, the *onkos,* and
perhaps a thick-soled shoe, the *cothurnus,* while the chorus wore low shoes.
In comedies the contemporary characters had only the usual common foot-
gear. Here we have the origin of the distinction between "sock and buskin"
—the ordinary shoe or slipper of comedy and the high-soled boot of tragedy.
Nobody knows at just what period these aids to impressive height first appeared. Padding prevented the actors from seeming thin as well as tall.

SCANT INFORMATION FROM VITRUVIUS

Almost all that we have written should have been liberally larded with
"supposedly," "it is said," and "probably." When we come to describing the
physical theater in which Greek plays were produced, we are on even
shakier ground. Only two ancient writers—Vitruvius and Pollux—have tried
to describe it in any detail, and Vitruvius wrote his *De Architectura* shortly
before the birth of Christ, while Pollux wrote his *Onomastikon,* a kind of
encyclopedia, in the second century of our own era. They often failed to
indicate clearly whether the theater they wrote about was Roman, Hellenistic,
or truly Classic. They were laboring under the gravest disadvantages in trying to study things long dead and gone. There was no printing press to
stimulate the writing of descriptive and technical books, or to preserve
diaries. Many old manuscripts have been lost, and some that Vitruvius
refers to as providing certain facts are among these.

In *De Architectura,* Vitruvius has a great deal to say about constructing
temples and baths and country houses, about water supply and clocks and

sun dials, about "stucco on damp places" and catapults and even astronomy. But, so far as theaters are concerned, most of what he writes deals with acoustics—"how to make the voices from the stage rise more clearly and sweetly to the spectators' ears." He gives as much space to "colonnades and passages behind the scenes" as he does to the proportions of the orchestras, to the seating arrangements, and to the height of the stages in Roman and Hellenistic theaters. He devotes only about sixty words to a scene-changing device of revolving prisms that still puzzles us. Since he calls such machines by the Greek name *periaktoi*, we may suppose that they came down from Attic beginnings. He is hardly more voluble—using some eighty words, all told—about what seemed of vast importance to the theater-folk of fifteenth-century Italy: the three types of scenery used in his own day for the forms of drama established by the Greeks—tragedy, comedy, and the satyr play. Vitruvius' only direct comment on the classic Athenian theater suggests that a man "who was in control of the stage" for a play by Aeschylus painted scenery in perspective. He writes, with some asperity, about a small contemporary theater in Asia Minor—which some think was not a theater at all but merely an assembly place—whose scenic background, painted in false perspective, was a jumble of mismated architectural forms. Pollux, writing in the days of the Roman Empire, merely lists some of the paraphernalia of the stage, including trapdoors, cranes, cycloramas, and lighting devices.

Aside from the obscurities of Vitruvius and Pollux, we have little other evidence except architectural ruins. We can see Roman auditoriums and pretty good indications of Roman stage walls in theaters from Asia Minor to France and Spain, and the ashes of Vesuvius have preserved, in Pompeii, paintings of Roman stages—and even of actors appearing on them. But the relics and records of Greek and Hellenistic theaters are not nearly so ample. The Hellenistic is, in fact, rather scanty, and the classic Greek almost non-existent.

THE SHAPE OF THE THEATER

We have reason to believe that in the days long before Thespis the dithyrambic chorus chanted and danced in the midst of townspeople and peasantry. We know that when the first Theater of Dionysus was created in Athens, the chorus appeared on a flat, circular area seventy-eight feet across; this *orchestra*—"dancing place"—has been found by archaeologists. But the first stone theater on this site, with a sixty-four-foot *orchestra*, was built more than a hundred years later, when the stage had become Hellenistic in form. The present structure dates from the time of Nero.

As to the auditorium, the place where the audience sat, we know nothing about it in the fifth century. We presume that some time before Thespis, it was found convenient to lay out the *orchestra* ring where two hills met and made a natural hollow, partly surrounded by sloping ground. The "theater in the round" was becoming less circular. We do not know when the Greeks began to dig into a hillside to make the auditorium, which seems to have surrounded two-thirds of the *orchestra* in the fifth century. (A hollow is called a *koilon* in Greek and a *cavea* in Latin. The latter became the Roman word for auditorium, while the Greeks dropped *koilon* in favor of *theatron*, or theater, derived from the Greek word meaning "to see.") At first, it is presumed, the spectators stood or sat on the hillside; next they enjoyed wooden benches. At Syracuse in Sicily, seats were carved out of the natural rock as early as the fourth century. When Lycurgus rebuilt the Theater of Dionysus about 333 B.C., he installed stone seats, a fashion that spread rapidly throughout the Hellenistic world. There are remains of glorious auditoriums from that later period—the beautiful, rock-hewn one at Syracuse, the well-preserved ruins at Epidaurus in Greece, and two in Asia Minor, the high sweep of seats looking out and down over a wide valley at Pergamum, and the chaste and almost miniature structure at Priene.

It is only the *orchestra* and the auditorium of the later Greek theater that seem at all definite and clear. Once we try to learn about the stage—even the Hellenistic stage—we are deep in probabilities and suppositions. As a matter of fact, it is dangerous to believe that any one form or any pattern of developing forms could have existed. The theaters we are concerned with —both Greek and Roman—were built over a period of 500 years. They were built in scores of cities and in many countries and under widely differing political and racial and cultural conditions. Diversity of structure, so far as the stage goes, was inevitable. So let's not look for something we can't find: one type of Classic theater, one Hellenistic type neatly developed from it, and a pure Roman variety. In addition, some authorities like to recognize a mixed type that they call Graeco-Roman, from the interaction of Hellenistic and Roman.

THE SKENE, OR STAGE BACKGROUND

In the course of time, Western Europe took *theatron*, the word that the Greeks used for the hillside hollow full of seats, turned it into the word "theater" and made it include the whole playhouse. We have done the same kind of trick with another Greek word, *skene*. What we call a scene in a play or a scene on the stage, or even painted scenery, comes from the word for a wooden hut or tent, *skene*. At Athens in 465 B.C., a *skene* was put up at the edge of the *orchestra* opposite the middle of the rows of seats. The common theory is that this was done to provide a dressing room for the actors and the chorus, and it was certainly a very handy place for a quick change of mask and costume when an actor was playing two or three parts. At any rate, the *skene*, or scene building, became a regular feature of all Greek theaters down through the Hellenistic period. We know that it had short wings at each end, that the wall of the *skene* was pierced, sooner or later, with three doors, and that there were side entrances between the wings

The Greek Theater. *Above, the Hellenistic playhouse at Epidauris with passage-way (called* parados) *between stage building and audience area. Below, a map of Hellenistic theaters. The sites of these theaters—some forty in number—are known either through ruins or historical allusions. Many more undoubtedly existed.*

A map of Roman theaters. These sites stretch from the neighborhood of London to North Africa and from Lisbon to Babylon. In addition to the more than 125 theaters shown here, the Romans erected numerous amphitheaters and coliseums for athletic events and spectacles.

of the building and the auditorium. But that is all we are sure of. We have no idea as to when the *skene* turned into a two- or three-storied structure.

There is even some confusion about the word *proskenion*—which finally turned into our "proscenium." *Proskenion* meant something in front of the *skene*. Sometimes this is taken to be the wall of the *skene* itself; sometimes, the playing space—or what we would call the stage—between the *skene* and the *orchestra*. Now the roof of the *skene* was certainly used in the fifth century as a place where a god could appear to resolve the difficulties of the plot, or from which he could be lowered in a crane. Some students who have tried to reconstruct Hellenistic theaters believe that this roof was converted into a second stage by having another wall at its rear, and some have provided a third story for the gods and the machine.

Of one thing we can be sure: the height of the stage floor at various periods. The classic stage was on a level with the *orchestra* or raised by only one or two low steps. The Hellenistic was about twelve feet high and the Roman about five. The Hellenistic was shallow, the Roman deep.

THE ROMAN PLAYHOUSE

We are on fairly solid ground when we come to the Roman theater. The Hellenistic had a full circle of *orchestra* in front of the *skene*. The so-called Graeco-Roman—which spread from one shore of the Mediterranean to the other just before the birth of Christ—thrust the stage of the *skene* over the edge of the *orchestra*. The Romans boldly joined the *skene* building to the auditorium, shrank the *orchestra* to a semicircle, and with their mania for arch-construction, sometimes built the whole theater as a free-standing structure on level ground. Chorus and actors were confined to a low stage, and the diminished *orchestra* became a place where movable seats were placed for Roman "brass" and distinguished visitors. A few steps led up to the stage, which was ornamented richly with columns, panels, and cornices, and had three doors along the back and one at each side.

The Roman Republic, with a tradition of almost Spartan simplicity, looked askance at the "degeneracy" of Greek art and most things that were Greek, and therefore frowned on the theater as a sybaritic and corrupting institution. The first theater was built of wood in 179 B.C. and soon torn down. In 55 B.C., when the Republic was turning into the Empire, Pompey ventured to build a permanent theater of stone, and got away with it by placing a temple to Venus Victrix above the last row of the auditorium. Thus the tiers of seats became steps leading to the altar, and the whole thing was disguised as a temple. (We are reminded of the famous and distinguished Boston Museum of Victorian times where proper Bostonians could freely go because they paid admission to see a museum of curiosities and got the play free!) Only two other permanent theaters were opened in the city of Rome before the huge Colosseum and its bloody shows dominated Roman entertainment, but scores of Roman theaters were built from England and Spain to Asia Minor. In many, the auditorium was sheltered by awnings, and the stage had a long, narrow roof. Later, at Pompeii and perhaps elsewhere, there were small theaters completely roofed in.

Long before the days of the Roman Empire, Italy had a much simpler and more popular theater. It was a theater of comedy, and comedy of the broadest sort. Some of its roots were Greek and some native. At Syracuse shortly before the time of Aristophanes, Greeks were writing farces that had no chorus and dealt at first with mythological figures, and later with everyday episodes such as domestic intrigue and knavery of all sorts. In southern Italy both the plays and the actors of such farces were called *phlyakes*, and today on ancient vases we find scenes that show the players on crude, low, wooden platforms, provided sometimes with a short flight of steps. There is every reason to believe that such stages existed for the rustic *atellanae* farces that originated much later in the Campania south of Rome, and dealt with stock characters of the day. In Rome, where comedy seems to have been better liked than tragedy, there developed the *fabula togata*—"fable," or comedy, "in native dress." From an Italian wall-painting, we know that Egyptian dancers appeared on rough platforms while a member of the company collected coins from the spectators.

SCENERY AND MACHINES

The Greek theater of the fifth century, as well as its Hellenistic descendants, was not so austere as to foreswear spectacle and scenic device. In 458 B.C., Aeschylus' hero Agamemnon entered in a chariot. There was some kind of painted scenery, for Aristotle credits it to Sophocles, and Vitruvius to Aeschylus. In Hellenistic times, scenery may have included ornamented panels set between the columns of the *skene*, and the *periaktoi*, or revolving prisms, mentioned by Vitruvius. There is some physical evidence of both. At Priene in Asia Minor there are ridges in the stage columns against which panels, or *pinakes*, must have rested, for there are holes for pegs to keep them in place. In two or three theaters, at the sides of the *skene*, there are stones with sockets in which the center beam of a *periaktos* may have rested. On each of the three sides of these prisms indications of scenes—probably stylized—were painted. Pollux writes of a "lightning machine" that may have consisted of a *periaktos* with zigzags of white painted on black. Nobody knows when the *periaktoi* were first used, but at least two other striking bits of stage machinery were introduced in the fifth century. These were the *eccyclema* and the *mechane*. Though by traditional rule murders could only be done off-stage, the resulting carnage could be exhibited to the audience by the *eccyclema*. This was obviously a platform that moved through a doorway, but we don't know whether it revolved on an axis or rolled out on wheels like a modern stage wagon. We know, however, that *eccyclema* came from a word meaning "to wheel out," and we have a scene from Aristophanes' comedy *The Archarnians* in which Dicaeopolis knocks on Euripides' door and demands that the dramatist come out. Euripides replies: "But I'm not at leisure." Then shouts Dicaeopolis: "At least be wheeled out!" "Well," replies Euripides, "I'll have myself wheeled out." The *mechane* was some kind of device for making a god appear on an upper stage or in the air, or for lowering him to the level of the human beings below—effects that seem to be called for in two of Aeschylus' plays and in many of Euripides'. Pollux describes a crane let down from above to remove a dead body or a living character. In Aristophanes' comedy *The Clouds,* Socrates seems to be suspended in such a machine, for he says, "I tread the air and contemplate the sun."

Scenic devices increase in number as we approach the Roman theater. Pollux lists nineteen—including trap doors and cycloramas—and almost all may have been used in Hellenistic times. Vitruvius describes three types of stage settings: for tragedy, "with columns, pediments, statues, and other objects suited to kings"; for comedy, "private dwellings with balconies and views representing rows of windows"; and, for "satyric scenes," "trees, caverns, mountains, and other rustic objects." Vitruvius' three kinds of sets correspond to the three forms of plays written and produced in the fifth century, but this does not mean that he is describing anything as early as the Hellenistic theater. Roman playhouses sported a curtain that hid the scene until the play began and then sank into a trough.

GREEK THEATER VERSUS GREEK PLAYWRIGHT

The purpose of any theater—its form, its scenic devices, and its actors—is to present the plays popular in its time. The value of any theater lies in its ability to present these plays effectively. Both theater and plays interact upon one another. The theater affects the plays, and the plays—within limits —affect the theater. Let us see how the classic Greek theater influenced the playwright, and how the playwright used the peculiar conventions of that theater to achieve dramatic effectiveness.

When the *skene* was no more than a dressing room at one side, the locale of the early plays of Aeschylus was open country. When the scene building with its three doors was introduced, plays could be laid in front of a temple or a palace. Sooner or later the central door was assigned to the hero, a side one was supposed to lead to the room of a secondary character or to guest chambers, and the other was used by a minor person, or represented a ruined shrine or a prison. The side entrances between the ends of the auditorium and the *skene* led in one case to the city and in the other case to the harbor or the countryside. The playwrights—who were resourceful directors and often actors—established these conventions to help make clear the action of their plays. They called into being the *eccyclema* and the *mechane,* and probably the painted panels and the *periaktoi* to ease some of the limitations of their stage. Like Shakespeare, they had characters describe things that the audience could not see but had to imagine.

LITERARY LIMITATIONS

The writer of Greek tragedy faced other limitations besides those of the physical theater. These were what we would call literary limitations. They were conventions of dramatic form carried over from the dithyramb. The most important of these conventions and the one that is hardest for us to understand and accept is the chorus.

To an audience that is used to intimate, personal drama, the chorus may seem an absurd interruption and therefore an impossible limitation on the art of the dramatist. When Gilbert Murray—translator of both Greek plays and the Greek theatric spirit—was lecturing on Attic tragedy about 1912, he described in somewhat the following words the absurdity of the chorus from the point of view of the present-day playgoer: When the heroine is engaged in some plot, arranging to murder her husband, or taking some step for the good of the community, fifteen visitors happen in. Sometimes they have a reason for coming, sometimes they don't. If there is one old gentleman, then there will be fifteen old gentlemen. And it doesn't help matters if the fifteen visitors start to dance.

Properly understood, Murray pointed out, the chorus appears as an aid, not a hindrance, to the Greek playwright. The chorus was neither actor nor bystander. It was, rather, a kind of link with the audience, making the spectator feel a closer participation in the drama. The chorus was an instrument for the expression of complete and ultimate emotion over great or terrible deeds. It translated the feeling of the actor into a different medium. It brought to the audience emotions that the characters in a play sometimes could not completely feel, or emotions that could not be expressed in ordinary words. The chorus turned crude suffering into poetry, even into soothing mystery. The chorus could, and did, "shake lyric splendor over the whole." Greek tragedy lived on two planes, in two worlds. First, the audience was interested in the individual and his personal feelings, then in the chorus and the sublimated emotion. The body departed, but the spirit remained. That was the secret of Greek tragedy.

Though the chorus linked the audience with the drama, it also separated scene from scene. The fact that the choral passages sometimes, but not always, divided the play into five scenes of personal action led the Roman poet Horace to believe that Greek tragedy was written in five acts, and caused Renaissance critics to assert that all plays must follow this pattern.

Lest you accept the further fallacy that Greek tragedy was bound by what have been called the three unities—the unities of time, place, and action—we must point out that Aristotle found only one unity in the dramas of Aeschylus, Sophocles, and Euripides. This was the unity that all good plays observe: the unity of action. As for time and place, some Greek tragedies had more than one locale, which meant, of course, that they could not observe strict unity of time.

THE FOUR FOUNDERS OF TRAGEDY AND COMEDY

There were writers of tragedy before Aeschylus (he was born about ten years after the first playwriting contest was established in Athens in 534 B.C.) and there were certainly many after Euripides. Yet there is only a single play in existence, *Rhesus,* that is not definitely assigned to one of the three great tragic writers, and some think Euripides wrote this rather inferior script. We have no comedies of the fifth century except those of Aristophanes, and only one complete play and a few scenes from the New Comedy of Menander. Few of the Greek plays were known to the Western world until 1453, when the Turks captured Constantinople and scholars escaping to Italy brought some play scripts with them. Others were found later among manuscripts in eastern Mediterranean cities. The reason that certain plays of Aeschylus, Sophocles, Euripides, and Aristophanes and not the works of lesser playwrights were preserved to us is, presumably, because they were most often revived and the manuscripts recopied, during the later Hellenistic period.

The three great tragic writers and their plays make a clear and interesting pattern. It is a pattern that follows developments and changes in Greek culture as well as in the theater. Aeschylus, pioneering, yet most bound by theatrical tradition, depended greatly on the chorus; half of his *Agamemnon* is lyric. His themes were traditional and deeply religious. He stuck close to the old ideas of a world in which Olympian law punished crime and protected the state. His plots were simple and his effects catastrophic. The plays of Sophocles were more intricate in plot, and he was more absorbed in the interplay of characters than in divine justice, though he gave more than lip service to religious tradition. Euripides pioneered in a different way from Aeschylus. He was deeply concerned with character and what were, for his time, unconventional and even impious ideas. In many ways a thoroughly modern man, he might be called the first realist and the first feminist. He forgot the broad issues of morality and religion while he explored what we would call abnormal psychology. If he dealt at all with social ideas, he was likely to write an anti-war play like *The Trojan Women* when his own city was locked in mortal combat with Sparta. Basically, Euripides preferred to probe the inner life of the individual. He changed tragedy from a conflict between man and the divine laws into a conflict in man's own soul between his good and his evil impulses. Though he dealt with mythological characters, he presented them realistically. From at least one manuscript, *Helen,* we know that Euripides attempted, probably for the first time, a kind of play that was neither tragedy nor comedy. He won far fewer prizes than either Aeschylus or Sophocles. In a very real sense he was ahead of his time, for the plays that the Athenians of the fifth century disliked and condemned were vastly popular with their Hellenistic descendants. That is why we have more manuscripts of Euripides' plays than all those of Aeschylus' and Sophocles' put together.

OLD PLOTS BUT NEW CHARACTERS

The plots of practically all Greek dramas were based on myths or legends familiar to their audiences, and many were used again and again. There were a few exceptions: Aeschylus' *The Persians* dealt with a war in which he had fought, and a playwright named Agathon tried unsuccessfully to use new plots about fictional characters. Perhaps because the Greek tragedies used stories hallowed by time, Aristotle wrote: "The plot . . . is the first principle, and, as it were, the soul of tragedy; character holds second place." Actually, so far as the audience was concerned, the very opposite was true. Old plots became exciting again because the dramatists handled the chief characters in fresh ways, gave them new emotional reactions. In *The Greek Way to Western Civilization* Edith Hamilton has demonstrated this brilliantly by analyzing the completely different ways in which Aeschylus, Sophocles, and Euripides presented Electra.

THE OLD COMEDY AND THE NEW

The comedy of Aristophanes—himself a conservative—lampooned the ways of Athens and its politicians, philosophers, and playwrights. This comic form was far more highly conventionalized than that of tragedy. Yet, within the complex and elaborate pattern, Aristophanes and his fellow-playwrights injected scenes that ran from political travesty and comic preachment to bawdy burlesque. *The Frogs* satirized Euripides; *The Clouds*, Socrates. Our nearest

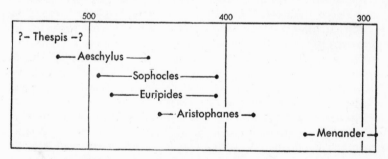

The Greek playwrights. *This, like the other time-charts in this book, shows the life-span of the writers, not their periods of playwriting activity. Some dramatists begin their important work while still in their twenties; Shaw was over thirty. Though these charts do not show the exact years of writing activity, they do indicate in a rough way the relationships in time among the various writers.*

approach to an Aristophanic comedy would be *Patience* if W. S. Gilbert had called one of the aesthetes Oscar Wilde and the other Burne Jones. *Lysistrata*, successful on Broadway in Gilbert Seldes' adaptation that somewhat curbed the chorus, had more of plot than satire behind its comic conception of how women ended a war by denying their favors to their husbands.

The contests in comedy began in 486 B.C., not quite fifty years after the first contests in tragedy. In only a little over a century, the Old Comedy of Aristophanes had disappeared, and the New Comedy of Menander had taken its place. Political and aesthetic satire had given way to comic plots from private life. Stock characters like the miserly old man and the scheming slave ruled the stage. They still wore masks, but the chorus was simply a group of caroling citizens who had nothing to do with the plot. Influenced no doubt by the *phlyax*, the New Comedy became, as one authority has put it, the model and the quarry for the Roman comedy of Plautus and Terence. Through antique comedy in Greece and Italy runs a pattern that ends in the *commedia dell'arte* of sixteenth-century Italy.

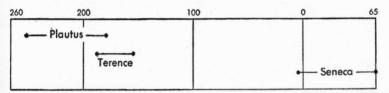

The chief Roman playwrights. *Plautus was dead before Terence began his comedies. Seneca did not write until almost two hundred years later. Rome had no permanent theaters when it had its two outstanding playwrights, and no playwrights except Seneca when it had theaters.*

Roman writers of tragedy simply translated or adapted Greek plays. A few, like Seneca, wrote original scripts, but they were generally content to have them read in private. The theater was too common and degraded an institution for the learned and well-placed.

The development of the Greek and Roman theater and its plays followed a familiar pattern, a pattern in which there is always hope and accomplishment and always disappointment and death. The theater began as a simple thing that imposed rather severe limitations and yet seemed to stimulate the playwrights through those limitations. Still more stimulating—and limiting, too—was the social and political and cultural atmosphere of the fifth century. Tragedy was born in the heroic times when Athens defeated the Persian invaders, and created the nearest approach to democracy that the world had known. Tragedy died in the spiritual confusions and decay that developed out of the Peloponnesian War. When the great playwrights of the fifth century were gone, and no one of equal stature came to take their place, the theater tried to fill the void with physical display and new ingenuities of production. The collapse of the Roman Empire carried down with it a theater that had fallen almost equally into decay. The theater of Dionysus died like its god, slain and torn apart by the enemies of its eternal spirit. It was to be born again, like Dionysus, in the spring of the Renaissance.

The RENAISSANCE THEATER

In ITALY

AFTER THE DEATH OF THE CLASSIC THEATER CAME THOUSANDS UPON THOU-
sand of religious performances in the cathedrals and the market places of
the Middle Ages. Oddly enough, while the Renaissance theater tried, in a fit
of scholarly devotion, to imitate the classic, it ended up as a new and almost
modern theatrical form.

As we have pointed out in *The Living Stage,* medieval drama was religious,
and it played in church and market place rather than in a theater. From
1450 onward we see the religious drama giving way to the secular, and its
backgrounds turning into a scenic stage that creates a new kind of playhouse.
The overlords of Italy—temporal and spiritual alike—provide theatrical performances of classic plays and pseudo-classic pageantry in courtyards and
great halls. Scholars search through ancient manuscripts for Latin and Greek
dramas, and act them as they are or adapt or translate them for performance.
Painters, rediscovering the laws of perspective, read what the Roman architect Vitruvius wrote about the classic theater, and create scenic miracles in
princely palaces. At last, in 1584, a group of scholars and aristocrats open in
the city of Vicenza what was probably the first real playhouse that Italy had
seen since the fall of Rome, the first one newly built and designed especially
for theatrical production and devoted to nothing else.

In just one way the theater of the Italian Renaissance was like the theater
of the Middle Ages. It left us no great plays. And so we may question whe-

ther it can be called a true theater. True theater means more than playhouse and actors and scenery. True theater cannot exist without plays that broaden and deepen human understanding, plays that arouse and quicken the spirit of man. From the time of those great poets and story-tellers Dante, Petrarch, and Boccaccio—precursors or begetters of the Renaissance—through the supreme years of the painters Leonardo da Vinci and Michelangelo, and on down to the invention of opera, Italy brought forth no fine, enduring drama. Therefore, in a true sense, the theater was not reborn during the Italian Renaissance in spite of all the lavish and magnificent activities of princes and popes, all the earnest and high-minded efforts of artists and academicians. There was no rebirth of the theater—as we know and revere the theater today—because there was no rebirth of the drama.

Yet, paradoxically enough, the modern playhouse with its canvas scenery and its miraculous machines was actually born in this time when men thought they were rediscovering and reconstructing the truly great theater of the classic world.

THE RENAISSANCE AND THE REVIVAL OF LEARNING

To understand what happened to the theater—and the drama—you must understand the Renaissance. It was not a simple and compact affair. It was not merely the Revival of Learning in the fifteenth century through the discovery of the classic past. The true Renaissance flowed out of the Middle Ages. Almost a hundred years before scholars awoke fully to the glory that was Greece, there were three great, original, and essentially modern writers, Dante, Petrarch, and Boccaccio. A literary revival came before the Revival of Learning. The writers did not imitate the beauty of the classic style. They created a new beauty in their own terms. Though these men wrote in Italian, they know the classics. In *The Divine Comedy* Dante chose Virgil as his guide to the other world; Boccaccio understood the significance of Greek literature; and Petrarch studied Greek as well as Latin. The three were portents of the coming age. Their work formed the broad basis of humanism—the new philosophy of life that denied the ancient dogmas of the church and the state, and exalted man as a creature of reason and free will.

Humanism grew and flowered as the discovery and study of classic literature in the late fifteenth and the early sixteenth centuries dealt the death blow to medieval domination over the minds of man. Conceived in "pagan" times, the great works of Plato, Aristotle, and other Greeks strengthened humanism as they undermined the authority of medieval mysticism. They proved the goodness and greatness of man in the past, and to the man of the present they gave confidence in his own abilities. As the new-found beauties and wisdoms of the ancient world provoked more and more inquiry, they destroyed the barriers to man's criticism of the present. To the Italian, seeing the continuity of human culture in the face of differing creeds and races, Greek civilization spelled out his right to spiritual freedom.

With humanism and learning came a great upsurge in painting, sculpture, architecture, and also in a few forms of literature—a swift expansion and perfection of the arts that we commonly think of as defining the Renaissance. Sometimes imitative of classic models and sometimes not, these arts achieved genuine and original creation.

Certain events did a great deal to stimulate and extend this cultural movement that one of its great students, Jacob Burckhardt, has called "the discovery of the world and of man." When the Turks captured Constantinople in 1453, eastern scholars fled to Italy, laden down with Greek manuscripts. When the Turks closed the road to India, Italians, Portuguese, and Spaniards were driven to discover and colonize the New World, and to circumnavigate the globe. Just a little earlier, the printing press—a German contribution to the many scientific developments of the Renaissance—gave the men of this age a unique and powerful new medium for the diffusion of their knowledge.

Yet even while churchmen, as well as laymen, lent their energies to classical research and became tolerant of humanism, the influence of the hedonistic and the pagan contributed to the moral decay of popes and princes. In addition, learning and scholarship turned too often into antiquarianism and pedantry. It is an unhappy fact that, though classical study recreated the playhouse, it stifled the play. And there was no great audience in Italy of the kind that we shall find in Spain and England to save the drama from the bookishness of academicians and the shallow ostentation of princes.

LINKS TO THE MEDIEVAL THEATER

The story of the theater of the Renaissance is no simpler than the story of the Renaissance itself. Part of the difficulty is a lack of exact information. Part is due to the fact that both were products of the transition from the Middle Ages, yet both leaped forward into a new interpretation of the ancient past. There seem to have been at least three links with the theater of other days.

The religious drama of the Middle Ages continued in Italy until at least 1454, when Florence saw in a *sacra rappresentazione* biblical scenes reenacted against twenty "mansions," or sets. The artist Uccello, who died in 1475 at the age of ninety-eight, executed on a wall of the ducal palace of Urbino a mural showing what seems to be a multiple setting for a mystery play; it includes three rooms connected by two doors, with a third door leading to a landscape. In 1471 a seventeen-year-old poet named Politian showed the temper of the new age by writing in Latin a mystery play in which the fables of classic mythology replaced the stories of saints and biblical figures that had furnished the plots of medieval drama. His *La Favola di Orfeo*—later produced in splendor by Ercole d'Este, Duke of Ferrara—is a link between the mysteries of the Middle Ages and two new art-forms that

Renaissance Italy was to develop. These were the pastoral play, which died in the English court masque, and the opera, which lives on today.

THE THEATER OF THE "ENTRIES"

Another link with the past may be seen in the "entries," the spectacular festivities that were staged to welcome royalty to a city. These were expensive but probably effective devices for impressing a conquered province with the power of its alien ruler, or assuring a native prince of the loyalty of his people. You may trace entries back to the processions of conquering generals returning in triumph to ancient Rome. Centuries later, in medieval London, houses were draped with flags, banners, rich tapestries, and glowing silks when kings like Richard I and Henry III celebrated a coronation or a marriage. By 1370, richly decorated floats, artificial arches, towers, and even stages for acted tableaux were added to the festivities, and entries became elaborate dramatic ceremonies. Their popularity was enormous, and by the time of the Renaissance entries were more numerous than monarchs Between 1443 and 1598 Italy enjoyed twenty-five entries, England and Flanders saw more than fifty, and France a hundred.

Sometimes an alien or a distrusted monarch showed the populace—his audience—a magnificent procession of costumed marchers and richly decorated floats. Far more often, however, a beloved monarch became himself the audience—a peripatetic one—as he passed a mile or more of spectacular displays that had been built and painted by a thousand or more workmen and artists. Among the sights to impress the eye of the sovereign were structures with one or more stages. Sometimes two stages shared a single platform; sometimes one was above the other. Thus, in a sense, the peripatetic pageant wagons of medieval England had become stationary, while the stationary audience walked or rode from one to another.

Upon these stages there first appeared dumb-shows, or *tableaux vivants,* sometimes with modelled figures, sometimes with living actors. Lettered scrolls presented what we might call "sub-titles" to the silent scenes. Later, English playwrights like Peele, Jonson, and Dekker wrote speeches and poems of welcome, and even little passages of dialog. In medieval times the subjects enacted were religious. Later, mythological figures welcomed the ruler.

Early in the Renaissance some of the entry stages displayed elaborate scenic effects. Clouds rose and descended with their divine freight. Curtains were used before they appeared in the Italian theater. Revolving stages turned the scene from a dead tree and a desolate landscape to a verdant prospect; this was half a century before the Renaissance artists introduced scene-changing devices in their theaters.

Entries often ended with a spectacular performance in the ruler's palace, along with a dance and a banquet. In 1489 such a show occurred in the Ducal palace at Milan to celebrate a noble nuptial. For *Il Paradiso,* a flattering mythological episode by an inferior poet, Leonardo da Vinci designed a mountain top the two halves of which split at the front and swung back to reveal a glittering heaven. Such were the spectacular pleasures of the court theater of the Renaissance, with or without the excuse of an entry or a wedding.

LATIN COMEDY FROM THE MIDDLE AGES

A third root of the Renaissance theater is long; it leads far back into the Dark Ages. Perhaps it is tenuous, yet it seems to account for the extraordinary speed with which the Revival of Learning swept Italy and most of Christendom, and it may explain why certain Roman plays were the first to be produced in the Renaissance and were long the most popular.

The dying Empire of the Caesars left Europe the legacy of an international language. The innumerable dialects of a disjointed continent could serve only the local peasants and craftsmen. Confined to small areas, these crude tongues were too limited in words and sentence-structure for the exchange of significant and sophisticated ideas. And so, churchmen and princes, wandering scholars and itinerant merchants, literate men of every part of middle and western Europe read, wrote, and spoke Latin.

It took no Revival of Learning to rediscover Roman comedy. Among the manuscripts slowly gathered together, first on monastery shelves and later in the universities during the Middle Ages, were eight plays by Plautus and six by Terence. Renaissance research added twelve more from Plautus, but scholars had read his *Menaechmi* (*The Brothers*) centuries before Ercole d'Este made it his second production at Ferrara, in 1486, and also Plautus' *Amphitruo*, which was his third.

In medieval days the ribald buffoonery of Plautus doubtless attracted the interest of the kind of young cleric who delighted in the Feast of Fools. The soberer brothers preferred the more refined Terence, and they often adapted his plays for performance in the schools. A German nun named Hroswitha seems to have been equally attracted by the pleasures of play-acting and the style of Terence, yet was fearful that the pagan plots would corrupt the sisterhood. Accordingly, Hroswitha wrote six Latin plays in the Terentian manner, but used for her characters such figures from Christian history as Abraham, Paphnutius, and Dulcitius. The churchmen of the Renaissance were not so righteously fastidious. Clerics laughed over Plautus's tales of bawdry when they saw them acted. Before Pius II was elevated to the papacy he wrote a witty and indecent comedy modelled on the Roman. Plautus as well as Terence was popular at the Vatican toward the end of the fifteenth century.

THE FIRST THEATER AND THE FIRST SCENERY?

It is easier to speculate over the medieval rudiments of the Renaissance theater than it is to describe accurately its beginnings in Italy. Who built the first temporary theater, and where? When did true scenery first appear? Who was the first producer—a prince of the church or a prince of the state? There are no good answers to any of these questions.

One authority says that "Alberti put a *theatrum* in the palace built in the Vatican for Nicholas V in 1452, but there is no record of its use for dramatic performances at that time." The writer doesn't cite his source for this, or explain that *theatrum* can mean a place for exhibition as well as a permanent playhouse. With no more evidence to go on, a second authority writes that "Alberti designed a theater proper for Pope Nicholas V." A third scholar implies that in 1486 Duke Ercole d'Este had his architect build a theater based on the writings of the Roman architect Vitruvius. A fourth identifies this playhouse with the one that seems to have been built for the poet-playwright Ariosto in 1532, and that burned down the next year, leaving not a trace of plans or sketches. All this confusion comes from the fact that many a nobleman or prelate had a habit of turning a great hall into a temporary showplace by putting a scaffolded stage and sometimes a proscenium frame at one end—while it all came down when the performance was over.

There is also some confusion over when scenery was first used and what it looked like. A Renaissance writer praised Cardinal Riario because he "first equipped a stage for Tragedy beautifully" in an outdoor production, probably between 1484 and 1486, and mentioned that the cardinal "first revealed to our age the appearance of a painted scene." But was this a true setting appropriate to the place and action of the drama? We know that a number of famous artists painted backgrounds that had no relation to the plays performed in palace halls. The elephant and the other figures in Mantegna's panels *The Triumph of Caesar* were no more appropriate than their title to the comedies of Plautus, *The Brothers* and *The Carthagenian*, which were acted in the great hall of the Marquis of Mantua in 1490, and for which the artist especially created these paintings on paper.

From a contemporary account we know that when the remarkable patron of the theater Ercole d'Este produced *Menaechmi* in 1486 it was in a courtyard and upon "a wooden stage with five battlemented houses. There was a window and a door in each. Then a ship came in . . . and crossed the courtyard. It had ten persons in it and was fitted with oars and a sail in a most realistic manner." The next year Ercole provided "a paradise with stars" for Plautus' *Amphitruo*. We have mentioned Leonardo's *Il Paradiso* of 1489. And in 1491 Ercole revived *Menaechmi* indoors and had Nicollo del Cogo paint "a prospect of four castles." Certainly as early as the fourteen-eighties scenery was achieving illusion.

ACADEMICIANS AS PRODUCERS

It was in this same decade that the Roman Academy began producing Latin comedies and an occasional tragedy by Seneca. Soon many other academies were set up in many other cities, most of them staging Roman plays or helping their princes to stage them. Within a century, a group of scholars and aristocrats, gathered together under the imposing title of the Olympic Academy, made the first enduring attempt to build a permanent theater on the classic model.

The academies of the Renaissance were extraordinary institutions, curious, powerful, and unique. Taking their title from the *Academia*—a grove near ancient Athens where the philosopher Plato taught—these dedicated bodies of scholars became the heart of humanism, the chief agents of the Revival of Learning. Their passionate zeal infected churchmen and nobles, and their discoveries of classic art, architecture, and literature turned the study of antiquity into a fashionable pursuit. Aided by the printing press, word of what the academies found and learned spread throughout Europe with amazing speed. Popular enthusiasm over the arts of the past may be judged from a single sentence in Gilbert Highet's *The Classical Tradition:* "When one particularly fine statue was excavated, it was carried in a special procession, with music and flowers and oratory, to be shown to the pope."

Unfortunately, these Italian scholars frowned upon their native tongue as a means of artistic expression. Deserting the language that had served Dante and Petrarch so well, they spoke only Latin in their meetings, and wrote their books and dissertations in the same ancient tongue. They even latinized their names; the leader of the Roman Academy, Giulio Pomponio Leto, became Julius Pomponius Laetus. This academic fervor for a dead language has left its mark today on the diplomas that certain universities give to "Jacobus Petrus Miller" and "Guilelmus Henricus McFadden."

Another peculiarity of these scholars was their extraordinary fondness for the drama. Pomponius Laetus launched the Roman Academy into competition with the Duke of Ferrara as the pioneer producer of Roman plays, and other academies followed.

We do not know for certain what kind of setting Cardinal Riario supplied for the performances of the Roman Academy on the Capitoline Hill or in the tomb of Hadrian, called the Castel Sant' Angelo, or within the cardinal's palace. Certainly scenic designers can't have gained much from Vitruvius, the Roman whose scanty contributions to our knowledge of the classic theater we have mentioned. His book on architecture, discovered by the Italians in 1414, and published in the original Latin in 1486, described houses with painted columns and other architectural details, but it told nothing about how they were arranged upon the stage. To solve that problem, the early scene designers seem to have turned back to the multiple stages and arcades used in the entries, and provided four or five curtained doorways under arches and separated by ornate columns. Thus each character had a "house" with his name neatly lettered above his door. In an edition of Terence published in 1493 there is a setting of this kind. One of the curtains is drawn aside to show an inner room with a window.

THE FIRST PERMANENT THEATERS IN ITALY

From this simple beginning it took long experiments in the designing of scenery, stage machines, and playhouses to bring forth the first modern type of theater, the Teatro Farnese of Parma, about 1618. After Ariosto's theater of 1532 in Ferrara, about which we know nothing, the next permanent building especially erected for the production of plays was the Teatro Olimpico in Vicenza. A distinguished architect, Andrea Palladio, designed it for the Olympic Academy of that city, and began its erection in 1580. It was the first attempt to recreate what the academicians thought was a Roman theater. The thirteen rows of seats followed the shape of an ellipse instead of a semicircle, thus providing better sight lines and more intimacy. There was a flat orchestra floor for the chorus and a raised and raked stage backed by a long wall with three doorways, flanked by two shorter ones, each with a single opening. For the central opening, Palladio adopted the triumphal arch that Roman conquerors built to celebrate their return from victorious campaigns. He probably intended to close the openings with curtains or doors, or perhaps to place *periaktoi* behind them. He died, however, in 1580, and the man who took over the completion of the theater, Vicenzo Scamozzi, made a radical change. Behind the five doorways he built short vistas of streets—three from the central arch—all radiating out like the spokes of a wheel. Built of wood and plaster, with three-dimensional ornament, they reproduced in violently forced perspective certain streets in a town of Boeotia in Greece.

The Teatro Olimpico was finished in 1584, and opened the next year with an elaborate production of Sophocles' *Oedipus Rex* in Italian and involving special music and a cast of 108. The building is a surprisingly warm and intimate playhouse where classics are now staged occasionally.

In the small town of Sabbioneta, Scamozzi tried an even more radical experiment. It was an experiment that seems to be the first step toward the modern theater with its single proscenium opening. At the end of the 1580's, Duke Vespasiano Gonzaga of Mantua, who had provided the town of Sabbioneta with a palace, a mint, and a printing plant, all on a small scale, decided to build a tiny theater for the *Academia dei Confidenti*. Because of the smallness of the structure—it seated only 250 against Olimpico's 3000—Scamozzi was apparently forced to give up multiple doorways in favor of a single vista that began at the very sides of the stage.

The theater in Sabbioneta may have influenced another architect, Giambattista Aleotti, when he designed the Teatro Farnese in Parma, twenty miles away. The auditorium was highly conventional. A horseshoe of raised seats held 3500 spectators, and between it and the stage was an orchestra floor that was used for spectacle and even flooded for at least one production. The stage, however, was almost modern in design. It had a wide proscenium and a deep stage behind. It is rather surprising that the Teatro Farnese had no curtain when it opened in 1618, for they had been often used in court spec-

An Italian Renaissance theater. *This is a plan of the Teatro Olimpico.* (*From Moritz,* Das Antike Theater, *and Cheney,* The Theater.)

The first theater with proscenium and curtains. *The modern picture-frame opening and curtain was built by the Prince of Parma in 1618 or 1619. The audience occupied the rising horseshoe of seats and the floor (which was sometimes flooded to make a sea for boats) as well.* (Drawing by Gerda Becker With.)

The Teatro Farnese in Parma. This theater, which marked the first use of the modern proscenium, may be seen in greater detail on the preceding page.

The theater in Sabbioneta. The smallness of the stage seems to have forced the architect to provide only one proscenium. Nearby Parma may have been influenced by this when the Teatro Farnese was built. (Both plans from Moritz, Das Antike Theater, and Cheney, The Theater.)

tacles. Ariosto had employed one in the production of his play *I Suppositi* at the Vatican in 1519. In his poem *Orlando Furioso,* he writes of what was to be seen "at the curtain-fall," because, as in ancient Rome, the curtains of the Renaissance usually descended into a trough instead of being raised.

The Teatro Farnese was a bombing casualty of World War II, but the theaters in Vicenza and Sabbioneta remain as living evidence—along with designs for scenery and contemporary descriptions of theatrical productions —of the energy that artists and academicians, princes and popes, devoted to their attempts to recreate the classic stage. Except on a very few occasions, their enormous and feverish activity brought forth a theatrical art that was not at all classic. Like other creators of the Italian Renaissance, they tried to emulate the ancients, and they ended by being highly original. The Teatro Olimpico was a plausible imitation of the past; the Teatro Farnese a startling preview of the future.

SCANT GUIDANCE FROM VITRUVIUS

The reason for the failure of the academicians as archaeologists of the theater and their success as originators of a new visual art lay in what we would now call lack of source material. Take Vitruvius and his *De Architectura,* which dominated theatrical theory for nearly three centuries. This revered book was almost the only key that the Renaissance had to the classic theater, and, as we have already said, Vitruvius supplied very little useful information. Yet his account of the *periaktoi* his observations about perspective in the theater, and his description of the three kinds of classic settings, were enough to set the greatest of Italian artists—Mantegna, Brunelleschi, Ghirlandajo, Michelangelo, Andrea del Sarto, Raphael, and Leonardo da Vinci—to painting scenery on many occasions. Lesser men like Bramante and Peruzzi, as absorbed as Paolo Uccello in thinking, "Oh, what a delightful thing is this perspective!" became scenic specialists.

SERLIO ON THE CRAFT OF THE SCENE PAINTER

In 1545 one of Peruzzi's pupils, Sebastiano Serlio, an architect as well as a painter, brought together in Book II of his *Architettura* what he believed was the nature of the classic theater, as sifted through Vitruvius, and what he knew were the stage practices of his contemporaries. He was the first to publish drawings of the three types of classic scenery: the tragic set with its lofty palaces, the comic set with its ordinary city houses, and the set for the satyr play with its landscape of trees, hills, and cottages. Far more important, he described how he—and, we may presume, the other designers—built and painted scenery.

Thus we know that the settings of his time combined false perspective with certain three-dimensional elements. The backing was flat, but the wings were bent at an angle like the splayed-out corner of a house, and they sported cornices and other architectural ornaments. "I made all my scenes of laths covered with linen, the cornice bearing out." The retreating sides of his wings were cut and painted in false perspective so that all the horizontal lines slanted backward and downward to the vanishing point of the scene painted on the backing. The wings toward the rear were treated somewhat differently from those farther "down stage." Serlio wrote: "if you make any flat buildings, they must stand somewhat farre inward, that you may not see them on the sides." These "up stage" wings had no raised cornices or other three-dimensional ornaments: "the Painting worke must supplie the place by shadows without any bossing out."

If the tops of the wings and the houses painted on them should slant downward to a distant vanishing point, why shouldn't their bases slant upward? In an effort to make false perspective as complete as possible, Serlio gave his stage what we call a "rake." The first few feet were flat; then the floor rose steadily toward the back. We do not know when raked stages came into general use, but they remained in fashion till late Victorian days. Slanting stage floors are still to be found in some old European theaters, and "up stage" and "down stage" remain part of the common theatrical vocabulary.

Serlio provided a good deal of information on how to imitate thunder and lightning and to move mechanical figures of men, animals, or planets on invisible wires. He explained how to create colored light by placing a bottle of red wine or colored water in front of a torch, and how to reflect it upon the stage by means of a "bright Basin" behind the torch.

From 1500 to 1650 Italian scene designers used other scenic patterns besides the angular, two-sided wings and the backdrop. One used prisms, or *periaktoi,* and another employed flat wings, and backings composed of two great screens. The prisms may have been used mostly in single pairs on the flat forestage with wings and backdrops on the raked floor behind them. But in 1583 an Italian, da Vignola, printed a stage plan with two *periaktoi* on each side of the stage and a very large prism taking the place of the backdrop. In 1632 the German architect Furtenbach recommended the use of *periaktoi,* and in 1638 the Italian Sabbatini provided detailed plans for their use.

THEATER PRACTICE ACCORDING TO SABBATINI

Sabbatini's book of 1638, *Pratica di fabricar scene e machine ne' teatri,* dealt elaborately with scenic perspective and machines for creating stage effects such as descending clouds and rolling waves. Sabbatini also explained various ways of making quick scene-changes. The three-sided *periaktoi* could be made even more versatile by fastening extra flats on the sides that had been seen and were now turned away from the audience. Painted cloths could be pulled across the two-sided wings. Sabbatini showed how groups of three or four angular wings could be nested behind one another along each side of the stage, and how the innermost wing in each group could be moved back to cover the front wing of the next group to the rear, thus changing the setting.

It seems likely that *periaktoi*—which presented great difficulties on a raked stage—were much less popular than the bent, or angled, wings, and, particularly, the flat wings which were introduced as early as 1600 and which continued in almost universal use well into the nineteenth century. To make quick scene changes, three or four of these wings were placed one behind another in groups on each side of the stage; when the down-stage ones were withdrawn the corresponding backdrop was "flown" or lowered into the basement, or, if it consisted of a great screen-like structure split in the middle, the two halves were pulled away to reveal a new pair. These flat wings were often set in grooves, which persisted down to 1900 in some small playhouses. At the turn of the century our theaters still used the "sky borders" invented during the Renaissance to complete the setting. Sabbatini and other artists went beyond this, however, when they used curved and slanting sections of sky-painted canvas six feet wide to form a series of arches over the stage.

Elaborate devices for quickly changing scenes bring up a point that has been curiously neglected. Until the last quarter of the nineteenth century, scene changing was done in full view of the audience. It was part of the entertainment. People enjoyed watching one scene magically dissolve into another. The idea persisted in the transformation scenes of extravaganzas and pantomimes not so many decades ago. Then why did the Roman theater have a curtain, and the renaissance and restoration theaters, too? It was there merely to hide the first setting and to close the play. Until about 1800 in England there was no "act curtain": the audience knew that the act was over when all the players left the stage. And in England until 1881 there was no curtain to hide changes of scene during an act; then Henry Irving introduced the so-called "scene curtain" to hide 135 stagehands, property men, and gas men who were involved with large set-pieces in *The Corsican Brothers*.

Illusion was the aim of the Renaissance designer. Whether or not he used three-dimensional ornament—"bossing out"—or angular wings for the corners of houses, he depended on the wonders of perspective to rival the reality that his audience saw and loved in the murals and canvases of great painters like Michelangelo and da Vinci. And yet, as time passed, no matter how deftly this flat scenery of wings and backdrop was painted in false perspective, it came to seem artificial and "theatrical." For the audiences of the twentieth century, the illusion was gone. Such settings were only for the ballet, and they had to be painted by as great a scenic artist as Leon Bakst of the Ballets Russes.

As a matter of fact, during the Renaissance such scenery was indeed painted by great artists, and it was used, in the main, for something quite as artificial as ballet.

ARTIFICIAL SETTINGS FOR ARTIFICIAL SPECTACLES

As we have told you, the academies and certain princes like Ercole d'Este made a great to-do about reviving Plautus, Terence, and Seneca, while Serlio, Sabbatini, and other designers claimed that they were reproducing the classic stage via Vitruvius. But most of the extraordinary scenes and machines of the Renaissance were not contrived for plays at all—whether Latin, Greek, or Italian. These Gargantuan marvels were lavished on court entertainments dealing with mythological or allegorical subjects, and made up of pantomime, dance, song, recitation, and pageantry. Sometimes the occasion was a state wedding or the visit of a foreign prince. Often the spectacular show was interjected between the acts of a Latin play; whether it was a tragedy or a comedy made no difference. These extravagant and amazing interruptions were called *intermezzi* or *intermedii*. One of the chief creators of such spectacles in the last half of the sixteenth century was Bernardo Buontalenti of Florence, who earned the nickname *delle Girandole* ("of the fireworks") because he turned his hand to pyrotechnic displays quite as readily as to the design of palaces and gardens, fortresses and military machines. Here is a description of one of his scenic effects:

In the third *intermedio* the scene represented a bare landscape as in a severe winter; beds of rivers and torrents, all dry and hard, were to be seen, when suddenly from the west Zephyr was seen to issue forth from a subterranean cave; she held the beautiful Flora by the hand, and sang a most lovely song with her; at the sound of this Spring appeared, with other festive deities, loves, winds, nymphs, and satyrs; and while all these together danced on the stage, the trees were seen to flourish again and renew their leaves.

Well into the seventeenth century this type of show lingered on as the chief vehicle of display for renaissance stagecraft. Since it was given by and for the court and not for the public, money was no object. Serlio advised his fellow-designers "never to take care what it shall cost." Extravagances reflect favorably on the prince, "for they are things which stately and great persons do, which are enemies of niggardliness." The ruler gave only three or four of these shows a year. For each production, the artist built a new stage in the great hall of the palace—or rebuilt the last one—only to clear it out when the performance was over. Under such conditions there could have been no true playhouse even if the artist-designer had not chosen—as he always did choose—to spill the entertainment off the raised stage and out onto the floor of the hall in a kind of dancing pageant. Here, too, they were following classic tradition. The Greeks danced in the *orchestra*.

"PASTORALS" AND OPERA

The scenic spectacles of the Renaissance found its most legitimate use in two new forms of entertainment. They were forms that came rather late, and they tended to confine the designer to a raised stage and a proscenium arch.

The first was the "pastoral," a poetic play on a rustic subject. Superficially it may seem an off-shoot of the sort of mythological fable that young Politian wrote for Ercole d'Este in 1471, and which others imitated. Actually it was a new kind of drama. Instead of following the loose form of the medieval mystery play, the author used a tighter, more dramatic structure. In general, shepherds and shepherdesses, nymphs and fauns, replaced the heroes and heroines of Greek mythology. The scenes became bucolic, and a myrtle grove or an Arcadian landscape with a humble cottage replaced a multiple setting of Olympus, Hades, an Attic palace, and so forth. Sometimes these plays were given in the garden theaters, with backgrounds and wings of clipped hedges, that graced the estates of great nobles in the sixteenth century. Pastorals became enormously popular with the aristocracy and courtiers; their ladies often played the parts of rustics and dryads. Torquato Tasso's *Aminta,* written and produced in 1573, and Battista Guarini's later pastoral *The Faithful Shepherd* were the most successful. Twenty contemporary translations of *Aminta* into French and nine into English testified to the popularity of this early form of the theater of escapism. In the seventeenth century, Inigo Jones, traveler as well as artist, developed from the Italian pastoral the elaborate court masque that Elizabeth I and James I delighted in.

Opera was the second new form of drama to come out of Italy. The earliest pieces seem related to Politian's *Orfeo,* to the pastorals, and even to the *intermezzi,* for all of these used music and song. But authorities claim that the birth of opera was a sheer accident. In 1595 a group of scholars and musicians, the Camerata of Florence, tried to imitate what they thought was Greek tragedy by telling, in *Dafne,* a mythological story in poetic dialog against a musical background. Other experiments followed *Dafne,* and opera became immensely popular with the common people after 1637, when Venice opened the first public theater. By 1700, Venice alone had built eleven more opera houses and produced some 360 operas, and this mixture of music, drama, and spectacle had spread triumphantly through all Italy to France, Austria, Germany, and England. An Italian enthusiast asserted in 1608 that in opera "the intellect and every noblest sentiment are fascinated at one and the same time by the most delectable arts ever devised by human genius." For over three hundred years opera has remained Italy's favorite form of theater art.

A MAGNIFICENT THEATER BUT NO PLAYS

Renaissance Italy produced great painting, sculpture, and architecture. It invented opera, and saw Claudio Monteverdi make it a respectable art-form through his revolutionary contributions to musical technique. Italians set the shape of the modern theater, and they were its first scenic designers. But, though Dante, Petrarch, and Boccaccio opened the Renaissance with immortal poetry and prose, Italy produced no plays of lasting value. Her playwrights held no more than a guttering candle to the scenic marvels of their stage.

There are a number of possible explanations. No one of them is wholly satisfactory. Added together they may solve this greatest of enigmas in the history of the theater.

Some believe that the Italian Renaissance produced no good plays because the theater placed too much emphasis on scenic display. They can quote from a writer of 1508 who commented upon a play by Ariosto:

> The subject was a most beautiful one of two youths enamored of two harlots who had been brought to Taranto by a pander. . . . But what was best in all these festivities and representations has been the scenery in which they have been played . . . a view in perspective of a town with houses, churches, belfrys and gardens, such that one could never tire of looking at it, because of the different things that are there all most cleverly designed and executed.

Not so many years ago critics who were hostile to the so-called "new stage-craft" assailed Adolphe Appia, Gordon Craig, and Max Reinhardt, along with modern devices for changing scenes, as destructive of the growth of true drama. Yet it was in this fifty-year period of scenic rejuvenation that dramatists such as Maeterlinck and Sartre, Shaw and Fry, O'Neill and Miller appeared, while the stage found new and more effective means to keep Shakespeare alive and vibrant.

In the very thing that stimulated and created the Renaissance theater—the rediscovery of the classic stage—lies another and a better reason for the shortcomings of Italian drama. Touched by the academic mania for Latin, many playwrights ignored their mother tongue. Worse still, they imitated the debased Roman drama instead of the Greek. Some turned out adaptations of the dry, rhetorical tragedies of Seneca. More of them imitated the comedies of Plautus and Terence, and pushed them further into obscenity. Academicians accepted what they thought were the "classic rules" of dramaturgy, added some misinterpretations of their own, and forced them on much of the drama of Italy and France through a good part of the sixteenth century.

Yet the sad state of the Italian playwrights cannot be blamed entirely on idolatry of the classics. Those who wrote in Italian and on Italian subjects were not much better than those who wrote in Latin. Their plays were more popular in appeal, but they were often shallow or vicious. After the insipidity of the pastoral *Aminta*, Tasso turned to the incestuous horrors of *Torrismondo*. Although Ariosto wrote plays of contemporary life he followed the patterns of Roman comedy and never approached the distinction of his own romantic epic *Orlando Furioso*. Machiavelli forgot all the academic rules, and wrote sharp, bitter comedies of his times; but, like the rest of the Italian playwrights, he lacked both compassion and imagination.

It was, perhaps, the social and political atmosphere of the Italian Renaissance that worked most heavily against the creation of a significant and lasting drama. Throughout the Renaissance, Italy was a country of petty states dominated by native autocrats and oligarchies, or ruled over by Spain, France, the Holy Roman Empire, or the Papacy. The closest approach to national peace lasted less than fifty years—from 1447 to 1492—and it was interrupted by intermittent local struggles between some of the city-states; at best, the despots built their power on corruption and cunning instead of open violence. In the fourteenth and the sixteenth centuries, the people were held in subjection by mercenary armies, and through half of the fifteenth by murder and guile. Against this picture of martial and political violence we must balance the courtly ideal of the perfect prince, exemplified by Ercole d'Este and Francesco Sforza. The prince and his courtiers aspired to the highest ideal of humanism: "the complete man," the embodiment of culture. But this was an idealistic conception that reached the people only through the magnificent palaces and churches and the beautiful paintings and statues that glorified the rulers of Italy and masked their political crimes. Where Italian princes ruled and the arts flourished, cruelty and corruption went hand in hand with culture. And because there was no free nation and there

Italians of the Renaissance. *Machiavelli's playwriting was confined to the last third of his life. Ariosto and Tasso began their work for the theater when they were about thirty.*

were no free cities, Italy had no staunch and patriotic citizenry. It lacked the sound, vigorous, self-reliant, and ambitious populace that loved and dominated the theater of Madrid and London.

For almost two centuries, the theater and its plays were dedicated to a very limited—and limiting—audience. It was an audience of scholars who were often pedants, churchmen who were sometimes far too worldly, and courtiers who were usually intemperate in all things. The audience broadened somewhat as Italian dialog replaced Latin, but it was never the vigorous and imaginative audience that nourished Lope de Vega in Spain and Shakespeare in England. The fine arts can flourish under princely patronage, for the artist works alone. But the dramatist can live only in the public theater where a play is a product of cooperation between writer, actors, and a vital audience. And when at last Italy built playhouses for the populace, opera took over.

THE PEOPLE'S THEATER

By 1550 scholars, painters, and poets—blessed and be-moneyed by the princes of church and state—had evolved a spectacular stage for an insignificant drama. In the next seventy years Italy built three permanent theaters, and accidentally invented opera. All this was the product of amateur effort, amateur in the worst sense as well as the best, and it was limited in vital quality and appeal. This aristocratic theater became professional and found a popular audience—two essential steps in the development of theatrical art —only when Italy began to spawn opera houses in the last half of the seventeenth century.

But another sort of professional theater was finding its popular audience around 1550. It was a theater of boards and trestles, and an audience that stood in the public square. Its actors passed the hat among the spectators, and then delighted the mob with improvised comedy. They had no written plays. But their brains as well as their bodies were so nimble, and their comedic art became so perfect, that they invaded Spain and the Teutonic countries, conquered Paris, and even played in London.

This theater was the *commedia dell'arte*. It got its name only when it was passing out of existence in the eighteenth century. The term *dell'arte* was a critical accolade. Those words signified that there was nothing of the amateur about the comedians and their comedy. Just as today the phrase "the profession" means people who know and practice the special art of acting, *arte* —as the English critic Allardyce Nicoll points out—meant the special art of playing these comedies.

There had been earlier names for this kind of theater, and they had defined its peculiar nature. One was *commedia all'improviso*, which meant that the plays were improvised. The other, *commedia a soggetto*, indicated that the actors improvised their comedies upon a "subject," or plot.

AN ART OF PLOTS AND "BUSINESS"

The *scenarios*, as we now call the plots of the *commedia dell'arte*, were bare outlines of the action. Each was the prompt book of the play and was posted backstage—when there was a stage in the modern sense—so that no actor might miss his cue or play the wrong scene. The head of the troupe went over the scenario with the actors when a new comedy was to be given or an old one revived. He explained the action, the pantomimic "business," and the use of the "props."

Fortunately two Italians wrote about the *commedia dell'arte* in the latter half of the seventeenth century when it was still alive, and we have reports or outlines of some 700 scenarios. Almost all are comedies. A few are pastoral in nature, and there are what we now call tragi-comedies. Only a few of the plots written down before 1600 have been preserved in manuscript, but, since most stage material was acted by troupes for generation after generation, many of the earliest scenarios may be among the 700 that we now have.

From the seventeenth-century writers we know that all the performance was not improvised. There were written prologs that had little to do with the plot, and there were also set speeches—delivered as soliloquies—with which an actor closed a scene or made an exit. These often ended in rhymed couplets such as we find in Shakespeare, while musical duets, interrupting the action, were written and rehearsed before production.

A writer of 1634 says that "the actors engage in study and load their memories with a great mass of matter, such as stock sentiments, conceits, love speeches, complaints, ejaculations of despair and madness, which they keep ready for all occasions." It is no wild guess that when a company had played an improvised comedy a number of times, most of the dialog had been committed to memory.

A curious feature of the *commedia dell'arte* were the *lazzi*—jokes of one sort or another interjected into the plot. Some of these were verbal.

The *lazzo* of Pulcinella's goodness is that he, hearing from the Capitano or another that they wish to kill him, and not being known to them in person, praises himself, saying "Pulcinella is a witty, straightforward, good fellow."

Most *lazzi* were physical—what we call "stage business." Often they had nothing to do with the action. While two lovers were engaged with their troubles, a comic servant might pretend to catch a fly, or eat imaginary cherries from his hat and flip the pits in the hero's face. A special way of tripping up an opponent was considered a *lazzo*. Here, in the words of an Italian comedian, is a specimen that might have come out of an American burlesque show:

I find Trivelin stretched on the ground. I think him dead and try to drag him to his feet; then I let my wooden sword fall down. He takes it and hits me on the buttocks . . . I seize and carry him; I lean him against the wings on the right-hand side of the stage. I look around at the footlights, and meanwhile he gets up and leans against the lefthand sidewings. This *lazzo* is repeated two or three times.

THE STOCK CHARACTERS

Two things gave the *commedia dell'arte* real distinction and even a kind of immortality. The first was deft acting; it was praised and imitated in Spain and France, where its impact was enormous. The other was the set of characters that the actors slowly created. Many of their names and figures are familiar today, and some have appeared in England's Christmas pantomimes. In somewhat the same fashion as the Italians, the comedians of our own radio, television, and burlesque shows build up individual characters that they play year in and year out.

Each of the seven men and three women that made up a typical company played a certain stock figure as long as he was young, or old, enough. Originally these characters had each been created by one particular actor. Gradually other actors gave them different dialects, and changed them in small ways. But certain types were unchanging, indestructible. The least interesting were the lovers—the *innamorati*. They looked and dressed like any young people of the time. Their names were usually the names of the actors and actresses who played them.

The comic characters were of many kinds. There were almost always two old men, close relatives of figures in Greek and Roman farce. One was Pantalone, a money-minded Venetian. He has come down to us in Shakespeare's "lean and slippered pantaloon" and Molière's Harpagon in *The Miser*. The other, Il Dottore, was a doctor of laws, seldom a physician. Always interfering with other people's business, he still appears in Rossini's *The Barber of Seville* and in Mozart's *The Marriage of Figaro*.

A group of *zanni*—from which we get "zanies"—were younger fun-makers and expert dancers. Arlecchino began as a stupid servant full of pranks. Later he became a smart fellow, and still later his patched clothes took on the decorative diamond patterns of our present day Harlequin. Pedrolino, another servant, became the French Pierrot, while Pulcinella was metamorphosized into the humpbacked English Punch. Other comic figure—like cowardly Brighella, Mezzetino with his red-and-white striped suit, and braggart Il Capitano—are to be found in Callot's engravings and Watteau's oils. In Colombina the Italians gave their heroines a confidante and mischief maker whom we have turned into Columbine. She was also the progenitress of our musical comedy soubrette.

A most peculiar feature of the *commedia dell'arte* was that all the comedians, and occasionally Colombina, wore masks. Sometimes the masks covered the whole face, sometimes half the face, and sometimes, as in the case of Arlecchino, Pedrolino, and Colombina, just the eyes. Since so many scenes in the *commedia dell'arte* depended on pantomime, it seems strange that the comedians should have sacrificed the mobile expressiveness of their faces. The masks, however, permitted stylized exaggeration of the features appropriate to the characters.

The various companies founded in the sixteenth century rejoiced in interesting names: I Fedeli (The Faithful), I Desiosi (The Desirous), I Confidenti (The Confident), I Accesi (The Inspired), and—the most famous in its time—I Gelosi (The Jealous). Today we have contracts signed by the actors of such companies, contracts that sometimes required periodic attendance at the confessional or prohibited swearing.

The lesser troupes traveled from town to town in Italy. The more renowned confined themselves to the larger cities. Traveling troupes usually carried their properties and simple stages with a curtain for backdrop. Whenever the strolling players had an opportunity to appear in real theaters, they made the most of scenery, stage machines, and the various special effects that Serlio and Sabbatini have described for us. There were difficulties, of course, when nobles invaded the stage to ogle the actresses, but at least one cardinal provided fines, stripes, or imprisonment for those who sat on the stage, stood in front of the actors, made unseemly noises, or threw "apples, nuts, or garbage at the comedians."

ITALY MAKES THEATER ABROAD

The *commedia dell'arte* was vastly popular with the Italian common people, but it had little effect on the Italian theater. Abroad the story was different. The influence of these comedians can be traced through France, Spain, and England, and, later, Germany. Italian companies won the favor of the French court as well as the Paris populace. They played with great success in the courtyard theaters of Madrid. They went as far as London to appear before Elizabeth I and James I. They influenced great playwrights abroad if not in their own country. In *All's Well That Ends Well* Shakespeare modeled Captain Parolles on Il Capitano. The plot of *The Comedy of Errors* is as typical of the *commedia dell'arte* as is the charming scene in *The Taming of the Shrew* between fair Bianca and Lucentio disguised as her music teacher. The characters and the stories of the Italians inspired Molière to create *Tartuffe, The Miser, The Imaginary Invalid, George Dandin,* and *The Rogueries of Scapin.* But it was not till almost a hundred years after Molière that Italian playwrights, Goldoni and Gozzi, began to draw upon the rich store of the *commedia dell'arte.*

Through entries, court spectacles, revivals and adaptations of classic plays, *intermezzi,* pastorals, operas, elaborate scenery and stage machines, theaters at Vicenza and Parma, opera houses, and performances of the *commedia dell' arte,* the Italian Renaissance developed and enjoyed more varieties of theatrical activity than any other period in the history of the world—all this in the face of national disunity and internecine strife. But, though Italy created the modern playhouse, it could not create fine and enduring plays. And so this Renaissance was not the rebirth of the true theater.

three

SPAIN'S GOLDEN AGE

IN SPAIN—AT LAST A FINE PROFESSIONAL THEATER

THERE WAS STRIFE IN SPAIN AND THERE WERE ALIEN CONQUERORS—JUST AS in Italy. But the Moors brought art and science with them in the Dark Ages of the eighth century, and only the ideological conflicts of Christianity, Judaism, and Mohammedanism stopped Spain from becoming a unified and glorious nation. And unity and glory were to come. For, while Italian princes intrigued for power or fought one another with mercenary armies, Spanish kings and the Spanish people drove down and out of Spain the followers of the Muslims who had conquered it seven hundred years before. In this struggle, peasants and townsmen won from their own native rulers a considerable amount of freedom through the abolition of serfdom, the granting of town charters, and the setting up of local and state legislatures called *municipios* and *cortes*. By 1492, the Spanish people were a united nation, vital and burgeoning. Then came imperial expansion and world-power— quickening and exhilarating at first, but, as always and everywhere, poisonous and fatal in the end. Resurgent Spain discovered America, and while she was conquering much of the New World, one of her kings—as Charles V of the Holy Roman Empire —ruled the Netherlands, a number of German kingdoms, Burgundy, Sicily, Naples, and Sardinia. He captured Francis I of France, drove the Turks down the Danube, conquered Tunis, and, with a mercenary army, sacked Rome in 1527. The imperial power of Spain in Europe, shaken by the defeat of the Armada in 1588, crumbled away after the loss of the Netherlands in 1609. Yet at home, in the realm of art and literature, a "golden age" persisted for half a century more.

THE GROWTH OF A NATIONAL THEATER

The medieval theater begins in Spain much as in France and England and Germany—largely religious but partly profane. Perhaps it is delayed a bit because of Moorish domination over much of Spain, and because of the early antagonism of the Catholic church. But, by the middle of the twelfth century, when half of Spain is freed, we know that someone has written a mystery play about the visit of the Magi to the new-born Jesus. Only 147 lines of dialog are left, but, like contemporary French scripts, they are written in the speech of the people instead of in Latin. In thirteenth-century Spain, just as in France, there are coarse and irreverent comedies. The Spaniards call them *juegos de escarnio,* or plays of mockery, and a king of Leon and Castile forbids the clergy to act in or even see them because they contain "much clowning and lewdness."

With the Renaissance, Spain breaks away to some extent from the Continental pattern. The power of the Catholic religion and the vitality of the Spanish people lie behind this. Sacred dramas continue until 1765—more than two centuries longer than on the rest of the Continent—many of them written by the best and most popular playwrights. The church frowns on humanistic worship of the pagan world, and the popular playwrights waste little time on sterile imitations of classic drama. But, above all, the Spanish audience is eager for romance and comedy and poetic drama, for heroic scenes out of Spanish history and legend, for "cloak and sword" plays laid in its own times, for comic and romantic intrigue, for anything of swift, theatric vitality. A number of secular plays appear before 1500, and within half a century their playwright-producers are creating a new kind of playhouse. Spain matches—and even anticipates—kindred plays and theaters of Elizabethan England.

SPANISH RELIGIOUS DRAMA—AUTOS SACRAMENTALES

In Spain the first religious plays, as well as the secular ones, were called *autos*—"actions" or "acts." The earliest sacred dramas seem to have been re-enactments of stories from the Bible or the lives of the saints. When the feast of Corpus Christi, celebrating the Blessed Sacrament, became the favorite season for the production of religious plays, their form had changed. Even the first of these *autos sacramentales* differ from the French mystery plays in a number of ways. They seem nearer to the English moralities in dramatic treatment and in methods of production.

The basic material of the *autos sacramentales* could be any sacred subject from the Creation, through the Nativity, to the Day of Judgment. But the playwrights treated these events allegorically instead of literally. They replaced re-enactment with a sort of dramatized imagery. A biblical figure became a man of the day. The devil turned into a pirate or a Moor. Abstract qualities or ideas took human form. Again and again we find characters called

Death, Virtue, Jealousy, or Pestilence—just as in the English moralities—or even the Days of the Week.

Many elements in the physical production of *autos sacramentales* were common enough in France, but many seem English—or purely Spanish. There were great processions to the church, but these in Spain often involved fantastic figures of giants and monsters moved and animated by men inside. At one time or another the guilds of craftsmen took over from the priests much of the responsibility and all of the labor of production. But the city fathers of Spain played a more and more important part, and in the sixteenth and seventeenth centuries they assumed authority and paid the bills, and also provided us with invaluable records. The *autos sacramentales* were never thrust out of the medieval churches as the French mysteries were; but, after the performance before the high altar, the actors gave the plays, in a more elaborate form, at various spots where the arms of the city had been placed on high. The early *autos* were acted by priests and guildsmen. But, as far back as 1454, town records show that three dancers and jugglers were hired to appear in a religious play. In the next two centuries the best of professional companies were engaged for special productions, and successful dramatists like Gil Vicente, Lope de Vega, and Calderón wrote hundreds of sacred *autos*.

One phase of the Spanish performances was peculiar to this nation that has always loved the dance. This was the introduction of dancing into the very church itself. At first a typical *auto* went somewhat like this: After the parade through the streets, a priest placed the Blessed Sacrament on the altar of the church. Then came the performance for the clergy and the town council. Following the usual religious service, dancers performed where the play had been given before the Blessed Sacrament.

THE SPANISH CARROS—LIKE ENGLISH
PAGEANT WAGONS

When the dance was over, another parallel with medieval England appeared. The *autos* not only presented abstract characters like those of the English morality plays. They resembled another kind of English religious play—the mystery—in their scheme of peripatetic presentation. After the performance in the church, the actors went from place to place in the city repeating the performances, and they rode, like the English actors, on wagons that carried the scenery. The Spanish called their pageant wagons *carros*, and their outdoor performance *La Fiesta de los Carros*—the festival of the carts. We should probably call these vehicles "wagons," or even "floats," for they must have been large and heavily built. Two features seem distinctively Spanish. At each stop the wagons were backed up against a platform on which the actors played important scenes. There was another kind of stage, which must have been used only in the parades, called *la roca*. This was a platform carried by twelve men, and on it stood Jesus, Mary, and various evangelists and saints.

Multiple sets appeared as early as 1400, and probably earlier. They grew more and more common in the fifteenth and sixteenth centuries and even continued into the eighteenth. Wagon and platform had often provided three or more settings on the same level, but by 1420 an *auto sacramental* was produced with five "mansions," or settings, built in the French fashion on a single long stage. In 1578 the city of Plasencia erected in the public square a huge platform that included a tank of water sixty feet long and twenty feet wide in which floated a sailing ship. There are records of productions with one setting above another, and of a single performance on three levels. Vertical and horizontal stages were very often combined during the fifteenth century. Doubtless the more elaborate multiple settings were confined to the street performances, but there is one mention of a dove descending from on high in the cathedral of Valencia, and another of scaffolds erected in two churches. The staging of the *autos* grew simpler when the sacred plays invaded the public playhouses after 1600. Today, however, at Elche and in many other towns, multiple stages are still used for popular religious performances.

A PRODUCTION ON WAGONS IN 1663

In George Ticknor's *History of Spanish Literature,* we have a description of the production in 1663 of an elaborate *auto sacramental* employing wagons, *El divino Orfeo.* The allegorical use of Orpheus and Eurydice springs from the influence of the Italian Renaissance.

It opens with the entrance of a huge black car, in the shape of a boat, which is drawn along the street toward the stage where the *auto* is to be acted, and contains the Prince of Darkness, set forth as a pirate, and Envy, as his steersman; both supposed to be thus navigating through a portion of chaos. They hear at a distance sweet music, which proceeds from another car, advancing from the opposite quarter in the form of a celestial globe, covered with the signs of the planets and constellations, and containing Orpheus, who represents allegorically the Creator of all things. This is followed by a third car, setting forth the terrestrial globe, within which are the Seven Days of the Week and Human Nature, all asleep. These cars open, so that the personages they contain can come upon the stage and retire back again, as if behind the scenes, at their pleasure—the machines themselves constituting, in this as in all such representations, an important part of the scenic arrangements of the exhibition. . . .

On their arrival at the stage, the Divine Orpheus, with lyric poetry and music, begins the work of creation, using always language borrowed from Scripture; and at the suitable moment, as he advances, each Day presents itself, roused from its ancient sleep, and clothed with symbols indicating the nature of the work that has been accomplished; after which Human Nature is, in the same way, summoned forth, and appears in the form of a beautiful woman, who is the Eurydice of the fable. Pleasure dwells with her in Paradise; and, in her exuberant happiness, she sings a hymn in honour of her Creator, founded on the hundred and thirty-sixth Psalm. . . .

The temptation and fall succeed; and then the graceful Days, who had before always accompanied Human Nature and scattered gladness in her path, disappear one by one, and leave her to her trials and her sins. She is overwhelmed with remorse, and endeavouring to escape from the consequences of her guilt, is conveyed by the bark of Lethe to the realms of the Prince of Darkness, who from his first appearance on the scene, has been labouring, with his coadjutor Envy, for this very triumph. But his triumph is short. The Divine Orpheus, who has for some time represented the character of our Saviour, comes upon the stage, weeping over the fall, and sings a song of love and grief to the accompaniment of a harp made partly in the form of a cross; after which, rousing himself in his omnipotence, he enters the realms of darkness, amidst thunders and earthquakes, overcomes all opposition; rescues Human Nature from perdition; places her, with the seven redeemed Days of the Week, on a fourth car, in the form of a ship, so ornamented as to represent the Christian Church and the mystery of the Eucharist; and then, as the gorgeous machine sweeps away, the exhibition ends with the shouts of the actors in the drama, accompanied by the answering shouts of the spectators on their knees wishing the good ship a good voyage and a happy arrival at her destined port.

DON QUIXOTE MEETS AN AUTO ON TOUR

The display of scenery and costumes varied from place to place and from time to time. Through at least four centuries the *autos sacramentales* used cathedrals and great plazas as their playhouses. But before 1580 there must have been humble troupes of strolling players taking crude productions from town to town. In that year Cervantes described one of these traveling companies:

Don Quixote was about to make a reply, but was interrupted by the sight of a cart crossing the highway, filled with the most varied and weird assortment of persons and figures that could be imagined. He who drove the mules and served as carter was an ugly demon, and the vehicle was open to the heavens and had neither awning nor framework of branches on which to stretch it. The first figure that Don Quixote beheld was that of Death himself, with a human countenance. Next came an angel with large and painted wings. At one side was an emperor with what appeared to be a gold crown on his head, and at Death's feet was the god Cupid, without a bandage over his eyes, but with his bow, his quiver, and his arrows. There was also a knight in full armor, except that he had no morion, or helmet, but instead wore a hat decked with vari-colored plumes.

Such a sight as this, coming as it did so unexpectedly, somewhat startled Don Quixote and struck fear in Sancho's heart, but the knight was at once cheered by the thought that this must be some new and perilous adventure, and with a mind disposed to confront any danger he stepped in front of the cart and called out in a loud and threatening voice, "O carter, coachman, demon, or whoever you may be! Tell me at once who you are and whither you are bound and who the persons are whom you carry with you in that wagonette, which looks more like Charon's bark than the kind of conveyance in common use."

Stopping the wagon, the demon gave him a most civil reply. "Sir," he said, "we are strolling players of Angulo el Malo's company. [He was a theatrical manager and playwright who was active about 1580.] This morning, which marks the octave of Corpus Christi [the eighth day after the festival], we have performed a theatrical piece in the village which lies beyond that hill yonder. It was a play [Cervantes uses the word *auto*] called *The Parliament of Death,* and we have to give it this afternoon in another village which you can see from here. Since the distance is so short, and in order to save ourselves the trouble of undressing and dressing again, we are traveling in the garments that we wear on the stage. That youth there is Death, the other is an Angel. That woman, who is the author's wife, takes the part of a Queen. This one is a Soldier, that one an Emperor, and I am a Devil."

COARSE COMEDY MIXED WITH HOLY EDIFICATION

The people of Spain loved the theater in all its forms, and they seem to have loved all its forms with equal enthusiasm. A public performance—no matter whether it was sacred or profane—combined the best features of a vaudeville show and what we used to call "the legitimate." Singing and dancing, monologs and comic sketches, even juggling, introduced or interrupted what was supposed to be the main attraction: the play itself. This may not have been true of all *autos sacramentales* produced in churches, but when they paraded out into the streets they were certainly just such a theatrical mishmash.

First there was a repetition of the same fantastic procession that had borne the actors to the House of God. After a prayer, the performance began with a prolog that often praised the show itself. In *El nombre de Jesús,* written by Lope de Vega, an actor and an actress play a villager and a peasant girl who run into each other after being separated in the crowd. The girl is so naive and loquacious that it takes only a little prodding to make her chatter on endlessly about the wonderful procession that she—and all the crowd, of course—have just seen. Next would come a short farce, one of the *juegos de escarnio* that the King of Leon and Castille had condemned in 1252, and then a sacred play. *Entremeses,* which were the interludes of comedy, dancing, and singing that were given between the acts of secular plays, seem to have interrupted in the same way the holy episodes of the *autos sacramentales.*

In 1601 a monk wrote about *"entremeses* treating of robberies and adulteries, which are ordinarily mingled with the *autos sacramentales."* Ten years later another cleric wrote indignantly about lewd and adulterous scenes acted out in church. The clergy attempted to curb these abuses both in and out of the cathedrals. In 1473 a church council issued a decree against the presentation of monsters, masks, bawdy figures, and "lewd verses, which interfere with the divine offices." There were probably many more decrees, but the ribaldries persisted—in the street shows if not in the churches. The seventeenth and eighteenth centuries saw the attacks increase. Laymen as well as priests inveighed against professional players in *autos.* An anonymous writer objected because an actress played the Mother of God, "and . . . having finished this part, the same actress appears in an *entremes,* representing an innkeeper's wife . . . , simply by putting on a bonnet or tucking up a skirt," and dances while she sings an indecent song. "He who played the part of the Savior in a beard takes it off and comes out and sings and dances 'Here Comes Molly.' " Priests echoed such attacks on the players. It was abominable that "the woman who represents the lewdness of Venus, as well in plays [in the theaters] as in her private life, should represent the purity of the Sovereign Virgin." Such attacks persisted until at last, in 1765, Charles III prohibited by royal decree the performance of all *autos sacramentales.*

COMEDIAS *AND THE FIRST PLAYWRIGHTS*

Charles III banned another kind of religious play. It was given only in the public playhouses, and it was called a *comedia de santos.* The words *de santos* are obvious enough—"of saints." *Comedia* seems to be clear, yet it isn't. Sometimes it applies to comedy, but just as often to melodrama or tragedy. (The word is also used for theater in a general sense.) Just as in the Middle Ages *auto* originally meant any play, whether religious or not, so in the late Renaissance *comedia* meant any play that was long enough to be given in three acts. For a few years some *comedias* were written in prose. In the "golden age" of Spanish literature—which runs from a little before 1550 to about 1650—all *comedias,* whether saintly or not, were in verse. In the dialog the writer was not restricted to a single type of poetry, as in our own blank verse dramas. Within the same play he would use different kinds of meter and various rhyme-schemes, giving each scene the lyric treatment that best suited it.

While Columbus was discovering and exploring the New World, the Spanish dramatist was discovering and exploring this new play form—the *comedia.* Or so a Spaniard wrote a hundred years later. Perhaps it is safer to say that the playwrights of Spain—and Portugal too—slowly developed a new type of native drama between 1500 and 1550.

The first playwright of this era and the founder of the Spanish drama was Juan del Encina. Musician, courtier, and actor too, he wrote chiefly on religious and pastoral subjects, yet he had humor and a real interest in contemporary society. By 1497 he turned out a nativity drama in which the shepherds spoke a local dialect and became the chief figures of the play. This *Égloga de Fileno, Zambardo, y Cardonio* was secular in feeling, and his later work became more and more an expression of his own times.

Most of the successful playwrights who followed Encina dealt mainly with contemporary life, and often humorously. Though Bartolomé de Torres Naharro spent much of his life in Italy, he escaped the worship and imitation of classic drama. He wrote a satire on an army of occupation, and laid a comedy in the servants' hall of a Roman cardinal. He developed a low comedy character, called a *gracioso,* that was widely used by later playwrights. Perhaps because Torres Naharro was aware of his shortcomings as a playwright, he introduced an *introito,* or prolog, in which he summarized the plot so that the audience would be sure to follow it. Later on the *introito* became a *loa,* often a monolog in praise of the play or of the city in which it was about to be seen. Seeking new matter for these inevitable *loas,* later playwrights fell upon such extraordinary subjects for commendation as the days of the week or even the letter A.

A more skilful dramatist, Juan de la Cueva, turned to national history for many of his subjects, characterized his people with more adroitness, and used popular verse-forms brilliantly. Another playwright, Gil Vicente, varied his work with comic scenes of everyday life. The fact that he was a Portuguese who wrote a quarter of his plays in Spanish shows the close ties between the theaters of the two countries.

LOPE DE RUEDA—POPULAR PLAYWRIGHT

Spain's first important dramatists—Encina, Naharro, Cueva, and Vicente —spent much of their time in Italy, and wrote primarily for the court and not for the people. Yet their plays had such fresh vitality that they were later acted by professional companies in many cities.

The first playwright who wrote directly for the popular stage was Lope de Rueda. He was the leading figure among the playwrights who were also actor-managers, toured from town to town, and dominated the Spanish stage until 1575. Because Rueda and his fellows supplied their companies with plot and dialog, they were called *autores de comedias,* but when their successors gave up writing and began to hire playwrights as well as actors, the words *autores de comedias* came to mean theatrical managers.

Until 1558, when Rueda left his job as a gold-beater and joined with a bookseller and a few friends in founding a company of strolling players, most secular drama had been performed only at court. Rueda was the founder of the Spanish national theater, both as popular playwright and as popular producer. He too, however, drew inspiration from Italy. The *commedia dell' arte*—as he saw it given by an Italian company that toured Spain—made him an actor. His comedies, six of them in prose and three in verse, followed Italian plots, but their form, their dialog, and their humor were thoroughly Spanish. It was Rueda who invented the *paso* (a comic sketch in prose used as an interlude between the acts) and excelled in this early form of the one-act play. The most famous was *The Olives,* in which a farmer who has just planted an olive shoot quarrels violently with his wife and his daughter over the price they are going to charge for the fruit that won't mature for five years. The idea must have been peculiarly amusing to a people bedeviled as the Spaniards were by rapid inflation.

When Cervantes was eighteen he saw a performance by Rueda's company. Fifty years later the author of *Don Quixote* wrote and published a brief description of the production. In the meantime public theaters had been established, the *autos sacramentales* had continued on their spectacular way, and Cervantes' memory of Rueda may have faded a trifle. Nevertheless, his picture of the crudities of these early entertainments was probably not far from the truth. The stage, he wrote, was made of four benches with planks across them a couple of feet off the ground. The scenic background was an old blanket. Behind it the actors put on their costumes and sang "some old ballad without the accompaniment of a guitar." The costumes and properties of such a troupe, when it was giving a shepherd's play, could go into a single sack, "and consisted of four white sheepskins ornamented with gilt leather, four beards and wigs, and four crooks." Recalling the scenic effects and stage machinery of his own day, Cervantes remarked that in a performance like Rueda's "there were no figures which rose or seemed to rise from the center of the earth . . . nor did clouds with angels or souls descend from the skies." For all that, Rueda "acted with the greatest skill and naturalness that you can imagine."

TOURING COMPANIES—RUEDA'S AND OTHERS

Strolling players like Rueda's company still toured Spain even after permanent theaters had been built in the sixteenth century. In 1603, Agustin de Rojas, who wrote many *loas* as well as *comedias,* set down an amusing catalog of the various kinds of troupes. He divided them into eight species. They increase in size, repertory, and prosperity. "A *bululú,*" wrote Rojas, "is a player who travels alone and afoot. He enters a village, goes to the curate, and tells him that he knows a *comedia* and a *loa* or two . . . he mounts upon a chest, and begins to recite, remarking as he goes on: 'Now the lady enters and says so-and-so,' and continues his acting while the curate passes round the hat. . . . A *raque* consists of two men; they enact an *entremes* or portions of an *auto* . . . they wear a beard of sheepskin, play a drum, and charge two *maravedis* . . . they contentedly sleep in their clothes, go barefoot, are always hungry, rid themselves of their fleas amid the grain in summer, and do not feel them in the winter on account of the cold." A *gangarilla* has three or four men, including a boy to play women's roles. They "borrow a woman's skirt and bonnet (which they sometimes forget to return). They play an *auto,* two comic *entremeses,* and charge four *maravedis.*" A *cambaleo* has five men and one woman who sings. "They have two *autos,* a *comedia,* and three or four *entremeses,* and a bundle of clothes that a spider could carry." They charge six *maravedis.* And so goes the list, adding players and plays, carts for chests, and donkeys to ride on, until Rojas arrives at the full *compañía.* Here he finds "every kind of grub and trumpery . . . very clever people among them, men much esteemed and persons well-born, and even very respectable women (for where there are many there must be all kinds). They take with them fifty *comedias,* more than 7000 pounds of luggage, sixteen persons who act, thirty who eat, one who takes money at the door (and God knows what he steals)."

PLAYS AT COURT AND IN SCHOOLS

Just as in Italy and England, some plays were written along classic lines, and were produced in palaces and universities. The first secular play of which we have a manuscript was in the Valencian tongue and staged in a Valencian palace in 1394. Sometimes the plays were in Spanish, sometimes in Latin, and sometimes they mixed the two languages. Translations of Greek tragedies appeared shortly after 1500. Certain universities required the students and faculty to produce two classic plays each year. The Jesuit colleges, as in Italy and France, used the drama for moral edification. But outside the palaces and the schoolrooms, there was no audience for plays patterned after the Greek and the Roman. The people preferred the followers of Encina, who wrote about contemporary life and followed the free form of the *comedia*.

It was at court that the scenic wonders of Italy first found lodging. In 1548, one of Ariosto's comedies was given in the royal palace at Valladolid to celebrate the wedding of a Spanish princess. The scenic display, done in true Italian fashion, so overwhelmed the man who wrote about the performance that he forgot to mention the name of the play. In the same year Philip II saw a comedy in Milan and, when he came to the throne in 1556, he brought an academician from Italy to produce Italian comedies at court. The king had spells of religious fanaticism, and in one of these—when he lay dying in 1598 —he suppressed the public theaters. Philip III imported Italian players as well as plays and scenic devices, and his queen, who was very fond of the drama, induced him to install a theater in the *alcázar*, or palace, in Madrid. *Autos sacramentales* were, of course, always welcome at court. Philip III engaged professional players to repeat before his courtiers the religious plays they had given publicly.

Philip IV, the last king of the "golden age," had a passionate love of the theater. During four months of his first year on the throne—he was only sixteen—he had forty-five plays presented at court, and between 1623 and 1654 about 300 *comedias*. Many of them were "command performances" by professional companies from all over Spain. He hired Italian architects to produce plays and spectacles in his royal gardens, with actors and audience floating on an artificial lake. In one extraordinary production he had the three acts of a *comedia* presented on separate aquatic stages, each by a different company. He spent as much as 500,000 *reales* on a single play. (It is hard to translate this amount into today's currency, but Cervantes tells us that a man could live—though probably not luxuriously—on a *real* and a half a day.) In 1632, when Philip IV built the palace called El Buen Retiro (The Good Retreat), he included in one of its halls a remarkable theater. When the scene was an exterior, an opening at the back of the stage turned the gardens of the palace into a far distant backdrop. Three years later he made Calderón, the last great playwright of the "golden age," the director of court performances.

THE COMMEDIA DELL'ARTE *IN SPAIN*

No one knows just when the ubiquitous comedians of the *commedia dell' arte* first reached Spain. As early as 1538 an Italian troupe was popular enough to be invited to appear in a Corpus Christi performance in the southernmost part of the country. This was in Seville, where Lope de Rueda was born and where he then lived. Rueda must have seen later Italian comedians before he left his work bench to become actor and playwright. Between 1538 and 1574, the next recorded date, these alien actors had won sufficient fame to be summoned to court. Alberto Ganassa—who was supposed to have created the character of Harlequin—appeared before Philip II. Shortly afterwards Ganassa and his company played at one of the public theaters that had opened during the past seven or eight years. The troupe gave performances in many other cities, both their own comedies and in the interludes of *autos sacramentales*. Speaking only Italian, but cannily emphasizing pantomime, they and their successors became so popular that in 1581 a censorious priest inveighed against "these foreigners who carry away many thousands of ducats from Spain every year." The effect of the Italian actors on both playwrights and actors was considerable.

PATIOS AND CORRALES—*THE FIRST PUBLIC THEATERS*

Until 1576 the actors of London put up their stages in innyards. In that year, when the manager of a company of players built the first public theater in England, he is supposed to have followed the pattern of the old innyards. It is important to note that Spain created playhouses rather like those in England, and it created them somewhat earlier.

During the sixteenth century, a good-sized house or inn in southern or eastern Spain was built around a *patio*. Like an English innyard, the *patio* was open to the sky; two or three galleries looked down upon it from all four sides, and there was a covered entry-way from the street. By putting a stage-platform against the inner end of a patio in an inn Malaga created a theater as early as 1520. Another appeared at Valenci by 1526, and a third in Seville by 1550.

In northern cities, where *patios* were unknown, the Spaniards made theaters out of courtyards formed by the backs of several houses. These hemmed-in spaces—usually filled with trash and refuse—were called *corrales*. By 1554, Valladolid had turned such a courtyard into a public theater. Barcelona did the same by 1560, Cordoba by 1565. Shortly after 1568 Madrid had five *corrales*. The word *corral* was soon applied to the *patio* playhouse of the south, and it gave way to *teatro* only after 1700 when Spain began to build Italianate opera houses.

In a typical *corral* of the sixteenth century, a broad stage without a front curtain stretched from one side of the courtyard to the other. The rooms and windows of the surrounding houses served as boxes for the more privileged spectators. The management rented the rooms, or the owners paid an annual fee for the exclusive use of these box seats. At the end of the *corral* opposite the stage a large upper room was set aside for women spectators, and was called—inelegantly—the *cazuela,* or stewpan. There were raised seats along the sides of the *corral* and in front of the stage. The "groundlings" stood in the remaining area. Because they were violently noisy in their applause and disapproval, they were called the "musketeers." (The violence of their disapprobation may be judged from Cervantes' boast in print: "I have written twenty or thirty plays, and they were all received without cucumbers or anything else that can be thrown.")

Because governmental authorities in Spain—as in France and England—made theatrical companies share their incomes with hospitals and charitable bodies, we know that at least six public playhouses were opened in as many Spanish cities between 1520 and 1568. As a matter of fact, the philanthropic institutions—*cofradias,* as they were called—actually controlled many of the theaters. We can't say that they built them, since these amusement places were at first merely *patios* and courtyards turned to a new use. But—and this is most important—these places were to be used for theatrical performances and nothing else, and they were gradually made over into a new and distinctive kind of theater where plays were staged very much as in Shakespeare's Globe. Moreover, whenever Spain built new public theaters, they all followed this same architectural pattern until after 1700.

THEATER MANAGEMENT IN SPAIN

As in London, the spectator paid a certain sum for general admission—unless, as sometimes happened, he could force his way in *gratis*—and, later, another and a larger fee for a seat on the benches or in the rooms above. Admission prices varied from time to time. When the court was in Madrid, they were higher than when the king was away. The theatergoer probably paid as much as he does today. In 1575 general admission was half a *real,* an armchair seat on the lower floor cost one *real* more, and a box seat six *reales.* A theater manager sometimes played the role of ticket speculator, and boosted the price of box seats to as much as thirty-two *reales.* By farming out the sale of the sixteenth-century equivalent of popcorn—fruit, water, and candy—the management added to its income. The playwright sold his work outright. The best got perhaps 300 *reales* for an *auto* and 550 *reales* for a *comedia.* He could live a year on the latter fee or buy ten donkeys. A new play was seldom given more than five or six performances in Madrid.

Performances took place in the afternoons. At first the theaters were open only on Sundays and feast days, later on Tuesdays and Thursdays also and sometimes on other days. But, between the interruptions of Lent, plagues, royal deaths, the heat of summer, and the rains of winter, hardly more than 200 performances could be given each year. Annoyed by the loss of business on rainy days, the Italian star Ganassa rebuilt Madrid's Corral de la Pacheca in 1574, adding a roof over the stage and the spectators' seats, and an awning over the area where the groundlings stood.

The next step in Madrid was the building by the *cofradias* of two permanent theaters, one in 1579 and one in 1583. In general they were much like the Corral de la Pacheca, but stairs were built to reach the galleries and boxes, and dressing rooms were provided back-stage. Gradually the older theaters in Madrid went out of existence. In the next few years playhouses were built in Toledo, Seville, Valencia, Granada, and Saragossa. The interior of a wooden structure in Seville—the Coliseo—had forty columns "with marble bases and capitals." It was rebuilt as a roofed structure in 1632, "holding between four and five thousand spectators, all of whom [by some architectural miracle] were equally able to see and hear." We can find no evidence that prosceniums and front curtains invaded the *corrales* of the "golden age." It is quite likely, of course, that they were used in the performances at court, for Philip III and Philip IV imported Italian architects to stage their shows. The only evidence, however, is rather late. The first public playhouse equipped like a modern theater may have been a temporary building in Madrid where an Italian company gave operas and *comedias* from about 1708 till 1719. On the same site, in 1738, a large opera house was completed under the guidance of the Italian diplomat from Parma, the Marchese di Scotti, and it opened with the opera *Armida Placita Demetrio*. The stage must surely have had a proscenium, a curtain, and all the other paraphernalia that Italian opera houses had been employing for a hundred years.

ACTORS, COSTUMES, AND SETTING

In many ways the theaters and the shows of Spain resembled those of England from 1580 to 1640. In many ways they did not. In London, boys always played women's parts until after the Restoration in 1660. As we have seen from Rojas' description of the Spanish companies, both boys and women appeared on the rude provincial stages. In Madrid, actresses were not licensed to appear in the public theaters until 1587. This official concession was forced by the competition of the Columbines of the *commedia dell'arte*. Thereafter women players became vastly popular. They invaded court performances, and under Philip IV they were almost worshipped. One of the best, "La Calderona," was the mistress of the king and the mother of his distinguished son, Don Juan of Austria, retiring at last to become the abbess of a convent.

Just as in London—and everywhere else until the end of the eighteenth century—the Spanish player wore on the stage the clothes of his own time. The only exception was when he played a Mohammedan in a historical drama, and even then the costuming could be sloppy. Lope de Vega complained that "the play of today is full of barbarous things: a Turk wearing the neck-gear of a Christian, and a Roman in tight breeches." Actresses wore breeches, too, whenever the playwright could manage it. Costumes grew more and more expensive as the "golden age" advanced. In 1636 an actor paid 3600 *reales* for a richly embroidered cloak.

If English theaters in the days of Elizabeth and James I followed the pattern now agreed on by most scholars, the *corrales* of Spain seem to have resembled them in their general arrangement, and their stages were used in much the same manner. They had no proscenium or drop-curtain. There were several doors for the actors to make their entrances, as well as a "trap" in the stage. A drapery hid or disclosed an inner stage at the rear. A gallery above provided a balcony or a parapet. There were curtains at the sides as well as the back, and these could be drawn away to reveal an object toward which characters in a play might be walking. There seem to have been crude "set pieces"—trees, for instance, painted on pasteboard or linen. But most changes of scene were accomplished, as at the Globe in London, by getting the actors off through one door, leaving the stage bare, and then bringing other actors on through a second door. Descriptive dialog helped out.

In Spain, the elaborate settings of the court performances may have invaded the theaters earlier than in England. In a prolog to a book of *comedias* published in 1622, Lope de Vega attacked scenery and machines through a dialog between a stranger and a character called Theater:

THEATER: Can't you see that I am injured? My arms and legs are broken. I am full of holes made by a thousand trap-doors and nails.
STRANGER: Who brought you to this miserable plight?
THEATER: The carpenters—at the orders of the theater managers. . . . The managers depend on machinery, the playwrights on the carpenters, and the spectators on their eyes.

It was this same de Vega who first said: "Give me four trestles, four boards, two actors, and a passion."

A SHOW OF INFINITE VARIETY

Compared with many performances at court and in the streets, productions in the earlier theaters must have looked pitifully bare and simple, but what the audiences listened to was the most complex sort of entertainment ever given in a public playhouse. First the musicians played. Then came a *loa*. It might be a simple monolog or, more likely, a skit in verse spoken or sung by two or more of the cast. After that came the first act, but sometimes there was a *paso* between the prolog and the play itself, or else a song and dance. Between the first act and the second and between the second act and the third, the audience enjoyed another *paso*, or *entremes*. These entr'act diversions might be supplemented by players who sang while they danced. And one of these *bailes*—as they called the dance numbers—ended the performance. The whole entertainment was probably as long as those interminable bills of our own Victorian stage that often included a tragedy, a short farce or ballet, a comedy or melodrama, and an epilog—and sometimes an "olio" of vaudeville turns.

CERVANTES, VEGA, AND CALDERÓN

It may seem extraordinary that the art of playwriting could flourish under such strange conditions. But the Spanish playwrights were extraordinary fellows. Most of them lived adventurously, and many of them transferred to the stage a good deal of the lustiness of their own lives.

Cervantes, the first notable playwright after Rueda, was both a soldier and a member of a holy order—like most of his fellows. He was wounded three times at the naval battle of Lepanto and lost the use of his right hand and arm. He spent five years in an Algerian prison, then fought in the Azores. Poverty dogged his heels and thrust him into jail. He joined the Franciscan order, and finished the last half of *Don Quixote* just before he died a poor man. Unfortunately, he gave more of his vitality to that great novel than to the thirty *comedias* and *entremeses* that he claimed he wrote. Compared with the work of Lope de Vega and Calderón, the plays of Cervantes—except perhaps for the *entremeses*—seem dry and formal.

The next important playwright, Lope de Vega, was as extraordinary in his plays as in his life, which is saying a good deal. He loved and lost wives, mistresses, and children. He sailed with the Spanish Armada and escaped its fate. For gun-wads he once used the same paper on which he had drafted poems to a fickle actress. Scurrilous verses about another lost-love and her whole family got him exiled from Madrid on pain of death. Within a few months, he had a son by a devoted wife, and another by an even more devoted mistress. When he was almost fifty, he joined a religious brotherhood. He continued to write plays and to have love affairs. But he did his religious devotions, scourged himself till the walls of his cell were spattered with blood, and helped burn a heretic priest at the stake.

Lope de Vega was the great inventor and pioneer of the "golden age" of Spanish drama. He shaped the final form of the *comedia* and gave it distinction. Instead of reworking the plots of others, he gave his rivals fresh stories to steal. One of his lighter plays, *Elacero de Madrid* (*Madrid Steel*), supplied Molière with the plot for *The Physician in Spite of Himself*. Sometimes, of course, Vega worked on old romances. He wrote historical pieces, including *The New World Discovered by Columbus*. Vega mixed tragedy with comedy and turned out the first social drama, *Fuente Ovejuna* (*The Sheep Well*). Like another of his plays, *El Alcalde de Zalamea* (*The Mayor of Zalamea*), it dealt sympathetically with the troubles of the lower classes.

Lope de Vega's output of plays was so enormous that Cervantes called him a "prodigy of nature." A year after his death in 1635, a Spanish writer credited him with 1800 *comedias* and over 400 *autos*, and we have records today of 431 of the secular plays. Lope said in print that "more than a hundred had passed from the Muses to the theater each in twenty-four hours."

In spite of Vega's fecundity, he seems to have maintained a high level of vigorous action and colorful romance, poetic effectiveness and rhetorical display. Like his audience, he was not interested in deep characterization. Somerset Maugham, in *Don Fernando,* gives us a key to the charm of the poetry that Lope wedded to his drama:

His plays . . . can best be appreciated if you look upon them as operatic "books" in which verse takes the place of music. He will write a bravura passage in which three persons, for instance, embroider upon an idea, each one ending his speech with the same refrain, so that you can almost hear the burst of applause that greets the ingenuity. Sometimes a character will present a theme in four lines and then enlarge upon it in stanzas each of which ends with one of the four lines. It is as much a set aria as "La Donna è mobile."

Calderón—last of many notable Spanish playwrights—conquered both court and populace. Knighted by Philip IV after he became director of the court performances, he was later made chaplain of honor to the king. Calderón served in three campaigns, died at eighty-one wealthy and esteemed, and left his fortune to the church for which he had written so many *autos.*

In his 200 *comedias* and *autos* Calderón borrowed freely from Lope de Vega and other playwrights, a theatrical habit of the Renaissance. The work of a truly religious man, his plays are distinguished by their high spiritual

The march of national drama. *The four chief dramatists of Spain, England, and France. The Spanish began earlier than the English, and continued longer.*

values, their sense of faith, as well as their lofty poetic quality. The modern world still admires Calderón's *La vida es sueño* (*Life Is a Dream*) and *El gran teatro del mundo* (*The Great World Theater*), as well as his own version of Vega's *The Mayor of Zalamea*, in which Calderón incorporated the theme of Vega's *The Sheep Well*. Goethe and Shelley wrote admiringly of Calderón. A number of his plays were translated by the German playwright Grillparzer and by Edward Fitzgerald, who immortalized *The Rubaiyat* of Omar Khayyam. In our own century, Max Reinhardt successfully produced *The Great World Theater* and also *La dama duende* as *Doña Diana*.

The originality of the Spanish drama is proved by its contribution of two great characters to the later theater of other lands. Guillén de Castro wrote a drama about a medieval hero of Spain which Corneille turned into *Le Cid*. Another playwright, Tirso de Molina, created the famous character of Don Juan. Writers in Italy, France, England, and the Netherlands translated or adapted many Spanish *comedias*.

SPAIN'S INSTINCT FOR DIALOG AND FREE FORM

There were two peculiarities about the writers of burgeoning Spain that made drama a natural form of expression and enabled it to be a truly popular art.

Spanish writers seem to have taken naturally to dialog. Even their novels —and Spaniards led in the development of this modern form of long narrative —relied heavily on conversation. *La tragicomedia de Calisto y Melibea* (commonly called *La Celestina* and published in 1499) seems like a long-drawn-out play. The "picaresque" novels of rascally adventure, starting in 1553, exploited dialog, and Don Quixote himself—as you may judge from the scene we have quoted—was fond of talking. Spoken drama was inevitable in Spain.

The Spanish playwright, like the Elizabethan, gained a great deal because he was free from the fetters of classical form. He ignored the unities of time and place, though he generally respected the unity of dramatic action. He never bowed before the idol of the five-act play. For a time he wrote in four acts, but soon he reduced his *comedias* to three. Cervantes claims the credit for this. Vega gives the distinction to his friend Cristobal Virués. In 1553 when Virués was not yet four years old, a playwright named Francisco de Avendaño wrote in three acts.

Our knowledge of the theater of Spain rests on the fortunate fact that its dramatists delighted to write about their craft. Many of these inveighed against the restrictions of the classic form. Tirso de Molina attacked the subject in his play *El vergonzoso en palacio*. Cervantes in the second act of *El rufian dichoso* has a character named Comedy tell Curiosity that she does not respect rules and there lies the only way to progress. Above all, Lope de Vega castigated the classic restrictions. Addressing in verse the learned Academy of Madrid in *The New Art of Writing Plays*, he said:

This subject seems easy, and it should be easy for any of you who have written few plays but know all about the art of writing them. I suffer from the disadvantage of having written them without any art. . . . When I have to write a play I lock up the [classical] precepts with six keys, and I banish Terence and Plautus from my study. . . . I know that, though they [my plays] might have been better if written in another manner, they would not have found the favor that they have enjoyed.

A FLOURISHING THEATER IN A RUINED NATION

The drama, says Maugham, "at no time and in no country has flourished so luxuriantly as in Spain during the hundred years that ended with Calderón's death." In 1681, when the last of the great playwrights died, Madrid had forty theaters. We know the names of over 2000 actors of the "golden age." Someone has estimated that 30,000 plays had been written and performed. Most of them must have been pretty poor by any standards, but many were distinguished, and some are now world-famous.

The story of the Spanish theater is all the more amazing because its drama mounted in vitality and importance as Spain sank. Playwriting began with the conquest of the New World. True drama developed, and better and more significant dramatists appeared even while Spain suffered from poverty and high prices at home, and while the wars in the Low Countries drained her dry. Thus, by a strange cultural lag, the stage and the fine arts increased in stature as the nation declined. In a ruined and hungry land—where a gallant gave his beloved presents of food instead of flowers—theaters multiplied and men like Lope de Vega and Calderón won immortality.

four

<hr>

The THEATER THAT
ELIZABETH I SUSTAINED

SHAKESPEARE CALLED ENGLAND "NEPTUNE'S PARK." "BOUND IN WITH THE triumphant seas," it found protection in "that water-walled bulwark." Many another Briton has hailed the isolation of this island kingdom. As a cold matter of fact, England's isolation has been relative rather than total. It has been merely convenient—in war and in the theater, too.

From 1600 to 1900 England spread an empire across the world. Before she took to the seas in global conquests, English bowmen had won the battle of Agincourt and Henry V, allied with Burgundy, had made himself heir to the French throne in 1420. Through the next hundred years of the Renaissance, English men of letters were visiting Italy, and Italian painters were attending court in London.

No, England was far from isolated. She knew the glories of the ancient world as she knew the glories of Agincourt. And for her scholars a most important part of the Revival of Learning was the revival of the classic drama. Yet England was so much England—so much a people living spiritually in its "other Eden"—that it could bring forth a very different thing, and a much better thing, than fake classicism. This was the unique playhouse of Burbage and the unique drama of Shakespeare.

RENAISSANCE STUDENTS PRODUCE PLAYS

England had heard as much as Spain or France about the concepts of the classic theater that existed in Renaissance Italy. The man who discovered the manuscript of Vitruvius was in England from 1422 to 1424. The man who translated the book into Italian came to London in 1548 to spend eighteen months as ambassador from the republic of Venice. Under Henry VII and Henry VIII, the English Crown employed at least nine Italian painters. Scholars and poets left England at that time to study humanism and the classics in Italy—many of them at the courts of Ferrara and Urbino where the theater flourished. What they learned in Italy brought playwriting and play-acting into the universities, the law schools, and even the schools for boys. The imitations of classic drama that they produced were shown at court.

The account books of King's College, Cambridge, show that something theatrical was going on there as early as 1482. There is the same kind of information from Magdalen College, Oxford, two years later. By 1512 the drama was so definitely a part of the curriculum that a certain student was granted a degree provided he wrote a comedy and a hundred songs in praise of the university a year after completing his studies. Cambridge went along with Oxford in believing that acting plays in Latin and Greek was an educational exercise. The 1546 statutes of Queen's College, Cambridge, required the performance of two comedies or tragedies in Greek each year; they set the time of production, and provided eight shillings and sixpence for expenses. A few years later Trinity College, Cambridge, required at least five plays a year. This attitude and practice continued into the seventeenth century. The young gentlemen who studied law at the Inns of Court in London also took to classic drama; they had long been required to study music and dancing, as well as divinity. As far back as 1526, the records of Gray's Inn list a "goodly disguising plaied." The classic drama also invaded the "grammar schools" of that time. We know that Eton spent money on two plays in 1525. The choir boys of St. Paul's played Terence's *Phormio* in 1528 for the king and Cardinal Wolsey. There are plentiful records of later performances.

Sometimes Elizabeth I journeyed to the schools and universities to see their productions, and visited the Inns of Court. Oftener the students and the young lawyers brought their plays to her palaces.

INTERLUDES BRING COMEDY AND INSTRUCTION

The Revival of Learning brought royal patronage to the interlude and developed a kind of comedy of admonition. At first, one-act pieces (that form a link between the Middle Ages and the Renaissance) were injected as comic relief in an otherwise serious play. Later they became a favorite form of relaxation between the courses of a state dinner. In 1493 Henry VII employed four men as the Players of the King's Interludes. Henry VIII increased the number to eight, while noblemen added similar troupes of players to their households. Instead of embracing the classical side of the Revival of Learning, the writers of interludes turned to humanism, and faced the new world rather than the old. Sometimes wisdom overshadowed wit. For instance, *Fulgens and Lucres,* an interlude of 1495 acted between courses at a feast in the great hall of Cardinal Morton, extolled the man who would "eschew idleness," who would devote his time to study, and who would promise his bride neither wealth nor ease, but "moderate riches, and that sufficient for us both."

Our knowledge of English drama in the early Renaissance is hampered by the fact that all but one play were never printed, and all but a few of their manuscripts have disappeared. We know, however, that John Heywood wrote a number of humanistic interludes that avoided allegory. The best liked appears to have been *The Play called the foure P. P.; a newe and a very mery enterlude of a palmer, a pardoner, a potycary, and a pedler,* and it was played at court in 1520. Generally known as *The Four P's,* the comedy had to do with a contest over who could tell the biggest lie, and the winner was the one who said he had never seen a woman out of temper.

Allegory, so popular in the morality plays of the Middle Ages, sometimes added instruction to comedy. Most of the plays were probably written for students to present in their schools or at court. *The Nature of the Four Elements* dramatized new discoveries in science and geography. *Wit and Science,* presented by the boys of St. Paul's in 1530, showed its student-hero courting Lady Science, overcoming the monster Tediousness, and taking part in a burlesque spelling lesson. Interludes, like morality plays, were always in the native tongue.

UNIVERSITY MEN BEGIN TO WRITE PLAYS IN ENGLISH

Even in the schools, England spent less time than Italy or France on exercises in classic dramaturgy. After adapting classic dramas and writing original plays in Greek and Latin, the schoolmasters and students turned to English. They clung to the proper academic form and borrowed a few characters from Terence or Plautus, but their plots and their dialog were original and thoroughly English. *Ralph Roister Doister,* written about 1553 by Nicholas Udall, who had taught at both Eaton and Winchester, and *Gammer Gurton's Needle,* produced a little later at Cambridge and credited to "Mr. S. M[aste]r of Art," are the earliest examples of native English comedy. Though the latter is written in rhymed doggerel, we can still produce and enjoy the comedy of the servant who finds an old woman's lost needle only by sitting down in the breeches she had mended with it.

Tragedy had a harder time than comedy in escaping from the bonds of Latin speech and classic themes and form. It is not till about 1560 that we have any record of a full-length tragedy in the English tongue. This play, *Gorboduc, or Ferrex and Porrex,* stuck fast to the rules of classic dramaturgy, but, besides using the language of the day, it substituted for the heroes of Greece and Rome mythical figures out of English history. In spite of its high success in school and court, and in spite of the imitations that followed, the play that hid a Latin form in the clothing of English speech never won acclaim with the populace and their professional players. Many academic scholars went right on translating Seneca and writing new plays in Latin until the coming of Shakespeare and his fellows.

Gorboduc is a very dull play in spite of a most violent plot. The younger son of a king kills his brother; his mother kills the son; the people rise in revolt and murder the king and queen; the nobles annihilate the rebels and then quarrel and slay one another over the succession to the crown. The authors—two young lawyers named Thomas Sackville and Thomas Norton —managed to make all this action tedious by talking it to death. They stuck to the classic rule that violence must happen off-stage, and they told about it through messengers with speeches running as long as a hundred lines.

Yet this dreary and gruesome contribution to a Christmas feast at one of the Inns of Court gave the Elizabethan stage something more than a tragedy written for the first time in the language of the people. It introduced blank verse to the stage. Hitherto, the poetry of Latin tragedy had been beaten out seven bars to the line—an even more awkward rhythm for dialog than the French alexandrine of six feet. Sackville and Norton had found their meter in the Earl of Surrey's translation of *The Aeneid,* published three years before. They used it stiffly and awkwardly, however, without any of the easy fluency that made blank verse the perfect form for poetic dialog in English. They missed Marlowe's "mighty line" and the lyric freedom of Shakespeare, but, at least, they showed the English playwright the road to dramatic poetry.

The other innovation of Sackville and Norton was a dubious one. They revived the "dumb show" used in the interludes of Renaissance Italy. In *Gorboduc* the action of the dumb show was symbolic: "first the music of hautboys began to play, during which time there came forth from under the stage, as though out of hell, three furies. . . . Hereby was signified the unnatural murders to follow." Subsequent Elizabethan playwrights—with whom the dumb show became unduly popular—showed in pantomime the same action that was later to be played with dialog. By the time of Shakespeare, the dumb show had lost its popularity; he used it only once, in the play-within-the-play of *Hamlet.*

PLAYS ACTED BY CHILDREN FOR COURT AND PUBLIC

The court's own contribution to Elizabethan drama was a curious one. But, then, it was a curious court. The nobles were eager and sensitive, as well as strong-mettled. Elizabeth I may have been a virgin, but she was no prude. You might expect from such folk a fondness for *Gammer Gurton's Needle* or, like Polonius, a "tale of bawdry." And ultimately, they did go for low comedy and high, for blood and thunder, for patriotic histories, and for everything else of vitality that the public theaters came to offer after the opening of Burbage's first playhouse in 1576. But in the earlier years of Elizabeth's reign, her courtiers had to look elsewhere for the refinements of dramatic art. Rather like some nouveaux-riches of our own time, they were out for culture. Face to face with the ambassadors of France, Spain, and Italy and their households of painters and poets, the English nobles wanted to be taught the refinements of life and literature, knightly chivalry and courtly love.

The royal troupe of interlude players developed by Henry VIII was pathetically short on refinement and sophistication; so it fell into disfavor in the second year of Elizabeth's reign, and never again appeared at court. There were a few refined and refining plays to be seen at the schools for lawyers. In 1566, Gray's Inn produced the second poetic tragedy in English, George Gascoigne's *Jocasta*, and also his comedy in English prose, adapted from Ariosto's *I Suppositi* under the awkward title of *The Supposes*. But, between 1558 and 1584, Elizabeth and her court mainly relied for the finer things of life—in terms of the drama—on a very different and a very curious kind of theater. This was the performance of mature plays by companies of young boys. They were the Children of the Chapel Royal, the Children of Windsor, and the Children of St. Paul's.

For many, many years, these youngsters had been merely choristers, but in the first quarter of the sixteenth century the Children of the Chapel began to act interludes at court. During Elizabeth's reign these boys, who were supposed to be giving all their time to musical studies and the three R's, took to play-acting with a vengeance. Along with the students of Eton and Westminster, the choristers gave far more plays at court than did adult actors. This peculiar mania for juvenile performances spread outside the court. When Burbage opened his first playhouse in 1576, Richard Farrant, Master of the Children of Windsor, took over a hall in what had been the Blackfriars Priory, and installed a company of boys to give public performances in what was called a "private" theater. Drawn at various times from Windsor, the Chapel, and St. Paul's, the lads gave the professional players serious competition from 1576 to 1584 and for the first fifteen years of the next century. During the latter period, Ben Jonson and other popular dramatists wrote plays for the children to produce.

The children of the Chapel played their part in turning the drama away from the classic form and toward the free-and-easy technique of Shakespeare's day. Richard Edwardes, the Master of the Children in 1564, was a playwright as well as a musician. So it was natural that, after he set the boys to acting other men's plays at court and in the lawyer's inns, he should produce one of his own. In the first of these, *Damon and Pythias*, a child-actor spoke a prolog in which Edwardes explained how necessary it was to blend comedy with tragedy. From the classical point of view, this was a heinous offence, but it became the heart of the later Elizabethan drama. The public flocked to *Cambyses,* a play that could be billed as "A lamentable tragedy mixed full of pleasant mirth." In *Hamlet* Shakespeare did not hesitate to place the comic scene of the grave-diggers just before Ophelia's funeral. John Lyly, a court playwright who served the children, wrote in stylized and precious prose, but he mixed comedy and tragedy, treated mythological characters romantically, and paid no attention at all to the unities of time and place. By 1588, when his *Endymion* was produced before the queen by the choir boys of St. Paul's, the court was going to the public theaters to see violent plays like Marlowe's *Tamburlaine* and Thomas Kyd's *The Spanish Tragedy.*

PROFESSIONAL PLAYERS AND THEIR EARLY PLAYS

While choir boys and school boys, students at the universities and lawyers at the Inns of Court, were producing plays, the professional actors were far from idle. On village greens and in banquet halls and inn yards they were giving shows that may have been crude at times, but that were usually popular. Some of the troupes may have danced and juggled better than they acted, but others must have had true skill. There were the players attached to such noble households as those of the Earls of Essex, Leicester, Derby, Worcester, and Warwick, and Lords Effingham, Hunsdon, and Clinton. The names of many of these actors are known, for they went on to play in the London inns and playhouses. Among them is James Burbage, who built the first theater and begat Richard, the best actor in Shakespeare's plays.

We know the titles of only a few of the plays that these companies acted in the provinces, and only a little more about the repertory of the London theaters before 1587. Around the middle of the century, touring troupes were still playing mysteries and moralities and John Heywood's interludes in the villages, the castles, and the city inns. They also gave *Ralph Roister Doister, Gammer Gurton's Needle,* and probably *Gorboduc.* Such fare, along with the comedy-drama *Cambyses* and farces padded out with song and dance, served the London playhouses until Christopher Marlowe came down from Cambridge to make English drama eloquent.

Another kind of play made its appearance before Elizabeth I ascended the throne, and it became extremely popular in the 1590's. This was the chronicle play. The first that we know about was *Kynge Johan,* produced in 1538 by its author, John Bale. A Catholic priest who turned Protestant, he wrote for his own touring company a number of pieces which twisted history to serve his new-found convictions. Other men wrote other chronicle plays—changing history to suit the stage and to show rulers less admirable than their Elizabeth. These dramas fed on English patriotism and particularly on the awakened sense of national power that grew out of England's "cold war" with Spain. Victory over the Spanish Armada in 1588 spurred on the playwrights. From the '80's we have about a dozen chronicle plays. In the '90's nearly eighty were produced. It was in those ten years that playwrights of skill and resource came to the London theater. Shakespeare probably began his work with *Henry VI* and *Richard III* between 1591 and 1593.

SUDDENLY—A GREAT THEATER AND GREAT DRAMA

During the last half of Queen Elizabeth's reign some quite extraordinary things happened to the English theater in an extraordinarily short length of time. First of all, in 1576 James Burbage designed and built a new kind of playhouse. In 1587 the first great playwright appeared—Christopher Marlowe with his *Tamburlaine*. Within fifteen years, London saw Shakespeare's *Richard III, The Taming of the Shrew, Romeo and Juliet, A Midsummer Night's Dream, Julius Caesar* and *Hamlet*. Before Elizabeth died, in 1603, the work of ten dramatists of stature had reached the stage. Five more, who were born in her reign, saw their plays done under James I. In a quarter of a century the English drama grew to full maturity.

Court and school contributed to the high distinction of the Elizabethan drama. The queen and her nobles accepted Shakespeare and his fellows with the same enthusiasm as the common people. The courtiers flocked to the theaters, and Elizabeth, who couldn't go to the public playhouses, saw the plays at court or in the lawyers' inns. The seats of higher learning contributed playwrights. Two-thirds of the dramatists—Shakespeare and Ben Jonson were the outstanding exceptions—had studied at Oxford or Cambridge. Some of the best of them turned actors. Almost all forgot their studies of the classic drama, and wrote freely and vitally.

MARLOWE LEADS THE WAY

Like many an Elizabethan playwright, Marlowe had a violent life and a short one. Son of a shoemaker yet a master of arts at Cambridge, he died in a tavern brawl before he was thirty. Rash and rebellious, a drunkard and a free-thinker, he left us characters and dialog as fiery, intense, and passionate as himself. The few plays that he wrote in his five short years of work may be uneven, but they scale the heights of poetic drama, and they opened the way for Shakespeare. Marlowe made blank verse a new, fluent, and powerful tool for the creation of true poetic tragedy. In a single play, *Doctor Faustus*, he brought splendor to the English stage. Here was lyricism at its peak:

> Was this the face that launched a thousand ships,
> And burnt the topless towers of Ilium?
> Sweet Helen, make me immortal with a kiss! . . .
> O thou art fairer than the evening air
> Clad in the beauty of a thousand stars!

True to the character of his Faust, the sceptic-playwright gave him these magnificent lines as the man faced damnation:

The stars still move, time runs, the clock will strike,
The devil will come, and Faustus must be damn'd.
Oh, I'll leap up to my God!—Who pulls me down?—
See, see, where Christ's blood streams in the firmament!
One drop would save my soul, half a drop: ah, my Christ.

SEVEN MORE ELIZABETHANS

No university man, Thomas Kyd shared Marlowe's violence as well as "vile heretical conceits denying the divinity of Jesus Christ." For this he was arrested and put to the torture. Released from prison, he was dismissed from the theatrical company of his patron, and died in poverty when not yet thirty-six. Before or about the time of *Doctor Faustus*, the "sporting Kyd"—as Ben Jonson called him—wrote *The Spanish Tragedy*. It was the first of a long series of "revenge plays" in which ghostly visitations promoted and punished violence. Shakespeare wrote several, including *Richard III*, *Titus Andronicus*, and *Hamlet*. Later came John Marston's *Antonio's Revenge*, George Chapman's *The Revenge of Bussy D'Ambois*, Philip Massinger's *The Roman Actor*, and one that has been revived in the twentieth century, John Webster's *The Duchess of Malfi*. Though *The Spanish Tragedy* was stiffly written, this harrowing play was the most popular and influential tragedy of Elizabethan times. Samuel Pepys, the Restoration diarist, saw it as late as 1668. It was played in Germany and Holland throughout the seventeenth century.

Robert Greene came down from Oxford about 1588, after deserting a wife and "having spent up the marriage-money which I obtained by her." He lived riotously and died at thirty-four after "a surfeit of pickle herringe and Rennish wine." Three times he published pamphlets repenting his sins, and in the last he attacked Shakespeare as "an upstart Crow, beautified with our feathers . . . in his owne conceit the onely Shake-scene in a countrie." Yet he had skill in humor and poetry, his novel *Pandosto* gave Shakespeare the plot for *The Winter's Tale*, and Greene's romantic comedy *The Honorable History of Friar Bacon and Friar Bungay* set a style and was still being played as late as 1630.

An Oxford graduate, George Peele lived till almost forty in spite of being dissolute and improvident. His good humor and his fresh skill in verse made his *The Old Wives' Tale* a success, and he wrote in *Edward I* one of the best of the chronicle plays that competed with those of Shakespeare.

Thomas Dekker and Thomas Heywood—not John, the writer of interludes —lived into their sixties and seventies, but left few more printed plays than the others. They were both victims of collaboration. When Heywood wasn't acting, he had what he called "either an entire hand or at least a main finger" in 220 plays, and Dekker was a "dresser," or play-doctor. Though Dekker was usually poor and spent six years in prison for debt, he had kindliness and charm and "poetry enough for anything"—as may be seen in his *The Shoemaker's Holiday*. Written in 1599, it is still revived occasionally in our universities. Heywood's fame rests—and rather securely—on a single play, *A Woman Killed with Kindness*. Produced in 1603 and dealing with contemporary people, it is the first middle-class tragedy.

BEN JONSON—SHAKESPEARE'S CLOSEST RIVAL

"Rare Ben Jonson"—another exception to the Elizabethan rule that good playwrights die young—all but bridged the time from Shakespeare's beginnings to the closing of the theaters by the Puritans in 1642. He wrote plays for a company of children at Blackfriars, and court masques for the scenic specialist Inigo Jones. Between 1605 and 1610 he did his best work for the theater in *Volpone, Bartholomew Fair, Epicoene, or the Silent Woman,* and *The Alchemist*.

Ben Jonson lived a varied life. For a time he was a bricklayer, and then a soldier in the Netherlands. He began in the theater as a poorish actor, but became a good coach, as well as an outstanding dramatist. His career was eventful and his mind disputatious. He killed an actor in a duel, served a short sentence, and was branded on the thumb. He was briefly imprisoned twice more for plays that met with official disfavor. In one case—an affront

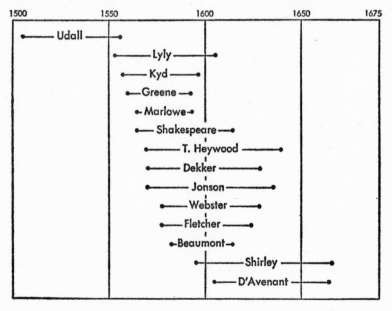

From school comedy to court masque. *The chief playwrights who lived from the time of Elizabeth I into that of James I died before the closing of the theaters in 1642. The years of the Commonwealth retarded playwriting for a generation.*

to the Scots—in which he only figured as a minor collaborator, he "voluntar-
ily imprisoned himself" when he might have escaped. This argues that his
attacks on other playwrights were neither malicious nor self-seeking. His
attitude toward his friend Shakespeare is typical. After the dramatist's
death, Jonson wrote to a Scottish poet that Shakespeare "wanted Arte."
When someone said that the author of *Hamlet* had never blotted (erased)
a line, Jonson said, "would he had blotted a thousand." Yet he wrote, "[I]
lov'd the man, and do honor his memory (on this side of idolatry) as much
as any." And in a poem that he composed for the Shakespeare folio edition
of 1623, Ben Jonson said, with rare divination: "He was not of an age, but
for all time!"

Through a grant from James I, Jonson became in all but title the poet
laureate of England. The honor might have gone equally well to George
Chapman. At the end of the sixteenth century he wrote for the public
theater, and in the next ten years for the children of Blackfriars and St.
Paul's—including the horrific revenge play, *Bussy D'Ambois*—but his fame
has rested for more than a century on Keats's sonnet celebrating Chapman's
translation of Homer.

JACOBEAN COLLABORATORS

The playwrights who wrote after the accession of James I in 1603 were
often skilful and polished, but they seldom showed the vitality and imagination of Shakespeare and certain other Elizabethan playwrights. Perhaps the
habit of collaboration—supported and enforced by a commercial manager,
Philip Henslowe—partly accounts for this. Certainly John Webster wrote
without assistance the best poetic tragedy since Shakespeare, *The Duchess
of Malfi*, and Philip Massinger was solely responsible for the best comedy,
A New Way to Pay Old Debts. The most successful collaboration was between Francis Beaumont and John Fletcher, with their *Philaster* of 1610 and
their *The Maid's Tragedy* of 1611, yet Beaumont wrote a better play, *The
Knight of the Burning Pestle*, before he began to collaborate with Fletcher
about 1608.

The evils of collaboration go beyond the matter of aesthetics. Because
so many men worked together openly or covertly on so many plays, credit
for authorship is often confused. Fletcher is an excellent example. Some say
he wrote five or six plays by himself; one authority gives him fifty-three.
Certain scholars believe he collaborated with Shakespeare on *The Two Noble
Kinsmen, Henry VIII,* and a lost play called *Cardenio*. Others send Philip
Massinger down to Stratford to help out the retired playwright after he had
exhausted himself over *The Winter's Tale* and *The Tempest*.

SHAKESPEARE—MAN OF MYSTERY

Shakespeare needed no collaborators. He had genius enough for two. Furthermore, as you will see later, he had the financial security and the aesthetic

freedom that came from being a partner, as well as an actor, in the most successful theater and the most successful company of players in London.

We know very little about the professional careers as well as the personal lives of many Elizabethan playwrights. Some died young. Some had only fleeting popularity. We know a good deal, however, about men of that time who lived as long as Shakespeare—fifty-two years—and had anything remotely approaching his success. Ben Jonson is a case in point. We know much more about his life than we do about Shakespeare's. This is only partly due to Jonson's getting into difficulties with the authorities, and borrowing money from manager Henslowe, who kept careful records. In the main, we know Jonson's life in considerable detail because of comments by his contemporaries, and because of the pamphlets he wrote and prefaces he prepared for his published plays. Shakespeare was curiously neglected by his friends, and curiously mum on his own part. He put forth no pamphlets and he wrote no prefaces for the two long poems or the eighteen plays that were published in his life time.

The life of the greatest dramatist of the Christian era is one of the most startling and provocative mysteries of literature. We know that he was born in 1564, and we suppose that he had a grammar school education in Stratford-on-Avon. At eighteen he married Anne Hathaway, a woman eight years his senior. His daughter by Anne was born half a year later, and twins arrived in 1585. He seems to have deserted his family at about this time, and disappeared. We know nothing more about him until 1592. Then, suddenly, he was prominent enough as an actor for Greene to call him "an upstart Crow," and a "Shake-scene." His first play, *Henry VI*, had reached the stage, for Greene parodied one of its lines—"O Tygers heart, wrappt in a womans hide!"—by writing of Shakespeare's "Tygers hart wrapt in a Players hyde." We can guess that this play and *Titus Andronicus* were acted by Lord Strange's men, just as we can surmise that Shakespeare saw the players of the Earls of Pembroke, Sussex, and Leicester perform in Stratford, or that he acted for Strange and for Leicester during the "lost years." In 1593 he published the poem *Venus and Adonis*, and the next year another one, *The Rape of Lucrece*. We know he joined the Lord Chamberlain's company in 1594, for official records show that he was among those paid for acting at court as one of the Chamberlain's "servantes" on December twenty-sixth and twenty-seventh. The next night *The Comedy of Errors* was presented at Gray's Inn.

Between 1594 and 1616 a little more than fifty mentions of the name of Shakespeare occur in print or in written records. No less than twenty-seven have to do with law suits or business matters, and six with close relatives. In a few cases he is mentioned as an actor in a play. There are three references to his owning a share in the profits of the Globe Theater and of Blackfriars. With one exception critical comments by his contemporaries are, as one authority puts it, "generally brief and either affected or conventional." We have no other facts on his personal life except some allusions to where he lived, two wills in his favor, his own will, and his death and burial.

The slight information that we have on Shakespeare's life and the dates of his plays has been gained by elaborately detailed studies pursued by a large number of scholars during the last two centuries. They have each played the role of a literary Sherlock Holmes.

THE PUBLISHING OF SHAKESPEARE'S PLAYS

No handwriting of Shakespeare's exists except for six signatures. These show four different spellings, and not one includes the "e" in "Shake." His name doesn't appear on the first six of his plays that were printed and published. After 1597, however, eight first editions bear his name. Oddly enough it is spelled either "Shake-speare" or "Shakespeare." Attracted by the martial glamor of a flourished weapon, printers or publishers gave the spelling "Shakespeare" to posterity.

They gave more than the spelling, of course. They preserved thirty-seven of his plays. Very few manuscripts exist of plays acted in London during the time of Elizabeth I, James I, and Charles I, and not too many dramas were printed. Of the 220 collaborations that Thomas Heywood boasted about, only one got into print. About 550 plays were published between 1559 and 1642, but one authority has calculated that almost 1500 were lost in manuscript through carelessness, or destroyed in theater fires. The reason that so few plays were published between the accession of Elizabeth I and the closing of the theaters was because the author sold all rights to an acting company, and the acting company sold a manuscript to a publisher only when its need for money was greater than its fear that a rival would pirate a play once it was in print. Authorities believe that some plays were stolen by the publishers through buying "parts" from actors, through paying them to recite the play from memory, or through having employees write down the dialog in shorthand. Copyright meant no more than that you could produce any play if you had a copy of the manuscript.

Among the eighteen plays published during Shakespeare's lifetime was *Pericles,* which is thought to be a collaboration. Another appeared in 1622. We should have only about half of his now known plays if two friends and fellow-actors, John Heminge and Henry Condell, had not gathered together all existing manuscripts and printed plays, and edited for publication in 1623 *The Workes of William Shakespeare.* This volume is called the First Folio. It is a "folio" because the standard sheet of printing paper was folded once, producing a page about thirteen and a half by eight and a half inches. The plays first published during Shakespeare's life—and published singly—are called quartos because the paper was folded twice—or quartered—producing a page about eight by six inches. The texts of some of the quartos are close to those in the folios—there were four folios printed between 1623 and 1685 —and some of the speeches in the quartos are better. But a number of these first editions are called "bad quartos," and were justly described by Heminge and Condell as "diverse stolne and surreptitious copies, maimed, and deformed by frauds and stealthes of injurious impostores." The thirty-six plays in the First Folio form the Shakespearean Canon, a parallel to the Church Canon of the accepted books of the Bible. The Third Folio added *Pericles* and six certainly spurious plays. *The Two Noble Kinsmen* was never given folio publication, but appeared as a quarto almost twenty years after Shakespeare's death.

SHAKESPEARE'S PROSPERITY

In Shakespeare's time no man could live by playwriting alone. Plays were sold outright for £6 or £8, which meant no more than $180 to $240 in the currency of today. Some playwrights may have received the profits from the second or third performances of their plays, but this can't have amounted to very much. The total income that Shakespeare received from the sale of his plays, spread over a little more than twenty years, was probably only about £300, or less than $10,000 in our money. Because of Burbage's liberality toward his most valuable associates, Shakespeare had, for many years, not only his salary as a player, but also a player's share in the profits, and, after 1599, he had an additional share as one of the ten owners of the Globe.

Shakespeare's financial security saved him from writing innumerable potboilers and collaborating or "dressing" other men's plays. Though many of his fellows wrote far more plays a year, Shakespeare's annual output of almost two plays each season, while he was with Burbage, is an impressive one by modern standards. He was able to do this by a kind of indirect collaboration with the historians, novelists, and playwrights of the past. He took large parts of his plots from older works. All but two of his plays have been traced to other sources than his own fertile mind.

Far more important, Shakespeare's secure position with Burbage's company saved him from the temptation to follow popular trends too closely, or to repeat his own successes. He may have written *The Merchant of Venice* —which uses material from two or three earlier works—because of the anti-semitism aroused by the trial and execution of a Jewish physician who was accused of trying to poison Elizabeth. He wrote "revenge plays" in *Richard III* and *Titus Andronicus*, but in between them came *The Comedy of Errors,* adapted from Plautus. *Much Ado About Nothing* and *Henry V* shared the same year. So did *Twelfth Night* and *Hamlet*.

THE ELIZABETHAN PLAYWRIGHTS IGNORE
CLASSIC RULES

The first great step forward for the Elizabethan drama was the designing and building of the unique Theater by James Burbage in 1576 and its companion, The Curtain, by another man the next year. They gave the playwrights a form of stage that suited their current needs, and led their successors to splendid new fecundity. A decade later came the first flowering in Marlowe's *Tamburlaine* and *Doctor Faustus*. Another ten years brought the full fruit of Shakespeare's plays from *Richard III* and *A Midsummer Night's Dream* to *Twelfth Night* and *Hamlet*. No dramatic era ever showed such swift, extraordinary progress.

While Shakespeare was still in Stratford, Elizabethan playwrights had broken with academic tradition. Like Lope de Vega, they had turned their backs on the classic unities and the dictums of Aristotle and Horace. In 1580 Sir Philip Sidney, poet, courtier, and critic, grieved over violations of the classic forms. If he had lived another five years, what would he have said of Shakespeare and his fellows—unless their poetry and power could have overwhelmed him? In Sidney's opinion, tedious *Gorboduc* climbed "to the heights of Seneca his style," and reached "the very end of Poesy." Yet he regretted that it was not "an exact model of all Tragedies. For it is faulty in both Time and Place, the two necessary companions of all corporal actions."

The Elizabethan dramatist not only forgot the unities. Unlike the authors of *Gorboduc*, he showed violent action on the stage, instead of merely talking about it. His violence approached atrocity; in *King Lear* Shakespeare showed the blinding of a man. Like the others, Shakespeare wrote what Sidney had called "neither right tragedy nor right comedy, mingling kings and clowns." Moreover, he mixed poetry and prose, and ignored the rule that verse should be reserved for the nobility and prose for the lowly. In *Twelfth Night* sea captains spoke blank verse, and the Countess Olivia descended to prose. Brutus delivered Caesar's funeral oration without benefit of meter, and Hamlet did likewise in his advice to the players. Half a dozen of Shakespeare's comedies have more lines of prose than of poetry.

FAULTS OF THE TIMES

The Elizabethan playwright was fond of some devices of an older stage that seem absurd or cumbersome today, but Shakespeare used them less—or better—than the other writers. He usually relegated the sub-plot to his comedies. To introduce a play or to bridge gaps of time, Shakespeare sometimes used the Prolog, Induction, or Chorus that seems to have come over from an Italian misconception of Greek tragedy. In *Henry V*, Chorus is a long but sturdy bridge of narrative and exhortation leading from one act to another. The speaker called Chorus in *Romeo and Juliet* bunglingly betrays the plot, but in only two places—before the first act and the second. (Modern producers often drop these speeches.) There are only three other Shakespearean Prologs. Shakespeare was chary of another device—the Epilog. He used only eight, none in his tragedies. One other feature of the Elizabethan theater that would seem absurd to present-day audiences was the "jig." A short song and dance probably closed even the performance of Shakespeare's plays—just as it did the shows in Spain. A Continental visitor to London saw a play about Julius Caesar, which may well have been Shakespeare's, and wrote: "At the end of the play two of the actors in men's clothes and 2 in women's clothes performed a dance, as is their custom, wonderfully well together." (Perhaps Shakespeare had objected to a song.)

The weaknesses of Shakespeare—beyond every playwright's normal chance of failure—were the weaknesses of his time and his audience. Elizabethan England loved allegory as much as violence, long-drawn philosophizing as much as soaring poetry. Too often, issues were all black and white, and characters either good or bad. Love at first sight seemed no more implausible than last-minute conversions with the good man turning to evil or the evil man to good. Audiences accepted magical potions as well as disguises that any child would see through. They were content with types instead of characters. It is to the great credit of Shakespeare that he gave us human beings like Hamlet, Henry V, and Catherine of France, Falstaff and Malvolio, Beatrice and Benedick, Richard II and Portia, Marc Antony and Brutus.

Now we must turn from dramatic literature to business, from playwriting to theater-building and theater-management. But we must consider, first of all, how the pleasure-loving authorities of the court fought for the theaters and their managers against the somewhat puritanical authorities of the City of London.

COURT AGAINST CITY OVER THE THEATERS

The city fathers began with a legitimate grievance. Whether the plays were given in innyards or in regular theaters, the crowds invited thievery. There were small riots, and the authorities were certain that, in this time of tension between the dominant Protestants and the suppressed Catholics, sedition flourished. Worse still, when the plague threatened London—as it did a good deal of the time—the gathering together of even small crowds helped spread infection. The Puritans had moral objections. A writer called actors "crocodiles which devour the pure chastity both of single and married persons." Their plays teach "all things that appertain to craft, mischief, deceits, and filthiness." "Whosoever shall visit the chapel of Satan, I mean the Theater, shall find there no want of young ruffians." Women cannot come from plays "with safe and chaste minds." Men in the audience "give them pippins, they dally with their garments."

With this, queen and court couldn't agree. They liked plays, and some were patrons of acting companies. So Elizabeth and her Privy Council fought back. In 1574 the queen won the first round by licensing a company called The Earl of Leicester's Men to play "within oure Citie of London" except during common prayer or the plague. The city acquiesced but inveighed against "eavell practises of incontinencye in great Inns havinge chambers and secrete places adjoyninge to their open stagies and gallyries,

inveglynge and alleur of maides." The city set up some rather mild regulations, but the net result was the building of playhouses outside the jurisdic-
tion of the city; at first they were to the north but later south of the Thames
in Bankside. For twenty years after Burbage built The Theater, the fight
between court and city continued, the queen going so far as to create her own
company. The conflict was highlighted by the closing down of the theater-
inns at certain times, by new regulations coming from both city and court,
and by the shuttering of the outlying theaters during plagues, as well as at
least once during normal times by order of the Privy Council.

The grim reality of the plague stands out in a city regulation of 1584 permitting the theaters to reopen only after the number of deaths in London—a
city of 200,000—had fallen below fifty a day for twenty straight days. The
plague closed the theaters almost all the time between January, 1593, and
the spring of the next year. This disaster forced the Strange-Derby company
to join the Admiral's Men under Alleyn and Henslowe in a touring venture.
After the plague was over, this joint company played a short engagement at
Newington Butts and then split up. Alleyn and the Admiral's Men went to
Henslowe's house, the Rose. When Derby died, his players found a new
patron in Henry Lord Hunsdon, became the Chamberlain's Men, moved to
The Theater, and acquired William Shakespeare and Richard Burbage.
Without the plague this great company might never have been formed.

CENSORSHIP AND MONOPOLY BEGIN

Regulations set up by the queen's Privy Council brought censorship to the
English stage—where it still exists—and also a kind of monopoly.

To overrule the city, a royal patent of 1581 centered all stage authority
in the Master of the Revels. This functionary in the office of the Lord
Chamberlain had long had the task of providing plays and other amusements
for the court. Now he was given national control over "showes, plaies, plaiers
and play-makers, together with their playing places, to order and reforme,
auctorise and put downe." This meant that all plays had to be approved
before production. Censorship was stricter on political matters than on moral.
In the light of their day plays were far cleaner than might have been ex-
pected. Adultery was a rare theme in comedy. In 1606 "An Acte to Restraine
Abuses of Players" was passed to curb blasphemy. One of its results was
that the First Folio of 1623 changed a speech of Shakespeare's merry Mistress Page from "what the devil" to "what the dickens."

Monopoly began in 1598 when the Privy Council ordered the companies
cut down to two—the Admiral's and the Chamberlain's. Others continued,
however, and within four years Worcester's Men were officially licensed.
James I took a firmer stand. He closed all but those under the patronage of
him and his family. The London stage was to suffer still more from such
restrictions in the eighteenth century.

THEATER-BUILDERS AND THEATER-MANAGERS

After Shakespeare and Marlowe—and far, far ahead of the earls and chamberlains and admirals who lent their patronage to the poor players— we must recognize James Burbage, carpenter-actor, and Philip Henslowe, speculator in almost anything, as the men to whom the Elizabethan drama owes its greatest debt. Close after them come Burbage's two sons, Richard, the actor, and Cuthbert, the business manager, and Henslowe's son-in-law, Edward Alleyn, who shared honors with Richard Burbage as Elizabeth's foremost player.

James Burbage was the pioneer. In 1576, when Shakespeare was barely twelve, this man built the first public playhouse in England. Not without right, he called it simply The Theater. His example inspired the building of the next theater, a year or so later, close by in Shoreditch, a northeast section of London. This theater—called The Curtain because it was built on a piece of land variously known as Curten Close and Courtein—produced some of the plays of Burbage's actor-dramatist, William Shakespeare, for Burbage once had an agreement to pool the profits of the two houses. In 1599 —two years after Burbage's death—the lease expired on the ground where The Theater was built, and Burbage's sons tore down the structure and used the lumber to build the famous Globe in the district called Bankside, south of the Thames. Later, in order to have a second playhouse—this one pro- tected against the rain—Burbage's sons turned into a "private," or roofed, theater a part of Blackfriars priory, which their father had bought shortly before he died.

Henslowe was a businessman. We would call him a speculator. He may have begun as either a dyer's apprentice or a bailiff's assistant, but he be- came a pawnbroker, a dealer in lime and leather, a buyer and seller of land, and a monopolist of bear-baiting. When he saw that, in ten years, the only two playhouses in London were on their feet as money-making ventures, he went into the theater business. In 1587—twelve years before the Globe was built in Bankside—Henslowe opened the Rose nearby, and in 1600 he put up the Fortune in northern London. When the first Globe burned down in 1613, he promptly turned his Bear Garden, south of the Thames, into the Hope theater. As theater-owner, or "housekeeper," he took his share of the profits from the companies that played his houses, but he also had personal and profitable relations with the actors and playwrights. To keep them in line, he became their generous and persistent banker. "Should these fellows come out of my debt," he wrote, "I should have noe rule over them."

Someone else might have built Henslowe's playhouses, but he might not have played banker and kept the records from which scholars have learned more about the history of the Elizabethan theater than from any other source. We are deeper in debt to this money-grubber than Ben Jonson ever was. Henslowe wrote in his so-called *Diary* the names and dates of many of the plays in his theaters, as well as the box office receipts and whether the plays were "ne," as he put it, meaning "new." Henslowe's contract for the building of the Fortune—which was modeled on the Globe, though square instead of many-sided—is the only detailed description of an Elizabethan theater.

It would be unfair to add to Henslowe's record of commercial canniness the fact that he got the capital for his speculations by marrying the rich widow of his first employer. The habit of marrying the boss's daughter was a common one in those days. James Burbage secured the money for The Theater from his wife's brother, a wealthy grocer, and the actor Alleyn got himself into partnership with Henslowe by marrying his step-child.

There were other theaters and theater-builders. By 1605 London had six public playhouses and a private one, Blackfriars. There was also a stage at Newington Butts, though this may have been merely in an innyard. Another public playhouse, the Hope—as we have already mentioned—was opened in 1613. Three "private theaters" appeared during the reign of James I and Charles I: Whitefriars about 1608, the Phoenix converted from the Cockpit about 1617, and the Salisbury Court in 1629.

WHAT WE KNOW ABOUT THE GLOBE

We know more about the kind of theater that Shakespeare commonly played in than we do about his life. And yet our knowledge of the so-called public playhouse is far from complete. Most scholars believe it took a unique form. This form was approached only by the Spanish *corrales*, which we described earlier, and it was destroyed by the Commonwealth and the Restoration. A few think that it may have been more like the Italian theater or a Dutch variant. This seems a bit far-fetched, for there were no permanent theaters in Italy before 1576, and a German who visited London in 1585 wrote that The Theater and The Curtain were "unusual houses, which are so constructed that they have about three galleries, one above the other."

The only definite evidence that we have on the shape of the Elizabethan theater and stage comes from four sources:

1. The great halls and innyards where plays were given before Burbage built the first theater in 1576, and the buildings for bear-baiting and bull-baiting.
2. Four sketches ranging in date from about 1596 to 1640.
3. The contract for the building of the Fortune.
4. Evidence drawn from the stage directions of Elizabethan plays.

The basic elements of the Elizabethan theater are a stage with a door at each side and a balcony above, to be used by the actors, and a flat floor and galleries at the sides and rear, to hold the audience. Some of these elements were to be found in the so-called great halls of palaces like Hampton Court, of the Inns of Court, and of colleges at Oxford and Cambridge. In the end wall of such a room there was a door at each side leading to the kitchen. These provided entrances for the actors, who played their scenes on the floor or on a low platform between the doors. Above, was the "minstrels' gallery," which served as an upper stage. There were sometimes galleries along the side walls, where some of the audience could sit, and usually a gallery at the back of the hall. The courtyards of the old English inns provided much the same elements. There were two or three galleries on all four sides, and doors that could be used by the actors. We presume that a stage was set up at one end, and that the players reached the stage by a few steps. The common people could stand in the rest of the innyard, while wealthier spectators could stand or sit on the galleries at the sides and at one end. For certain scenes the actors could use the gallery over the stage.

We know that professional actors gave plays in the great halls from time to time. After the first theaters were built, there are records of frequent performances in the courtyards of the Bell Inn, the Bel Savage, the Cross Keys, and others. Some of these may have been used earlier; others certainly were. In 1557 a play called *A Sackful of News* was suppressed after being given at the Boar's Head. At the Red Lion a play called *Samson* was acted in 1567, and the Bull Inn was used for plays before 1576. There are two reasons why companies still played in innyards after theaters were available. First, there were more troupes than playhouses. Second, the inns—with warm rooms and drink to be had—were more comfortable in the chilly and rainy English winters.

South of the Thames there were buildings that may have suggested to Burbage a way of improving on the innyards. These were structures for bear-baiting and bull-baiting. This popular pastime consisted in watching mastiff dogs attack a tethered animal or one another. Maps of 1560 and earlier show two circular buildings used for these purposes, and each appears to have galleries from which the spectators could watch in safety. The close relation of the baiting places and theaters is obvious, for when Henslowe made the Hope theater out of his Bear Garden, he installed a movable stage, and used the building both for plays and for what the Elizabethans called "sport."

DRAWINGS OF ELIZABETHAN PLAYHOUSES

We have not more than four old pictures that purport to show the interior of an Elizabethan theater. Only one of these can be depended upon, and it shows merely a part of the total stage space.

A Dutchman named de Witt visited London about 1596. He was much impressed by the city's "four beautiful theaters," and he described and sketched "the finest and the largest," the Swan. Unfortunately his description is very brief and means little, while his sketch was lost and all we have is a copy supposed to have been made by a fellow student. The doors are too close together to fit the stage "business" indicated in most plays. Above them there are boxes for spectators where most authorities think there was an upper stage.

The next sketch is from the title page of a play called *Roxana,* a tragedy in Latin, printed in 1630. It shows curtains and a raised stage, but, again, spectators appear in two boxes where scripts often seem to indicate an upper stage. As *Roxana* was in Latin and first acted at Trinity College, Cambridge, this sketch may show a university production.

The nearest approach to what scholars consider the Elizabethan stage is a drawing reproduced in *Messalina,* a play printed in 1640. Here we have a raised stage with painted curtains behind it. Above is a very shallow stage —hardly more than an unrailed gallery—behind which we see a curtained opening. The drawing isn't wide enough to show entrance doors at the sides. It is more than possible that the artist sketched an actual stage of a theater in London.

The last drawing is late. It appeared in 1672 in *The Wits, or Sport upon Sport,* a collection of "drolls," or short comedies acted here and there between 1642 and 1660 while the theaters were banned by the Puritans. The footlights, the candelabra, and the spectators above the stage suggest that this is a joint-product of the artist's imagination and a performance in a private hall.

THE CONTRACT FOR THE FORTUNE THEATER

To Henslowe, the careful businessman, we owe the only record of the size, shape, and parts of an Elizabethan theater. When he decided to build the Fortune in 1600, he made—and time has fortunately preserved—a contract with a carpenter to put up a building resembling in all but one detail "the late erected playhouse . . . called the Globe." The difference lay in the fact that the new house was to be square—an idea that Henslowe abandoned when he rebuilt the Fortune after it had been burned to the ground. The contract specified that the building was to be eighty feet "every way" and fifty-five feet within. There were to be three stories with galleries providing "convenient divisions for gentlemen's rooms" and "twopenny rooms,"—the first story twelve feet high, the next eleven, and the third nine. The stage was to be forty-three feet wide, and it was to extend half way across the open yard, making it twenty-seven and a half deep. There was to be a "shadow or cover over the said stage," and a "tiring house," which may have included an inner and an upper stage as well as rooms in which the actors could change their attire. As Henslowe specified "convenient windows" in the tiring house, we may suppose that among these were ones used for balcony scenes, as in *Romeo and Juliet.*

WHAT THE STAGE DIRECTIONS TELL US

Henslowe's contract fails to list many possible features of the stage, falling back on "to be in all other proportions contrived and fashioned like unto the stage of the said playhouse called the Globe." We may presume that there were side entrances even in the early Theater, or Shakespeare would not have written such a stage direction in *Richard III* as: "Enter on one side, Queen Elizabeth, Duchess of York, and Marquess of Dorset; the other, Anne, Duchess of Gloucester. . . ." In conflicts, opposing forces come in through opposite doors: "Enter on the other side of the field, Richmond, Sir William Brandon, Oxford, and other Officers."

There is no mention of an inner stage in the Fortune contract, but scholars think they have found plenty of evidence even in the early plays: With the curtains closed, the stage could be a street, a country road, a battle scene. When they were open, the inner stage could become a tent, a room in a tavern, a cave, a shop. If the inner stage was occupied by a throne, then that area and the main stage became a palace.

This theory of a permanent inner stage, or "study" as it is often called, was attacked in 1953 by an Englishman, C. Walter Hodges, and an American, Leslie Hotson. They made the same point, and it is a telling one. No sane author or director would let an important scene be played in an alcove far back of the great platform-stage. It would be too remote, and the sight-lines would be bad. On the other hand, scenes of great significance *were* played "within." Hodge's suggestion was that for a play like *Antony and Cleopatra* there would be a special structure built out from the back wall, and easily seen by everyone.

Hotson was much more radical. He found in the records of the court around 1600 charges for "a broad stage in the middle of the haull" when a play was done in the palace of Whitehall. He concluded that plays at court were staged with multiple sets in the midst of the audience, and then declared that they were done the same way at the Globe. So, wrote Hotson, Shakespeare had a "theater in the round." It was a conclusion that ignored what pictorial evidence we have.

There were certainly upper stages. A narrow gallery shows in the *Messalina* sketch. This could serve as a battlement, the top of a hill, or any high place. In *Richard III* we read: "Enter Gloucester, in a gallery above, between two Bishops." According to most authorities, curtains behind the gallery could be drawn aside to reveal an inner stage. In *Antony and Cleopatra* it is a tomb. In the stage directions we find: "Enter Cleopatra and her maids aloft," and "They heave Antony aloft to Cleopatra." In the last act, "Proculeius and two of the guards ascend the monument by a ladder, and come behind Cleopatra. Some of the guards unbar and open the gates, discovering the lower room of the monument." Hodges' suggestion of a temporary structure works as well as a permanent one.

Shakespearean authorities believe that there were two other stages on the level of the gallery. These had the "convenient windows" of the Fortune contract, and they were placed above the two side doors to the main stage. In the first balcony scene of *Romeo and Juliet* we read, "Juliet appears above at a window." If this window were merely imagined as part of the gallery, then Romeo would have to speak the lines of his love scene with his back to most of the audience. There are other windows called for in Elizabethan plays, and other balcony scenes with rope ladders for the hero to climb up and come down.

Above the balcony was a still higher stage for the musicians and for scenes far aloft, as, for instance, at a ship's masthead. Thus the Elizabethan theater appears to have had seven useable areas: the main stage, an inner stage on the same level, the gallery, an inner stage on that level, the two windowed stages at the sides, and the high place for the musicians. Naturally, the three levels had to be connected by back-stage stairs. There were also stairs to the "cellarage" under the main stage, or platform, and to the "hut."

The hut was the top of the tiring house, and it had room for cannon and other sound machines. From it actors could enter the "shadow," or "heavens" —which was the roof over the stage—and be let down through a trap door. Thomas Heywood in *Apology for Actors* wrote of the heavens "where upon any occasion the gods descended." In *Alphonsus, King of Aragon* a stage direction runs: "After you have sounded thrise, let Venus be let downe from the top of the stage." In *Doctor Faustus,* Marlowe asks for "Musicke while the Throne descends." In the prolog to *Every Man in His Humor,* Ben Jonson, who was not too fond of scenic machinery, wrote sarcastically of the kind of play in which a "creaking throne comes down the boys to please."

The main stage seems to have had a number of traps. In the last act of *Hamlet* there must have been a "grave trap." Witches and spirits could rise up through this trap in the main stage, accompanied by smoke. In *The Brazen Age,* Heywood requires openings in both the heavens and the stage: "Jupiter strikes him [Hercules] with a thunderbolt, his body sinks, and from the heavens descends a hand in a cloud, that from the place where Hercules burnt, brings up a starre, and fixeth it in the firmament." Some think the upper stage had a trap, too.

A FLEXIBLE THEATER FOR FREE-RANGING PLAYS

A study of any Elizabethan play shows how flexible the stage had to be to accommodate the many changes of scene—no less than forty-three in *Antony and Cleopatra.* Yet, at the same time, the playwrights had to take more trouble over certain things than the later men who wrote for a stage with a curtain. Unless a death took place on an inner stage—which was impossible to such a violent and corpse-filled scene as the last in *Hamlet*—the author had to devise some reason for carting off the mortal remains. When all the actors left the stage a scene in one locale was over, and a new setting was to be seen or imagined when another group of actors entered. This meant that an actor could not end one scene with an exit and come back at the beginning of the next; someone else had to begin the new scene. Thus, at the end of the first scene in *Hamlet,* Horatio and his friends leave the parapet to tell Hamlet about his father's ghost. The next scene begins with the entrances of the king, the queen, Hamlet, Laertes, and Polonius, and continues for almost 160 lines before Horatio enters to talk with Hamlet. With such dramaturgy and such a stage, free and wide-ranging plays could be acted with great speed and effectiveness. If there were intermissions, there is no textual evidence that these were necessary, except as a relief from the tension of the play or to give the management a chance to sell food and drink to the audience. There are no indications of acts and scenes in almost all of the Shakespearean quartos. Though most of the First Folio plays are so divided, six do not show even act divisions. The Elizabethan playwright did not *think* in five acts, like the classicists of the Renaissance, and his scenes ran along much like those of a motion picture.

Sir Philip Sidney, who must have seen performances at The Theater and The Curtain as well as at court, was much irritated by the way the playwrights threw scene after scene upon the stage:

Where you shall have *Asia* of the one side, and *Afric* of the other, and so many under-kingdoms, that the Player, when he cometh in, must ever begin with telling where he is; or else the tale will not be conceived. Now we shall have three Ladies walk to gather flowers, and then we must believe the stage to be a Garden. By and by, we hear news of shipwreck in the same place, and then we are to blame, if we accept it not as a Rock.

THE AUDIENCE

The audience doesn't seem to have been bothered by all this. It accepted the conventions of the Elizabethan stage just as the Greeks had accepted the conventions of the Greek stage. Shakespeare's audience was a mixed one. In the "gentlemen's rooms" of the gallery, there were lords and ladies just as intelligent as Sidney, just as wise in knowledge of the classic stage. In the "pit"—that flat area between the gallery walls, where the "groundlings" stood almost surrounding the stage—there were tradesmen and apprentices, servants and mechanics, soldiers and sailors. Too often this audience has been pictured as ignorant and rowdy and altogether undesirable. This was certainly the opinion of the puritanical city officials who wrote of "sondrye robberies by pyckinge and Cuttinge of purses." Our unfavorable picture of the audience in the pit is due largely to what the playwrights wrote about them. Hamlet says that the groundlings "for the most part are capable of nothing but inexplicable dumb-shows and noise." Peele disliked writing for the "penny knaves delight." Jonson said that "the beast, the multitude . . . love nothing that is right and proper." The playwrights said almost as much about the actors, but they must have been much more annoyed at the habit of apple-eating, nut-cracking, and beer-drinking that apparently went on throughout the performances. We must remark however, that Nell Gwyn began her career by selling oranges in the Restoration theaters, while English audiences today drink coffee or tea and eat biscuits or ice cream in the intermissions.

Contemporary drawings of the Elizabethan stage. *Above at the left is a sketch made from a description by de Witt after he had visited the Swan about 1596. Next to it is a cut from Roxana, published in 1630. At the left is a scene from* Messalina, *printed in 1640.*

The elements of Shakespeare's stage. *These drawings accept the concept of inner stages. Upper left, the "study," or inner stage, set for the grave scene in* Hamlet. *Upper right, the chamber above the study, as it may have been used for* soliloquy in Macbeth. Lower left, one of the window stages, used with the main stage for the balcony scene in* Romeo and Juliet. *The last, the main stage and "tarras," or balcony, for a scene in* Henry VI, *"Loe, where George of Clarence sweeps along."* (Drawings by Gerda Becker With, after those of Maurice Percival in Watkins, *On Producing Shakespeare*.)

James Burbage made no mistake when he kept the "pit" that had been inevitable in the innyards. Thus he insured a much larger audience than could have been seated; some think the Globe held 3,000 spectators. It was also an audience that must have grown highly critical when a poor scene made them conscious of tired feet. The high quality of the poetic drama from Marlowe through Shakespeare proves that the Elizabethan audience had sensibility and native intelligence. Few could read, of course, but an audience that couldn't read could have very sharp ears and an eagerness for ideas and emotions that could come only from the stage.

THE "PRIVATE" THEATERS

Beginning in Elizabethan times there was a curious and a vague distinction between the "public" theaters that we have described and the "private" ones. Anyone could buy admission to a private theater, but, because the price of seats ranged from sixpence to two shillings instead of from a penny to a shilling, the audience was a bit more select. In a private theater everyone had a seat. Certain gallants paid an extra twelvepence for stools on the stage until this became such a nuisance that Charles II stopped the practice in his time; it took another century and the authority of a David Garrick to finally do away with it.

Public theaters *versus* private theaters may seem a distinction without a difference, but it was a very real one. The title page of *The Duchess of Malfi* reads: "As it was Presented privately, at the Black-Friers; and publiquely at the Globe, By the Kings Majesties Servants." In an early and defective edition of *Hamlet*, Gildenstern explains to the prince that the actors have left their theater because "the publicke audience that came to them, are turned to private playes, and the humor of children."

The concept of a private theater may go back at least as far as 1574. In that year the London authorities made regulations for the innyard performances, but exempted those "withoute publique or common collection of money." They were thinking of the Inns of Court, plays in noblemen's houses, and sporadic appearances of the child-actors. Perhaps the term "private theater" arose about 1576—after the opening of The Theater and The Curtain—when Richard Farrant, Master of the Children of Windsor, decided to give performances by his choristers and the Children of the Chapel at Blackfriars. Since this was a rather radical step, and since the theater and its actors were still close to the line of vagabondage, Farrant may have thought it wise to announce "private" performances in a "private" theater, though he took money from the public in advance.

The popularity of the child-actors and their private theaters was great but intermittent. At various times they had private theaters at Whitefriars, at St. Paul's, and at Porter's Hall, as well as at Blackfriars. James Burbage bought part of Blackfriars in 1596 and made it over into a theater. He died the next year, however, and his sons leased it to the Children of the Chapel.

The children fell out of favor with the court, and in 1608 or 1609 Black-friars became the winter home of the players of the Globe. Like other private theaters, its repertory leaned toward sophisticated comedy.

An outstanding difference between the public and the private theaters was that the latter were roofed and used artificial light. Where public theaters had to open by two in the afternoon, the others could play later and into the evening, as, for instance, when the queen of James I appears to have engaged the Blackfriars and its actors to entertain her and her guests on certain nights in the 1630's.

DID THE ELIZABETHANS USE SCENERY?

There seems to have been a good deal of scenic display in Elizabethan plays done at court or even in the lawyers' inns. Records of the Revels' Office list money spent for a "citie" and a "battlement," for "canvas to cover divers townes and howes and other devisses and clowds," for "the Clowdes and curteynes," for "one great city, one senate house," for "vii Cities, one villadge, one Country howes, one battlement," for "great cloths" and "greate curteynes." Many productions probably showed different "man-sions" at the same time, after the fashion of the medieval stage, though it may be argued that the court adopted Serlio's scheme of a single setting for a street or a woods.

With James I, Italianate scenery and scenic devices definitely began to invade court performances. Beginning in 1605, they were employed in the "masques" staged by Inigo Jones, as we shall see later. Toward the end of the reign of Charles I, scenery seems to have spread from court performances to those in the private theaters. In 1636 the queen was so impressed by what she heard about a production of a play at Oxford that she borrowed the costumes and scenery for her own players. The university authorities sent the "Cloathes and Perspectives," and requested that they should not "come into the hands and use of the common Players"—which suggests that the private theaters had begun to use such scenery. A writer remarks that a play produced at Blackfriars in 1637 had scenes such as "were only used at Masques." There are two or three other allusions to painted settings at that private theater between 1638 and 1640.

The public theaters, however, used very little in the way of scenery. There were probably some suggestions of settings on an inner stage—hangings or set pieces for rooms, trees for a wood. Romeo "climbs a wall and leaps down within it." But Henslowe's records list only properties:

> i rock, i cage, i Hell mouth.
> i tomb of Guido, i tomb of Dido, i bedstead.
> i wooden hatchet, i leather hatchet
> Iris head, & rainbow; i little altar.
> i copper target, & xvii foils.
> iii timbrels; i dragon in Faustus.

i Pope's miter.
iii Imperial crowns; i plain crown.

Some believe that, at one time, there may have been lettered signs, or "local-
ity boards," over the side doors of the stage, as there were in the drawings
of scenes from Terence. Sidney wrote: "What Child is there, that, coming
to a Play, seeing *Thebes* written in great letters upon an old door, doth
believe that it is Thebes?"

"GORGIOUS AND SUMPTIOUS APPARELL"

Productions at theaters like the Globe and the Fortune must have been
elaborate and impressive in two respects—music and costuming. Henslowe
lent money for the purchase of instruments, and stage directions called not
only for "flourishes" at the entrance of royalty and generals, but also music
to accompany songs, dances, and even whole scenes. As for costumes, in
1577 a clergyman attacked the "gorgious and sumptious apparell" on the
stage, a Swiss visitor wrote in 1599 that the players were "very expensively
and handsomely dressed," and an Italian—who should have been highly
critical—commented on "the sumptuous dresses of the actors."

Most of the costumes must have been of the type then worn in court or
in private life, but there were attempts to imitate foreign or class dress.
Among other costumes, Henslowe inventoried a Moor's coat, a dress for Neptune, and two Danish suits. A line in a play by Kyd mentions a "Turkish
bonnet." Shylock wore a Jewish gabardine. A 1595 sketch of a scene from
Titus Andronicus shows Turkish trousers on one actor, and an attempt at a
Roman cloak. The best of materials had to be used because an actor on the
center of the platform was within sixty feet of the most distant spectator,
while hundreds stood close to the stage. Though the cost of theater-building
may seem low to us—Henslowe paid only £520, or not more than $25,000
today, for the first Fortune and about twice as much for the second one
built of brick—good cloth was very expensive. Velvet cost a pound a yard,
or about $50. There was one way, however, of getting good secondhand
clothes. A continental visitor reports that "when distinguished gentlemen or
knights die, almost their best clothes are given to their servants, but as it is
not fitting that they should wear them they sell them cheaply to the
actors."

THE ELIZABETHAN REPERTORY SYSTEM

The playwrights, the public, and the actors had one great advantage in
Shakespeare's time that they do not share today in England or the United
States. This was the repertory system. There were no long runs. The bill
changed nightly, but plays were repeated over and over again at various
intervals. For thirty performances in the season of 1593-94 Henslowe lists
thirteen plays, most of which were acted twice and some three or four times.

A popular play was often given over many years. A play that would have failed if it had been produced for a run could be nursed along through a number of well-spaced performances. The playwright received no royalties, but at least he had the satisfaction of knowing that even his comparative failures drew good houses from time to time.

Because a permanent company was part of the repertory system, the actors improved their technique by constantly working together on a wide variety of plays. The playwright gained from their increased skill. He also profited by being able to develop parts to suit the abilities of the players. Because an actor in such a company was able to play a "fat" part two or three times a week, he was probably willing to give his talents to a smaller part every now and then. Will Kempe, the greatest comic actor in London, who may have acted Falstaff and Bottom, played the tiny role of Peter, the servant of Juliet's nurse.

FROM ROGUES AND VAGABONDS TO THE QUEEN'S MEN

The story of the Elizabethan actors is an interesting one. It is also complex and confusing, and, at times, pretty vague. Quite early, one fact stands out: companies of players had to have the patronage of a noble man if they wanted to tour in comparative safety. The reasons for this were probably many. At a time when drama was coming to life again through the Revival of Learning, vanity might urge a king or an earl to keep a troupe of actors among his household servants, and to let them spread his name across the countryside. The actors profited by reflected glory. They drew larger crowds when they came to a town as the Earl of Leicester's Men than if they were billed as Burbage's Players. Further, they sometimes had a measure of financial support when they wore the livery of a nobleman's servant. Behind all this, however, there must have been a holdover from the feudal way of life which was still of recent memory. At the end of the Middle Ages there was no such thing as a "masterless man," unless he was a fugitive from justice or from his lord. There is a whiff of this in the Tudor Poor Law of 1572 that classed as "rogues and vagabonds" all "Common Players in Enterludes & Minstrals, not belonging to any Baron of this Realme or towards any other honorable Personage of Greater Degree."

Records are scanty, but the Earl of Worcester seems to have had a company of players as early as 1555, the Earl of Warwick and the Earl of Leicester in 1559, and Lord Strange, the future Earl of Derby, in the sixties, and the Baron of Effingham in the seventies. Other noblemen followed the fashion. One authority lists twenty-three companies under noble patronage during the reign of Elizabeth I. Having dropped her own players of interludes in favor of boy-actors, she turned back to adults in 1583 and set up the Queen's Men, a brilliant company in their red liveries, who played at court, in London inns, and on tour till about 1590.

THE ACTING COMPANIES

The history of the individual troupes is hard to follow. Companies passed from one nobleman to another. The death of patrons, defection among players, and, worse still, the calamitous plagues that harried England from time to time disrupted old companies and created new ones. Even in London the facts are often dim. Between 1559 and 1586, when there were adult performances at two theaters and no one knows at how many inns, we have records of some dozen companies. In the last fifteen years of Elizabeth's reign most of these disappeared and five new troupes were added. The most successful companies in the 1580's and the early '90's were the Queen's Men, with the famous clown Tarleton, Leicester's Men, with whom Richard Burbage played for a time, and the troupe of Lord Strange, who became the Earl of Derby. Out of these, only Derby's survived long, and only under two new names. On Derby's death, they became the Chamberlain's Men, and James I made them the King's Men after his coronation. This troupe, for which Shakespeare wrote and Richard Burbage acted, had only two real rivals. One was the Earl of Worcester's Men, with whom Edward Alleyn had acted before coming to London. The other was made up of the provincial players of the Baron of Effingham, later the Earl of Nottingham. It was called the Admiral's Men because Effingham was Lord High Admiral when he defeated the Spanish Armada. Marlowe wrote—all too briefly—for this company, Alleyn was its star, and Henslowe its landlord and banker. All three companies appeared at court and probably toured from time to time, certainly when plagues swept London.

James I and his family took a hearty interest in the theater. When he was not only heir to the English throne but also king of Scotland, he borrowed Elizabeth's players to help celebrate his marriage by performances in Edinburgh. On his accession, he took over the Chamberlain's company as the King's Men, and turned Worcester's into Queen Anne's, and the Admiral's into Prince Henry's. Later, two other of his family maintained troupes. One was his daughter Lady Elizabeth and the other his son Prince Charles, who was to lose his head to the Puritans seven years after they closed down his company.

ECONOMICS IN THE ELIZABETHAN THEATER

The economics of the various acting companies was as complex as their history. Sometimes, but probably not too often, they had a certain amount of support from their noble patrons. Henslowe, however, lent money to the Admiral's company. When companies appeared at court they were paid for "plaieing and other feates of activity." In most cases, troupes were stock companies—in the financial as well as the theatrical sense. Some ten to fifteen players would buy shares at about seventy pounds apiece, a considerable amount in our money. This capital went mainly for plays and costumes.

The sharers hired other actors at sixpence a week. The boys who played women's parts were apprenticed to the sharers, who were paid a few shillings a week for the lads' appearances.

Most companies in London rented theaters from their owners on a curious basis. They were entitled to all the penny fees collected at the door. The owners got all the money paid by spectators for moving out of the pit and standing or sitting in the galleries. In many cases, as the popularity of the company increased, the sharers got half of the gallery receipts. The men who collected money at the main door, and at the two doors leading to higher-priced seats were called "gatherers." They were ordinarily paid by the actor-sharers, but in Henslowe's theater, that canny man insisted on hiring his own. The money was dropped through a slot in a box—to which we owe our term "box office." The position of the sharers was improved by Cuthbert and Richard Burbage when they decided to build the Globe. We know that they paid half the ground rent, and that five of their actors, including Shakespeare, paid the other half. We may presume that the building was financed in the same way, and that the five players got half of the theater's "take" as well as their proportion of the acting company's share.

ACTING IN SHAKESPEARE'S DAY

The Elizabethan actor began as rogue and vagabond and ended under the patronage of royalty. When the first companies toured in interludes and rough comedies, six men might have to play twenty-five parts. When the Globe and the Fortune flourished there were well-balanced companies of about twenty skilled and respected players. The livery of earl, queen, or king became them well.

There is a great deal of argument about the style of acting in Shakespeare's day. One group of scholars claims that it was formal and rhetorical; another, that it was natural. Some believe that it varied or developed from one to the other. We know that it must have been spirited and deft, or else the long and intricate speeches that occur so often in so many plays could not have been understood and enjoyed. Gesture and movement must have been important. The actor-playwright Thomas Heywood warned his fellows "not to use any impudent or forced motion in any part of the body, no rough or other violent gesture; nor on the contrary to stand like a stiff starched man."

There are two powerful arguments in favor of the so-called natural acting seen today in performances of Shakespeare at the Old Vic. The first point is the intimacy of the public theaters. The whole of the Globe could be dropped into the auditorium of the average Broadway theater without touching the stage. It was a quarter the size of the opera house type of auditorium where actors like Robert Mantell played Shakespeare around the turn of our century. The actors at the Globe needed to "project" their voice far less than actors in most of our theaters. The second reason for believing that companies of good and popular actors in Shakespeare's day weren't oratorical and didn't rant rests on what that dramatist had Hamlet say in his advice to the players: "Speak the speech, I pray you, as I pronounce it to you, trippingly on the tongue . . . o'erstep not the modesty of nature; for anything so overdone is from the purpose of playing, whose end, both at the first and now, was and is, to hold, as 'twere, the mirror up to nature."

A very curious feature of Elizabethan acting was the popularity of the boy-player. It went further than the productions of the various companies of children. Women's parts on the professional stage were played by boys up to the closing of the theaters in 1642 and even in the early years of the Restoration, when Pepys wrote in his diary: "One Kinaston, a boy, acted the Duke's sister, but made the loveliest lady that ever I saw in my life." Many women went to the public theater—as Shakespeare attests in three epilogs addressed to them—but they were banned from the stage. When two French companies appeared in London, the first in 1629 and the second a few years later, their actresses were hissed and pelted with rotten apples. The appeal and the skill of the best boy-actors may be guessed from the epitaph that Ben Jonson wrote for Salathiel Pavy of Queen Elizabeth's Chapel, when he died at thirteen. Among his lines were these:

> 'Twas a child that so did thrive
> In grace and feature,
> As heaven and nature seemed to strive
> Which owned the creature.

ACTORS NOW REMEMBERED

By its very nature, acting is the most ephemeral of the theater arts. Until the coming of the phonograph record, the silent film, and finally the talkies, we had no record of an actor's art except portraits, and the descriptions and opinions of his contemporaries. Shakespeare, Marlowe, Thomas Heywood, Jonson, and Webster were actors, but we really know them only as playwrights. Six other players have a life of their own. Two, Heminge and Condell, immortalized themselves by editing the First Folio of Shakespeare's plays. Richard Tarlton and William Kempe shared in man's love for great clowns and comedians. Tarlton was "the Queen's Majesty's jester, . . . gracious with the Queen, his sovereign, and in the people's general applause." Kempe was, at one time, a member of the "English Comedians" who toured Holland, Denmark, and Germany, and he wrote a little book about how he danced from London to Norwich. The last pair that we will mention were the greatest actors of their time, Richard Burbage and Edward Alleyn; but we know more about them for what they did off the boards than on. After their deaths, Ben Jonson celebrated both men in verse. He said of Alleyn, "others speak, but only thou dost act." This supreme adulation did not prevent Jonson from writing of Burbage:

He's gone and with him what a world are dead,
Which he revived—to be revivéd soe
No more young Hamlett, ould Heironymoe,
King Lear, the grevéd Moore, and more beside,
That lived in him, have now for ever died.

Both men, Burbage and Alleyn, live for what they did in theater management. Burbage shared with his best actors the ownership of the Globe and Blackfriars. Alleyn joined with Henslowe in theater-building, bear-baiting, and other speculations, and would have died a millionaire if he hadn't preferred to found and build Dulwich College—where, incidentally, the records of Henslowe were preserved.

THE COURT MASQUES OF INIGO JONES AND BEN JONSON

The last form of theatrical entertainment that was developed in the time of Elizabeth and perfected under the first two Stuart kings is the "masque." Its roots are in the court shows of the Italian Renaissance. On Twelfth Night in 1512 young Henry VIII "with xi other wer disguised, after the manner of Italie, called a maske, a thynge not seen afore in Englande." There had been "disguisings" and ballroom pageantry before this, but now for the first time royalty took part in the entertainment. Henry's daughter Elizabeth also enjoyed the masque—a name borrowed from France—and her shows, like her father's, were mainly pantomime. It was James I, abetted by Ben Jonson and Inigo Jones, who turned them into a peculiar sort of lyric entertainment backed up by elaborate scenic display. The Stuarts produced at least a hundred of these expensive spectacles before Cromwell and Parliament curbed their extravagances.

Some of the masques were given at the Inns of Court, but most of them in the royal palaces. Sometimes they celebrated a betrothal, a marriage, an accession to power, or the visit of a foreign prince or minister. Often there was no more excuse than princely display and the adulation of royalty. Courtiers as well as trained singers and dancers took part in them. Prince Henry "walked on" in the silent title-role of *The Masque of Oberon*, and Charles I and his queen played parts in some of these spectacles. James I's Queen Anne loved masques even more than the theater, and blacked her face to play one of twelve Negresses in *The Masque of Blackness*. She induced Ben Jonson, as court poet, to write some thirty masques. And, in order to have a proper stage designer, she brought from her brother's court in Copenhagen the English architect Inigo Jones, who had studied the scenery and machines of Italy.

The scripts that Jonson wrote—Milton, too, and half a dozen successful playwrights—were quite short. They make only eight to twelve pages in modern print. Most of the characters were mythological or allegorical— Diana, Boreas, Neptune, Reason, Splendor, Love, and Revel, but Merlin and

Arthur got into one of the casts. Lord Bacon—who wrote a masque himself—lists among the choruses and dancers "Satyres, Fooles, Wildemen, Antiques, Ethiopes, Pigmies, and Beastes." Here are a few characteristic titles: *The Masque of Blackness, The Masque of Beauty, The Golden Age Restored,* and *Pleasure Reconciled to Virtue.*

ITALIANATE SCENIC MARVELS IN ENGLAND

The chief distinction of the masque was that it introduced Italianate scenery and stage machines to England—and the proscenium, too, for Jones designed a new frame of symbolic figures and ornament for each of his productions. At first he used the multiple stage with its "mansions"; then the single stage set of Serlio. But because he liked startling changes of scene, he leaned more to the revolving prisms called *periaktoi,* together with the bent, or angled, flats, and groups of wings that moved in grooves. Instead of using a front curtain drawn to each side to expose the first scene—which had been done as early as 1565—he introduced a drop curtain painted with designs. At first he let this fall into a slot, *à la* ancient Rome, but later he raised it aloft by a drum and ropes and pulleys. It was never used to hide a change of scene, for Jones delighted in making magical transformations in full view of the audience:

The part of the scene which first presented itself was an ugly Hell; which flaming beneath, smoked unto the top of the roof . . . on a sudden was heard a sound of loud music, as if many instruments had made one blast; with which not only the hags themselves, but the hell into which they ran, quite vanished, and the whole face of the scene altered, scare suffering the memory of such a thing; but in the place of it appeared a glorious and magnificent building, figuring the House of Fame, in the top of which was discovered the twelve Masquers, sitting upon a throne triumphal, erected in form of a pyramid and circled with all store of light.

A courtier who saw *The Masque of Blackness* described one of the elaborate devices that astounded the audience and at the same time introduced Queen Anne as part of the show:

There was a great engine at the lower end of the room which had motion, and in it were the images of sea-horses, with other terrible fishes, which were ridden by the Moors. . . . At the further end was a great shell in the form of a scallop, wherein were four seats. On the lowest sat the Queen with my Lady Bedford.

The very nature of the masque prevented Ben Jonson from using his full talent as a dramatist. His poetry was lost and forgotten in the extravagant display of pageantry and spectacle. A man of his temper was bound to revolt. In 1631 he quarreled with Inigo Jones. Jonson called him a "maker of properties . . . whirling his whimsies." He satirized Jones and masque-making in a play called *The Tale of a Tub.* In his *expostulation with Inigo Jones,* Jonson wrote: "Painting and carpentry are the soul of masque."

Painting and carpentry were expensive. Not counting the elaborate costumes furnished by the nobles who took part, the production of *The Masque of Oberon* cost almost £1500—three times as much as the Fortune theater had cost to build the year before. In 1618 James I spent £4000 on a single masque.

Scenic wonders, as we have said, were invading the private theaters in the late 1630's. But, when Cromwell curbed the court and closed the playhouses in 1642, the war between scenery and the Shakespearean stage was ended almost before it had begun. During the truce of the Commonwealth, a writer of tragedies and masques, William D'Avenant, pondered the future of scenic display and brought forth English opera. When the theaters opened again in 1660, the Red Bull playhouse fought, for two or three years, an unequal battle with the new stages. Perhaps Inigo Jones had doomed the Globe and the Fortune before the soldiers of the Commonwealth pulled them down.

five

The BAROQUE THEATER
Of FRANCE

THE THEATER OF FRANCE HAD A STRANGE KIND OF CONTINUITY FROM THE
twelfth century to the end of the eighteenth—and, indeed, down to our own
time. Well into the Renaissance, the people of the provinces saw medieval
mystery plays given in open fields, public squares, Roman amphitheaters,
palaces, and even cemeteries. In Paris an amateur company began, in 1402,
to produce mysteries in a hall of the Hôpital de la Trinité. It is in the story
of this group, the Confrérie de la Passion, that we find a clear thread leading
from the medieval drama to the theater of Napoleon's youth.

After a hundred and fifty years of producing mysteries, the Confrérie de
la Passion built a playhouse of its own in the ruins of the town house of
the Duc de Bourgogne. Forbidden to give religious plays, the brotherhood
turned unsuccessfully to farces, comedies, and tragedies. By 1578 they had
begun to lease their stage to professional companies of players who were
touring France. The Hôtel de Bourgogne continued as an active, producing
playhouse until 1783. Thus the stage of France, through a single theater,
flows on for 235 years in unbroken continuity from medieval religious drama
to what we might almost call the modern stage.

FROM A MEDIEVAL PLAYHOUSE TO A RETARDED
DRAMA

If we put aside—as indeed we must—the converted hall of the Hôpital de
la Trinité and the still more make-shift *patios* and *corrales* of Spain and

innyards of England, we may say that the Hôtel de Bourgogne, opening about 1550, was the first public playhouse built since the fall of Rome. Yet this does not mean that the theater of France came to its full perfection before the theater of Spain and England. It was not till 1634 that Paris had a second theater for the paying public. Italianate scenery and machines did not appear till 1641. And it was only between 1637 and 1677 that France had notable native playwrights. Contrast this with the swifter progress of Italy, Spain, and England. As early as 1538 Italy was sending abroad companies of exceptionally trained actors. By 1570 Spain could boast numerous popular theaters and a significant drama, and by 1600 London had six playhouses and William Shakespeare.

France had two excuses for being laggard in the theater—just as it was laggard in the fine arts—through the fifteenth and sixteenth centuries.

The first was war—war on its own soil as well as outside its borders. From 1346 to 1450 English armies conquered or harried much of Northern France. For another hundred years France fought intermittently and none too successfully with other European kingdoms and principalities. The disaster of religious civil war crippled France in the last half of the sixteenth century. Unity, power, and a century of prosperity came to France first through Cardinal Richelieu, who made Louis XIII supreme over his nobles as well as his people, and then through Louis XIV, who left France the dominant power in Europe when he died in 1715.

The second hindrance to theatrical progress was monopoly. Through the Middle Ages and the Renaissance, many a monarch and many a municipality liked to give a favorite courtier or a favored group the sole right to make or sell or manage this or that at a nice profit. The theater of France did not escape the blight of such monopoly. Until 1634 there was, officially, only one public playhouse in Paris because the Confrérie had enjoyed for a hundred years the exclusive privilege of producing plays or licensing their production in the chief city of France. Until Paris began to have other companies in competing playhouses, she had no dramatists of enduring merit.

PLAYS AT FAIRS AND IN TENNIS COURTS

Monopoly is not an easy thing to maintain when you have to deal with people so zealous and unaccountable as actors. The Confrérie found it particularly difficult. The brotherhood had to spend a great deal of time and energy running down, suppressing, or taxing random companies of actors. The great fairs of Saint-Germain in the winter and Saint-Laurent in the summer were particularly troublesome. There touring companies gave fly-by-night performances, and often blew town before the Confrérie could prosecute them. Finally, an edict of 1595 legalized plays at the fairs. Then a touring company moved into the Hôtel d'Argent, and others into various tennis courts, all paying the Confrérie a fee for each performance.

The French tennis court made no worse a theater than the hall of an *hôpital.* This place of sport was a long, roofed structure of considerable size. As the popularity of the game slackened somewhat in the fifteenth century, many traveling companies used these quarters as temporary theaters all through provincial France. From the Paris fairs, it was only natural that the actors should move over into Paris tennis courts. The first troupe that was set up in legitimate competition with the actors at the Hôtel de Bourgogne used one of these structures for two years while they built a permanent house on the site of another tennis court. This was the Théâtre du Marais, which opened in 1634 under the direction of the fine actor Guillaume Montdory and the powerful patronage of Cardinal Richelieu.

Obviously, there was a political background to the Confrérie's loss of its monopoly. This lay in the tensions and jealousies of Louis XIII and his great prime minister. The king—not content with plays at court—had been supporting at the Hôtel de Bourgogne a company of actors known as the Comédiens Ordinaires du Roi or the Troupe Royale. Richelieu, who was responsible for the growing power of both France and its monarch, liked to irritate his "master" in petty ways. One of these was the backing of Montdory and his Théâtre du Marais. Louis replied by drafting some of Montdory's best players to augment the Troupe Royale.

The next step for Richelieu was to become playwright and producer. He forced five writers—including Pierre Corneille, who had won fame with comedies and tragedies at the Théâtre du Marais—to collaborate with him on some plays that, not unnaturally, proved rather poor. Richelieu provided the plot, and a different dramatist wrote each of the five acts. In 1641, the year before the cardinal's death, he opened a small but beautiful theater in his palace, later known as the Palais-Royal. There, on a stage equipped with Italianate scenic devices, he produced a spectacle called *Miramé.*

COURT THEATERS TURN PUBLIC

There were court theaters before Richelieu and Louis XIII, and after them. Kings and courtiers delighted in balls, ballets, and spectacles, but they also liked actors and opera. As early as 1577, the Gelosi troupe of Italian comedians appeared in what may be called the first court theater of France, in the Salle du Petit-Bourbon. In 1645 Cardinal Mazarin, the Italian-born prime minister of Louis XIV, brought from Venice the greatest scenic magician of his time, Giacomo Torelli, to stage operas at court. For the cardinal, he reproduced a spectacular Italian opera, *La Festa theatrale della finta pazzia,* and for the seven-year-old king he added such engaging furbelows as a ballet of monkeys, flying parrots, and mechanical ostriches. To celebrate the wedding of Louis XIV in 1660, Mazarin built a theater in the Tuileries, one of the royal residences. The name of this theater—the Salle des Machines—indicates the kind of shows he provided.

The attitude of Louis XIV toward his court theaters and the Parisian public was a remarkable one. In his palaces, from the Louvre to Versailles, he provided all manner of performances for his courtiers and their ladies. But—and here he was unique among princes—the king turned over the Petit-Bourbon and the Palais-Royal to acting companies that played month after month to the general public. In addition he gave goodly subsidies to his Italian players to the Troupe Royale, to Molière and to the company at the Théâtre du Marais.

HARDY—FIRST PROFESSIONAL PLAYWRIGHT OF FRANCE

The drama of France from 1500 to 1700 comes in curious compartments. They seem almost sealed off from one another. First there is the native farce, rooted in the Middle Ages and withering in the Renaissance. Next, scholars and schoolmasters imitate the classic drama of Rome. The first popular playwright, Alexandre Hardy, works in and for the theater, pays scant attention to the classic form, and seems nearest in impulse to Lope de Vega and Shakespeare. Then Corneille and, later, Racine revive the unities of time, place, and action, write mainly on classic themes, and win a popular audience. Sandwiched between these two neo-classicists comes Molière with his comedies of contemporary life. He observes the unities and he writes in verse, yet almost all his characters are of his time, and his dialog is natural as well as witty. In spite of his enormous success with king and commons, the other playwrights do not imitate him.

Lope de Vega of Spain—William Shakespeare of England—Alexandre Hardy of France. In 1600 these were the oustanding playwrights of the three nations. They had turned their backs on the classic drama. They wrote free-ranging plays of many scenes and vivid action. They were popular at the box office. If Hardy had had the genius of the other two, France might have bred a somewhat different drama from that of Corneille and Racine in the seventeenth century.

Hardy worked for the touring company of Valleran-Lecomte, but never as an actor. His job was to turn out plays. As the first professional playwright of France, he was prodigious in output. Some say he wrote 600 pieces; some, 1200. He alone supplied most of the pieces produced by the actors of Valleran-Lecomte after the company invaded Paris by taking over the Hôtel de Bourgogne sometime between 1600 and 1610.

Hardy wrote all manner of plays: tragedies, tragi-comedies, melodramas, and pastorals, everything but comedies. Like any proper classicist, he divided his plays into five acts. In his earlier tragedies he often used the great figures of Greek and Roman times, and he even employed a chorus. But he ignored the unities of time and place, and he showed—often in violent scenes—the episodes that occurred off-stage in Greek and Roman plays and that classic playwrights brought to the audience only through narration. The result was a more vigorous drama. Like Lope de Vega and Shakespeare—and Corneille and Racine, too—he wrote in verse, but his dialog, like Molière's, was direct and almost natural. His speeches were never long-winded. His chief contribution to the dramatic form was to invent a new one. It was new at least to France, if not to England and Spain. This was tragi-comedy. According to Aristotle and his garbled echo Horace, tragedy dealt with the kingly and the well-placed; comedy, with lowlier folk. Hardy mixed the two. The ending might be happy or unhappy, but high affairs shared the stage with comic incidents.

CORNEILLE—THE CLASSICIST IN SPITE OF HIMSELF

In Rouen, when Pierre Corneille—greatest poet-dramatist of France—was not yet twenty-four he saw some of Hardy's plays acted by Charles Lenoir and Guillaume Montdory. Affected by the plays and the performers, Corneille turned to the theater, and he became, like Hardy, a successful professional playwright. In 1630 Lenoir and Montdory produced Corneille's first play, *Mélite*, in a converted Paris tennis court. Lenoir and several other actors deserted to the Troupe Royale at the Hôtel de Bourgogne. But the success of *Mélite* and the backing of Richelieu encouraged Montdory to found the Théâtre du Marais in another tennis court. Corneille wrote loyally for Montdory's playhouse, as Hardy did for the Bourgogne some years before.

Corneille was not at first, or by instinct, a classicist. That was to come later. He began by writing five comedies of contemporary life, and turned out a tragi-comedy, *Clitandre*, before he wrote his first classic tragedy, *Médée*, in 1635. The Spanish drama attracted him greatly. You can see its influence in his next play, the comedy *L'Illusion comique*. Nine years later he made his finest comedy, *Le Menteur*, out of Alarcón's *La verdad sospechosa*. In between—late in 1636 or early in 1637—he scored an enormous success at the Théâtre du Marais with *Le Cid*. This play, too, had a Spanish original, and was free in form and romantic in feeling.

Before the production of this "cloak and sword" drama, Corneille could see no more reason for writing as a neo-classicist than for following the freer form of Hardy. The "classic regulations" had not yet set their stamp on French drama. But, in spite of the popular success of *Le Cid*—it was acted in London within a year—a storm of fierce criticism descended on Corneille for not having observed the classic rules. Corneille withdrew to Rouen for three years, and weighed the virtues of his artistic convictions against the advantages following the rules dear to potent Richelieu. The result was *Horace*, dedicated to the cardinal, *Cinna, Polyeucte*, and *Le Mort de Pompée*. They all followed the regulations. He relapsed with *Le Menteur*, but turned again to classic tragedy, and was elected in 1647 to the sacred French Academy. Definitely he was now not only the leading dramatist of France, but also the major classicist of its stage.

Corneille had a long and full career. He outlived his close friend Molière, and wrote his last play only three years before Racine, his newly ascendent rival, retired from the theater. Corneille contributed to France a new form of play in his comedies of intrigue. For Louis XIV and Mazarin he wrote the "machine plays" that climaxed the baroque theater, and led the way to French opera. Over and above *Le Cid*, his reputation rests on developing classic tragedy. He did more than anyone else to establish the classic regulations. Yet he did not obey them as closely as his followers. He saw larger values in the theater.

RACINE—HIS WORK AND HIS WAYS

Jean Racine came to the theater at a fortunate moment. When Molière gave this young man his first production in 1664, Corneille had already won popular acceptance for the kind of drama that Racine knew how to write with consummate skill: classic tragedy. Racine's first two produced plays, *La Thébaïde* and *Alexandre le Grand*, had a mild success. *Andromaque* established him as the leading playwright of France. The next year he turned to a satire on lawyers, *Les Plaideurs*, modeled on *The Wasps* of Aristophanes. After that, Racine kept to tragedy. In 1670 he clashed directly and successfully with his only rival. His *Bérénice* was produced a week before Corneille's *Tite et Bérénice*, and won greater popular and critical acclaim. A similar conflict occurred seven years later, when Racine's finest tragedy, *Phèdre*, competed not too successfully with a play of the same name by an inferior but popularly sentimental playwright.

Piqued by this, Racine accepted appointment as court historian to Louis XIV, retired from the theater, married a rich wife, and devoted himself to a life of domesticity and devoutness. Just before his death, he returned to the stage most discreetly and privately. Mme. de Maintenon—first the mistress and later the secret wife of Louis XIV—asked Racine to write biblical plays for a kind of finishing school for young ladies in St. Cyr. He agreed on condition that the plays should not be publicly produced. The result was the fine and sensitive dramas *Esther* and *Athalie*.

Racine played a most important part in the great days of the French drama, which began with *Le Cid* in 1641 and ended with *Phèdre* in 1677. Except for his comedy *Les Plaideurs* and two oriental plays of contemporary feeling, all his work was on classical subjects. When he departed from the 'regulations,' it was only in details. He gave more emphasis than Corneille to love and pity. His poetic style was more precise and brilliant. But his range of interest was narrower, and he lacked the originality and the warm imagination of his great rival.

In spite of dubious doings in the world of the theater, Racine maintained the highest principles in his plays. He gave virtue an exalted place and he pointed out in a preface to *Phèdre* that "the slightest evil is severely punished; the very thought of crime is made as horrible as the commission of it. . . . We should like our work to be as solid and full of useful instruction as were those of antiquity." Racine and Corneille accepted the aristocratic world as it was. No hint of social criticism crept into their plays.

Molière, on the other hand, though he supported the king, and the king supported him, wrote of ignoble aristocrats and ridiculed the falsities of their life. Occasionally his valets showed some discontent with their station. And when Molière defended the salutary purpose of comedy, in his preface to *Tartuffe,* he wrote: "I do not see why there should be a privileged class."

MOLIÈRE—FROM AMATEUR TO IMMORTAL

The comic genius of Molière ennobled the theater of Paris from 1658 to 1673. For ten years it interrupted and overshadowed the development of classic tragedy. Fresh, tonic, and bracing, his work gave the French stage its true distinction between the rich vitality of Corneille in *Le Cid* and *Le Menteur* and the tragic perfection of Racine in *Andromaque.* Even as he was dying in 1673, Molière wrote and acted *Le Malade imaginaire.* This was, as John Palmer has said, "a supreme gesture of the comic spirit—the play in which the great comedian passed from a counterfeiting of death to death itself." No playwright has made so glorious an exit from the stage.

Molière began as an actor—an amateur actor—in 1644. His group was made up mainly of the younger people of two households, and was sometimes referred to as Les Enfants de Famille. The actors seem to have preferred to call their venture the Illustre Théâtre. A group of *commedia dell'arte* per-

French playwrights and the Spanish. *This chart, repeated from our discussion of Spain in the Renaissance, shows how the writers of France came late enough to borrow from Cervantes and Vega as well as Calderón.*

formers would have been content to name their troupe "The Illustrious," and use the streets as a playhouse. But Molière and his friends hired a tennis court in 1644. After some disastrous performances there, they tried another site. It all ended in Molière's being clapped in jail for debts to a candle merchant, among others. His father, Jean Poquelin, subsequently paid the claims, perhaps out of gratitude for his son's having assumed the name of Molière when he went on the stage. After the unhappy experience of Molière and his friends in Paris, they turned to the provinces and spent thirteen years on tour.

Before the movies killed the American touring system, "the road" would often accept what Broadway had rejected. Something like this must have been true in seventeenth-century France. We know all too little about the career of Molière and his fellow-actors in the provinces. But we do know that they left Paris late in 1645 and that they didn't return until 1658. We also know that, on leaving, they immediately acquired a patron, the Duc d'Epernon, and that in 1653 they were taken under the wing of a new one, the Prince de Conti, who had been a fellow-student of Molière's at the Jesuit college. Like a dozen or more of their competitors, they gave French tragedies, Italian farces, and Spanish plays of intrigue and derring-do. Toward the end, Molière turned playwright and added some Italianate farces and comedies to the repertory. Two of these, *L'Étourdi* and *Le Dépit amoureux,* must have been quite popular, for he revived them later in Paris.

There can be no doubt that the company grew in stature as time went on. New actors joined them, their performances improved in skill, and Molière's plays grew popular. Toward the end, the troupe was hired on a number of occasions to give plays while the *États,* or local legislatures, were in session, and, at least in one case, we know that they were paid rather handsomely. The best evidence of their progress is that when the Prince de Conti turned puritanical and withdrew his patronage, the Duc d'Orléans, brother of the king, presented Molière and his players before Louis XIV and his court in the guard room of the Louvre in Paris.

MOLIÈRE'S MOST DRAMATIC HOUR

It was a critical day for Molière, this twenty-fourth of October, 1658. Now almost thirty-seven—with half of his creative life behind him in the provinces—he was to appear before a twenty-year-old king who was already the arbiter of theatrical art in France. Through Molière's choice of a vehicle for his actors, he doomed the company to failure, but through his resourcefulness and wit he turned the evening into a triumph.

Tragedy had been the chief fare of the Illustre Théâtre. It had figured prominently in the provincial repertory. Molière loved the dark muse with such passion that he did not consider how hopelessly mediocre his troupe would seem in tragedy when compared with the actors of the Hôtel de Bourgogne—who, incidentally, were in the audience at the Louvre. Instead of playing one of his own comedies—which were to make the fame of his company in Paris—he chose Corneille's *Nicomède*. The results were dire. Obviously, "Monsieur" (as the brother of the king was officially termed) had made a grave mistake.

Before the play was over, Molière had sensed defeat and had determined on a line of counter-attack. When the polite applause ended, he stepped forward and spoke to the king with dignity and grace, with pride as well as a certain pleasant irony. Here is an account of part of his speech as reported by La Grange, an actor who joined Molière the next year:

After thanking His Majesty in modest terms for the kindness with which he had overlooked the deficiencies of his company, which had appeared only with the greatest misgivings before so august an assembly, he assured His Majesty that the desire which all had to amuse the greatest King in all the world had caused them to forget that His Majesty had in his service excellent originals of which they were but feeble copies. Since, however, His Majesty had been so good as to suffer their country manners, he begged very humbly to be permitted to present one of the small diversions which had acquired for him a certain reputation and with which he had been accustomed to amuse the provinces.

The small diversion was *Le Docteur amoureux*. The success of Molière, his acting, and his play was electric. Ignoring the failure of the company in *Nicomède*, Louis XIV let the Troupe de Monsieur share the Salle du Petit-Bourbon with his Italian players.

For the first weeks of Molière's stay at the Petit-Bourbon, that stubborn devotee of the tragic art repeated the same mistake he had made at the Louvre. He played five tragedies by Corneille, and starved at the box office. Then he revived his provincial hits *L'Étourdi* and *Le Dépit amoureux*, and Paris flocked to his theater. From then on, the success of Molière was the success of his own plays. As they grew in number, they grew, too, in quality.

MOLIÈRE AS SOCIAL SATIRIST

Many of the comedies of Molière—the best of them, in fact—brought trials and tribulations as well as success. The first play that he wrote in Paris, *Les Précieuses ridicules* (*The Affected Ladies*), stirred up a hornet's nest among the smart and powerful poseurs of the court. Only the intervention of the king, who happened to be out of Paris at the time of its production, saved this first comedy of manners from suppression.

As Molière grew more caustic in his comedies, as he wrote more keenly and discerningly of the foibles of society, of the injustices done women, of the hypocrisy of some members of the clergy, attacks upon him and his plays increased. So, fortunately, did the prosperity of his troupe. In 1662 he was accused of licentiousness and impiety because in *L'École des femmes* (*The School for Wives*) he attacked the right of a guardian to marry off his ward against her will. In his version of the Don Juan story, *Les Festin de Pierre,* he pictured a wicked marquis. Immediately the courtiers accused him of attacking the nobility, and of agreeing with the sentiments and behavior of his libertine-hero. Again the king supported Molière. To make the royal attitude clear, Louis XIV took over the company from his brother in the summer of 1665, called it the Troupe du Roi, and gave it a subsidy. The greatest of Molière's difficulties arose over *Tartuffe,* and lasted from 1664 till 1669. The first three acts of this attack on a religious hypocrite were given as part of a festival at Versailles, *Les Plaisirs de l'isle enchantée.* The onslaughts of many of the clergy and the courtiers became so violent that Louis XIV did not dare license the play for public performance, but he had it read and acted in his palace and other homes of royalty. He secured the endorsement of a legate of the Pope, but others in the Catholic hierarchy denounced Molière as a devil in human form, and the king dared not move till 1667. Even then the troubles of *Tartuffe* were far from over. When it was produced at the Palais-Royal—where Molière had moved from the Petit-Bourbon—the king was out of the city, and the president of the Paris parliament closed the theater. The archbishop of Paris banned the acting or seeing and the reading or hearing of the play, either in public or in private, on pain of excommunication. Louis had to defer another licensing for eighteen months. Then, in 1669, *Tartuffe*—with its name changed to *The Impostor*—became a great and deserved success.

COMEDY-BALLETS TO PLEASE THE KING

The support that the king gave Molière in the battles over these four plays was not due entirely to Louis' good sense. The king valued the plays for what they were—works of comic genius—but he also valued Molière as a man who could write and stage superb entertainments at Versailles and other pleasure places. From 1662 to 1670 he gave a good deal of his time and energy to pleasing *le Grand Monarque* in this fashion. Molière showed great ingenuity in devising spectacular shows and at the same time injecting into them his own plays. He invented for this purpose a form called the comedy-ballet. The first production was actually commissioned by the prime minister Fouquet for his gardens at Vaux-le-Vicomte, but its huge success put ideas in the king's head. Thereafter Molière was to work only for the glory of Louis XIV. The entertainment at Vaux was spectacular in over-all effect, for Torelli provided stage machines, the architect Le Brun painted the setting, and Lully composed the music, but the king got quite as much pleasure from the satire around which it all revolved. In *Les Fâcheux* (*The Bores*) the amorous dalliance of two lovers is interrupted by the advent of one bore after another. Through these *fâcheux,* Molière satirized a dozen facets of society, and the delighted king suggested that the playwright add another bore, the Royal Master of the Hunt. In 1664, Molière wrote a second comedy-ballet, *Le Mariage forcé,* in which the king danced as an Egyptian.

Two theaters of Spain's "golden age." *Above, one of the* corrales *of central and northern Spain, probably the* Corral de la Pacheca of Madrid *as it appeared in 1574.* (Drawing by Gerda Becker With, after a sketch by Comba.) *Below, a drawing of a scene from Calderon's* La Fiera, el Rayo y la Piedra, *given at Valencia in 1690. Note the flat wings.* (*From Valbuena,* Literatura dramatica español, *courtesy the Bibliotec Nacional, Madrid.*)

Two French theaters. *Above, the first theater built in Paris, the Bourgogne, as it was in 1645. Below, the open air theater at Versailles built by Louis XIV. Here Molière appeared on the night of his death in 1673 in La Malade imaginaire.* (Drawings by Gerda Becker With, after engravings by Chauveau, Le Pautre.)

The best of half a dozen more was *Le Bourgeois gentilhomme*, produced in 1670.

Having amplified the old equipment of the Palais-Royal, Molière tried his hand, in 1668, at a type of entertainment called the "machine play." Rocks that opened into heavens, flights of demi-gods, palaces that became grottos, living dragons and centaurs—these had entertained Italian princes for more than a century, and Mazarin and Torelli had brought them to Paris twenty years before. In writing and staging *Amphitryon*, Molière showed his usual moderation and good sense. He confined the mechanical contrivances to the prolog, in which Mercury was seated on a cloud and Night appeared in an aerial chariot, and to the last act, in which Mercury flew aloft and disappeared in a cloud.

MOLIÈRE'S ONE TRAGEDY

Molière's love of tragedy made him, in 1660, write one play in that *genre*. This was *Don Garcie*. It was obviously a failure, and, though he obstinately kept it in his repertory for three years, he never published it, and he finally borrowed some of its best verse for his *Le Misanthrope*. The failure of Molière and his company in tragedy lay in the fact that he disliked the declamatory bombast of the day, and preferred a simpler and more natural kind of diction and performance. For the last production of *Don Garcie* he wrote a little play, *L'Impromptu de Versailles*, attacking the tragedians of the Hôtel de Bourgogne. Perhaps if Molière had been an Elizabethan playwright, his love of both tragedy and comedy, coupled with his equal facility in poetry and prose, would have made him a rival to Shakespeare.

A MAN OF MANY PARTS

The bulk of Molière's plays can be divided into three forms: farce, comedy-ballet, and comedy. But in spirit, content, and style they often overlap.

From Molière's days in the provinces until two years before his death, he was the master of the farce of intrigue. Most of these plays, including *Le médicin malgré lui* (*The Doctor in Spite of Himself*), *L'Avare* (*The Miser*), and *Les Fourberies de Scapin* (*The Rogueries of Scapin*), were based on Italian or Roman originals, yet the best of them present human failings or satirize social pretensions.

Many of his comedy-ballets are farcical, but many present some of his finest and purest comedy. *Georges Dandin* and *Le Bourgeois gentilhomme* included ballets and were produced in court spectacles. *L'École des maris* (*The School for Husbands*) is a brilliant comedy of manners, like *L'École des femmes* (*The School for Wives*), which followed in 1662, and *Les Femmes savantes* (*The Learned Ladies*) of 1672. *Tartuffe* and *Les Misanthrope*, perhaps his greatest comedies, showed, like so many of his other plays, Molière's aversion to both bigotry and excess. The last of his social comedies, *Le Malade imaginaire* (*The Imaginary Invalid*), has been called "the history of the death of Molière." Touched by family tragedy and gravely diseased, he wrote gaily of a man who only imagined himself to be ill. It was a gesture of courageous detachment seldom if ever equalled by any other writer.

Molière died immediately after his last appearance as the imaginary invalid. Partly because he was an actor and had not repented that sin, but chiefly because he had been a keen critic of life, he was refused Christian burial until Louis XIV's last intervention for his friend and the true genius of his reign. Molière was buried after sunset, without ceremony, and with only two priests in attendance. There is even doubt as to whether his body was interred in consecrated ground. The grave of the greatest playwright of France is unknown and unmarked.

PLAYHOUSES AND SCENERY

We know very little about the theater buildings of the time. All we can guess about the Hôtel de Bourgogne is based on a fan-shaped drawing made in 1645, a contract for the theater's reconstruction a few years later, and an eighteenth-century plan. The theater hall, located on the second floor, was forty feet wide. The total length was ninety-six feet, which included a stage thirty-three feet deep; later this playing space was deepened by ten feet. The raked stage was six feet high at the front so that those who stood on the floor of the "pit" could see better. Toward the rear the auditorium floor rose in several levels where there were benches. A row of boxs hung out from the side walls and continued along the back. There may have been another row of boxes above, and even an open gallery with benches still higher. The stage had no formal proscenium arch until after the remodeling. The Théâtre du Marais is supposed to have been made over in Italian fashion from an old tennis court. We know very little about the Petit-Bourbon except that the stage was shallower than at the Bourgogne. There were two halls in the Palais-Royal that could be used for plays. One seated six hundred and the other three or four thousand. It must have been the latter that Richelieu used for his spectacular *Miramé* in 1641. The stage of the Salle des Machines, which Mazarin built for another Italian designer, was fifty-nine feet high in order to house the machinery for flying backdrops—there were 144 of them, each seventy-five feet wide—and for lifting actors on clouds and chariots. The Guénégaud, an opera house, could hold 1500 people, and the theater erected for the Comédie-Française in 1689 had room for 2000. Neither played to much more than half capacity.

During the eighteenth century France saw all manner of scenery. In the provinces and at the fairs there was often just a rough curtain behind a stage set on barrels. In the 1640's Richelieu and Mazarin introduced huge Italianate settings painted in false perspective and changing magically before the eyes of the spectators. During the first half of the century, the Hôtel de Bourgogne continued to use the multiple set of the Middle Ages, with as many as five locales visible at the same time. Then when classic tragedy with its unities of time and place became popular, a fourth kind of scenery appeared. This was a single setting, usually the front of a palace. The Italians used a more or less permanent street setting, and most of Molière's comedies were played against a single background.

THE COMÉDIE-FRANÇAISE—LOUIS XIV'S FINAL CONTRIBUTION

The death of Molière altered the fortunes of the four Paris companies. The King, who did not believe that the Troupe du Roi could live without Molière, gave the Palais-Royal to Lully for opera. Molière's actors moved to the Guénégaud. (Just a few years before, in 1671, this house had been built by a nobleman for the Académie Royale des Operas, an institution that ignored Lully.) Through various pressures Louis combined the French-speaking company at the Bourgogne with the actors at the Guénégaud and the Marais. Thus—except for the Italian company that had shared the Bourgogne—Paris in 1680 had only one playhouse, but France had its first —and the world's first—national theater. Gradually it came to be called the Comédie-Française in contradistinction to the Comédie-Italienne. In 1689 it moved into a new playhouse, the first to be built with a horseshoe-shaped auditorium. Today the institution is also known as the Théâtre-Français and in addition—to honor the man who trained so many of its first players—the House of Molière.

THE FIRST PARIS THEATERS

1402	*Hôpital de la Trinité*	Confrérie de la Passion
1548	*Hôtel de Bourgogne*	Confrérie de la Passion c. 1600, Troupe Royale (Hardy) 1670, Italian players
1577	*Petit-Bourbon*	Italian players 1645, Torelli productions 1658, Italian players and Molière
1634	*Théâtre du Marais*	Montdory and his company
1641	*Palais-Royal*	Miramé (Richelieu) 1660, Molière and Italian players
1660	*Salle des Machines*	Spectacles for Mazarin
1671	*Guénégaud*	Opera 1673, La Grange and Molière's company 1680, Comédie-Française

This last major gesture of Louis XIV toward the theater was grand, dangerous, and characteristic. It was grand because it created a strong theater supported by the state. It was dangerous because it was a creature of absolutism, a monopoly barring healthful competition. It was characteristic because it expressed the king's love of ordered power as well as his love of the theater. The Comédie-Française has always maintained high standards in its acting and its classic repertory. It has often blocked progress in playwriting and in production.

Throughout the baroque end of the Renaissance, France failed to create the free and imaginative drama of England and Spain. Yet the clarity and logic of the Gallic mind, working through polished poetry, drew from the classic concept of tragedy a notable, if special, form of drama, and the genius of Molière broke the bounds of a rigid verse-form and a narrow social environment.

six

The NINETEENTH CENTURY

—A TIME Of CHANGE

In EUROPE

IF WE LOOK AT CENTURIES AS PERIODS OF SOCIAL AND ARTISTIC DEVELOPMENT —or, at least, change—we find that they are seldom limited to an even hundred years. This was particularly true of the nineteenth century.

Of all centuries, it was the century of revolution—political revolution and industrial revolution. And these movements appeared before 1800. Political revolution began in 1776 and 1789, and it continued through 1830 and 1848 and 1871, each rebellion breeding reaction as well as progress. Industrial revolution may be said to have started in 1765 when James Watt made a steam engine that could drive machinery, and this revolution ran a steadier course. The outcome of all these upheavals was a slow march toward political and social democracy. There was slower progress in public education, while the population of capitals and manufacturing cities grew enormously.

A CENTURY OF PROGRESS IN THE THEATER

The theater was greatly affected by the peculiar nature of the nineteenth century. There was revolution in playwriting, and there was reaction, too. Creative minds sought fervently for change and betterment. Minds of another sort exploited the new audience of the uncultured who now had money to spend. Playgoers—and theaters—grew in numbers as industrial development swelled the ranks of the middle classes. The vast bulk of these new audiences was under-educated, and looked to the stage for an escape from the world in which they lived and worked. Between the years of Sheridan and Beaumarchais and the years of Ibsen and Shaw, the state of the theater may seem, on the whole, depressed and depressing. Yet the story of the theater through the full nineteenth century—which we will cover in this essay and the beginning of the next—is a story of definite and important progress. It is progress that can be matched only in the fifth century before Christ and the centuries of the Renaissance.

Playwrights moved from classicism to romanticism and to realism; some few moved toward the poetic, and even toward a hint of the expressionistic. Theaters increased in number and—more important—they shrank in size. Acting advanced from bravura display of star talents to well-rehearsed ensembles and to a natural style of acting that suited the realistic play. Science provided the stage with gas, limelight, the arc, and the incandescent bulb. Scenery, along with costumes, became historically accurate. The stage gave up wings and backdrops, and achieved the realism of the box set. At the same time, theories of more imaginative staging developed.

THE ROMANTIC MOVEMENT IN GERMANY

The romanticism of the early nineteenth century had its roots in Germany and in a new literary movement called *Sturm und Drang*, or Storm and Stress. Taking form in the 1770's, it glorified the individual and exalted emotion as against the rationalism of Voltaire. In the theater its writers abjured the classic rules of French drama, and, though they worshiped Shakespeare, most of them wrote in prose instead of verse. If their dialog had a certain quality of naturalness, the feeling and atmosphere of their dramas breathed romanticism.

In 1773, Johann Wolfgang von Goethe's *Goetz von Berlichingen*—rich in medieval color and romantic in action—helped to break the path for Shakespeare and to establish Storm and Stress as an important movement in the theater. The last important play of this type was Johann Friedrich Schiller's *Die Räuber* (*The Robbers*) of 1781.

GOETHE AS DRAMATIST—AND MORE

As dramatist and director, Johann Wolfgang von Goethe gained in stature from his accomplishments in many other fields. He was, first of all, Germany's greatest poet. He was a leader of thought in the natural sciences, and he studied occult philosophies. He knew much about agriculture, forestry, horticulture, and mining. He drew and painted with skill. Through more than half a century Goethe acted as chief counselor to the Duke of Weimar, and for twenty-six years he was director of the ducal theater.

In spite of Goethe's long experience in the theater, his plays are less actable than any that approach them in thought or poetic expression. He confessed that he had "written in opposition to the stage." As director of a playhouse, he was successful within the limits imposed by a small community. His theories of acting were old-fashioned, but he worked assiduously. All in all, he provided some 4,000 different bills, a third of them devoted to opera or operetta. He designed stage settings and theorized on their nature. At the same time he was occupying important posts in the government. From his very considerable labors, he escaped through a two year's sojourn in Italy, a land whose spiritual and physical warmth has always fascinated Teutonic peoples.

During 1786 and 1787, when Goethe was in Italy, a change came over him as a playwright and a philosopher. In the presence of the vast ruins of the Roman world, he turned away from the reality of the emotions, which was the base of Storm and Stress, and began to seek a reality of spirit that, he felt, could be best achieved through a classic and severe approach. *Egmont*, which he finished in Italy, is in prose, and it retains some of the earlier feeling. Then Goethe gave up prose, and rewrote his *Iphigenia* in blank verse. *Faust*—his most renowned and, perhaps, least actable play—is a product of both artistic periods. He began to write it in the first days of Storm and Stress, and he finished the second part of this Gargantuan drama only three months before his death in 1832. The tragedy of Gretchen comes out of his youthful impulses; some of Part One and all of Part Two are a product of his new classicism.

SCHILLER—GREATEST OF GERMAN PLAYWRIGHTS

When Goethe brought him to Weimar in 1799, Schiller was already famous as a playwright and within seven years of his death from tuberculosis. In 1781, when Schiller was only twenty-two and a doctor in the army of the Duke of Wuerttemberg, he wrote his first play, *The Robbers*, a drama of fierce resentment. The next year Schiller's own resentment against army life made him go AWOL to Mannheim, where the play had been produced. There Schiller lived under an assumed name and earned his living as court playwright and stage manager. Then followed *Kabale und Liebe*, an attack on the morals of the nobility, and *Don Carlos*, a plea for tolerance. For the next twelve years the stage saw no new plays by Schiller. As a university professor during this period, he gathered material on the Thirty Years' War, material that he was to use in his great trilogy on the warrior Wallenstein. Schiller completed his work in Weimar, and wrote four more plays before he died: *Maria Stuart*, *Die Jungfrau von Orleans* (*The Maid of Orleans*), *Die Braut von Messina* (*The Bride of Messina*) and *Wilhelm Tell*, his greatest feat of craftsmanship.

Both Schiller and Goethe strove to achieve an ideal beauty, but Schiller was a more powerful dramatist. Most of his plays are less classic in form or feeling than Goethe's, though his *The Bride of Messina* employs lyric choruses and is the nearest approach of his time to ancient tragedy. His plays have the drive and vigor of Storm and Stress, but they move from a glorification of individualism toward something approaching social drama. Goethe's early plays and most of Schiller's anticipated the romantic movement that reached the French stage almost fifty years later.

In Austria and Germany romanticism had two other men of great talent. The Viennese Franz Grillparzer found success in his first play, *Die Ahnfrau* (*The Ancestress*), produced in 1817. He wrote with warmth about Sappho and about Jason and Medea. He turned Calderón's *Life Is a Dream* into *Der Traum ein Leben* (*Dreaming Is Life*), which provided an excellent part for the distinguished German actor Adalbert Matkowsky at the end of the nineteenth century. Grillparzer had a knack for comedy. So had Heinrich von Kleist, who began by writing a "fate drama" at the end of the eighteenth century, and achieved fine humor a little later with *Der Zerbrochene Krug* (*The Broken Pitcher*). It was in his serious plays, however, such as *Penthesilea* and *Die Hermannsschlacht* (*The Battle of Arminius*), that he showed his dramatic power as well as his command of vivid dialog. Bedeviled by graver obsessions than the romanticists' fondness for sleepwalking scenes and savage passions, Kleist has been called the unconscious father of the modern psychological drama. His tragedies went almost unnoticed until the Duke of Saxe-Meiningen revived a number of them seventy years after Kleist had committed suicide in 1811.

HUGO AND HERNANI

There has been a great deal too much ado over Victor Hugo's battle for romanticism in the 1820's. As we have pointed out, medieval and renaissance melodramas had flooded the French stage for more than two decades. The fact that the audience on the opening night of Hugo's *Hernani* in 1830 rioted for and against the play has made most critics think of it as the first romantic drama of nineteenth century France. Actually, it was merely the

The romantic movement. *The impulse came from the Storm and Stress movement of 1771 to 1781; the climax was French. This chart leaves out the inferior and more popular writers of romantic melodramas—Kotzebue, Pixerécourt, Knowles.*

first success by a really distinguished writer. There would probably have been no ruction if Hugo had not attacked the classical unities in his preface to *Cromwell*—fifty years after Lessing—and if *Hermani* had not been produced in the one remaining home of classical tradition, the Comédie-Française. Like Hugo, the elder Dumas is better known for his novels, particularly *The Three Musketeers*, than for his best play *La Tour de Nesle*.

Alfred de Musset, a far finer and more sensitive playwright than Hugo or Dumas or any other Frenchman who had written since Molière, was a romantic, but not in the current fashion. He glorified his passionate affair with the feminist authoress George Sand in *One Does Not Trifle with Love*, but he also wrote with humor. His first group of one-act plays, *Comedies and Proverbs*, have something of the flavor of Molière. He turned his back on the stage after the failure of his first drama, *La Nuit Venitienne*, in 1830, and wrote only for publication. In the poetic mood of two of his plays, *Fantasio* and *Lorenzaccio*—set in no definite time or place—de Musset is close to the *symbolisme* of Maeterlinck and later French writers.

ENGLISH ACTOR-MANAGERS OF MERIT

All was not dark on the English stage in the first half of the nineteenth century. There were good actors besides Mrs. Siddons and John Philip Kemble, who had ornamented the eighteenth. Another brother, Charles, and his daughter Fanny played with distinction. The greatest actor was the tempestuous Edmund Kean; Coleridge called his romantic performances "like reading Shakespeare by flashes of lightning." There were two subtle comedians: Charles Mathews, who, in his *At Homes*, played all the characters in short satiric pieces, and his son Charles James, who acted with and married that remarkable actress-manageress Mme. Vestris. William Charles Macready, the only rival of Edmund Kean, was scholarly and idealistic as well as hot tempered. He hated his profession, but he acted Shakespeare's plays almost as they had been written, and he produced poetic tragedies by Byron, Browning, and Bulwer-Lytton. Samuel Phelps, like Macready, preferred Shakespeare to his adaptors. At the Sadler's Wells Theater he produced all but seven of the poet's plays between 1844 and 1862.

HISTORICAL ACCURACY IN COSTUMES

The first half of the nineteenth century saw some important developments in costuming, scenic design, and devices for changing sets.

It took the European theater about seventy-five years to accept completely the obvious idea—carried out by Macklin in 1773—that the costumes of a historical play should agree with the times and people it presented. Twentieth-century producers have done *Hamlet* and other old plays in modern dress and in modern scenery as daring experiments. "Modern dress," along with conventional scenery, was the general custom until the second half of the eighteenth century. And it was only between 1810 and 1850 that historical accuracy gradually became established.

Attempts at accuracy of costuming came first. In the 1750's, Diderot praised Mlle. Clairon for discarding her hoop skirts in a Chinese role. A few reforms followed, yet in her *Memoirs*, written twenty-five years later, she was urging actresses to give up massive and monstrous hair-dos and adopt "the costume of the role one is playing." Only Talma and the French Revolution could put Clairon's ideas into more general practice in Paris. The German Heinrich Gottfried Koch used medieval costumes in *Goetz von Berlichingen* as early as 1774. And six years later Goethe played Orestes in a kind of classic garb.

The major credit for establishing true historical accuracy in London must go to a remarkable man of French descent, J. R. Planché. He wrote innumerable burlettas and extravaganzas, and he was an accomplished musician. But it was through his scholarly interest in the past that he contributed most notably to the artistic progress of the London stage. In 1823 he persuaded Charles Kemble to mount *King John* in really authentic costumes—"the precise habiliments of the period," as the playbill proclaimed. Planché's *History of British Costume* made a theatrical stir in 1834, and to this we may credit in part the excellence of Macready's costuming. (Macready also sought for accuracy of setting; while Kemble's *Coriolanus* had shown a Rome of imperial marble, Macready's reconstructed the ruder republican city of five centuries before.) Planché's greatest contribution, however, lay in the part he played in the launching of Mme. Lucia Vestris as an actress-manageress who was to establish the vogue of naturally acted comedy and the realistic box-set on the London stage.

MME. VESTRIS—PIONEER

Before the extraordinary Mme. Vestris opened her own theater in 1831, she had sung in opera, played Shakespeare and Sheridan, and made a name for herself as the most celebrated player of "breeches parts" since Nell Gwynn and Peg Woffington. The charm of her singing and dancing were excelled only by the naturalness and vivacity of her acting. But the most remarkable thing about the young woman was her refurbishing and management of the Olympic Theater. She turned a rather disreputable playhouse into the only theater except the King's—which was devoted to opera—where the smarter and more intelligent public of London felt at home. A critic saluted her "little back drawing-room of a theater. . . . Hail, thou sublimation of little laughs! thou bit of the millinery part of heaven!"

Mme. Vestris and Planché brought a curious sort of comedic realism to the Olympic's productions. This lay partly in the fact that the director took advantage of the intimacy of the little house to give the acting a quiet naturalness. A distinguished critic wrote that the players seemed "oblivious of the footlights." Instead of the absurdly stylized costumes always worn by such characters as the serving maid and the young-man-about-town—hitherto as fixed as the wardrobe and masks of the *commedia dell'arte*—Mme. Vestris introduced varied and appropriate costumes of the day. Furniture took on a natural appearance. There were antiques where needed, and all modern pieces where appropriate. Hitherto, the only chairs on the London stage were those that actually had to be sat upon because of the action of the play. Others were painted on the wings or the backdrops; this was going on in other cities as late as 1868, if we credit a sketch for *Faust* at the Hanover Court Theater. In addition to dressing her rooms with as many pieces of furniture as such rooms would normally have, Mme. Vestris played a most important part in introducing the modern type of box-set in London.

THE BOX-SET ARRIVES

No one knows just when wings parallel to the footlights were first replaced by continuous walls for the right and left sides of rooms. Eighteenth-century plans show wings so hinged that they could be aligned from the proscenium to the backing. At the Court Theater of Mannheim, Germany, in 1804, a stage designer joined pairs of wings with flats that contained practicable doors or windows. About that time the French stage must have had something like the walls of a box-set; for in 1811 Goethe inveighed in his autobiography against the French stage for "shutting up the sides of the stage and forming rooms with real walls." There is good evidence that Mme. Vestris used a box-set in November, 1832, for a critic wrote that the stage's "more perfect enclosure gives the appearance of a private chamber, infinitely better than the old contrivance of wings." In 1834, when Drury Lane produced a new play by Planché, a reviewer reported that the "stage was entirely enclosed," and even suggested that there was a ceiling instead of a row of hanging "borders."

The box-set won complete success when Mme. Vestris put on Dion Boucicault's comedy *London Assurance* at Covent Garden in 1841. Critics wrote of the realism of its rooms with their heavy moldings, real doors with doorknobs, ample and correct furniture. For many years, however, scholars gave credit for this reform to the playwright and director Tom Robertson, whose comedies were presented with great success by the actors and managers Squire Bancroft and his wife, Marie Wilton, between 1865 and 1870. Bancroft not only claimed that the settings had "for the first time, ceilings." He said that they had door "locks and similar matter never before seen upon the stage."

HISTORICALLY ACCURATE SCENERY

Settings as well as costumes began to be genuinely accurate around 1810, when Josef Schreyvogel became director of the Burgtheater in Vienna. Count

Brühl, in charge of the Royal Theater in Berlin, followed Schreyvogel's example in 1817 with *Henry IV*. Shortly after the middle of the century, two actor-managers in London at last succeeded in bringing historical accuracy to the plays of Shakespeare.

Charles Kean was a far less talented actor than his father Edmund. He made up for this through his ability as a director. His actors were always well cast and well rehearsed. He achieved more of an ensemble than anyone since Mme. Vestris. With the zeal of an antiquarian, he saw to it that his scenery fitted the period of the play. He did the same with the costumes, except for an occasional lapse such as when his wife in *The Winter's Tale* wore a correct Greek dress over a crinoline. Perhaps Kean's most noted revivals were *King John, Macbeth, Richard II,* and *Henry VIII.* While he made lavish spectacles of the last two plays, he gave *Macbeth* the rude atmosphere of its time and place.

Charles Fechter may have been born in London, but his parents were French and he spent more than half his life in Paris. Before he was thirty, he had created the role of the lover in *La Dame aux camélias (Camille)*, and, for a time, he was co-director of the Théâtre de l'Odéon, the second state playhouse of France. After playing briefly in Germany and eight years in London, he came to America to work only half a dozen years before he died. His French accent did not prevent the success of his *Hamlet* at the Princess's Theater, London, in 1861. Perhaps it gave an added novelty to a picturesque and highly accented interpretation that was called "revolutionary" and also "gentlemanly melodrama." Like Laurence Olivier on the screen, Fechter played Hamlet in a blond wig. Fechter's massive settings and his medieval costumes outdistanced those of Charles Kean in authenticity and effectiveness. At the Lyceum, he depressed and subdued the footlights. He used ceiling pieces instead of borders, and he originated or developed a new method of scene changing.

SETS UP FROM THE BASEMENT

Before the box-set developed, changes of scene were made quickly before the eyes of the audience by the use of shutters or wings and drops. Curtains to mark the ends of acts probably did not appear in England until about 1800, and there were no scene curtains until 1881 in a production by Irving. On pages 29-31, 53, and 102-103, we have explained some of the ways of changing scenes that developed in the Renaissance. Backings could be raised or slid aside like shutters. For the sides of the set, *periaktoi* could be turned or wings could be "nested"; on the Continent, "chariots" in the basement carried the wings in and out through slots in the stage floor, but England preferred to slide them in grooves.

In 1863, Fechter tore out the grooves in the Lyceum. Some accounts say that he installed the Continental "chariot and pole" system; others say that he divided the stage into a jigsaw puzzle of sections that could be lowered

.for scene changes. During the last quarter of the nineteenth century in a number of European and American playhouses, the entire stage was divided into traps through which sections of settings could be raised from the basement. In some cases—and perhaps in the theater of Fechter—there were long narrow openings called "cuts" which ran along each side of the stage from the front to the rear; perhaps through them the side walls of a box-set could be brought up to the stage level and joined by a backing. Thus science developed more—and not the last—of those stage machines that have been called the largest and most elaborate tools ever employed in art.

GASLIGHT DIMS THE AUDITORIUM

Historical accuracy and box-sets, ceiling pieces and "cuts," were not the only changes in physical production during the first three-quarters of the nineteenth century. Another was the introduction of gaslight on the London stage in 1817. In one way, this was a dubious improvement. The number of theater fires increased greatly. Nearly 400 theaters burned down in America and Europe between 1800 and the coming of electricity. Gas had two great advantages, however, over candles and lamplight. Conveyed by flexible rubber tubing—literally miles of it—from a central source to footlights, borders, and house lights, the flow of gas could be controlled, and the lights dimmed in any part of the theater. After about 1860, lights could be completely extinguished, and then relit by electric sparks. For the first time the auditorium could be darkened and all light concentrated upon the stage—a reform advocated by an Italian in 1598 but not generally practiced until Henry Irving's productions in the last quarter of the century. The brilliance of gas made it possible to do away with borders and all but the first row of border lights, and to use ceiling pieces.

Oil lamps and even candles continued in use for a number of generations in smaller theaters, while two other forms of very brilliant illumination appeared between 1800 and 1850. About the same time as gas came "limelight." It was an intense, white light produced by heating a piece of limestone with a very hot combination of gases. Used with a curved mirror, it became a spotlight of great brilliance. Somewhat the same effect was produced by the arclight, first introduced at the Paris Opera House in 1846. Made by an electric current heating two rods of carbon to incandescence, this early form of the arc suffered from flicker and noisiness.

VICTORIAN PLAYWRIGHTS

Too much credit went to Robertson and Bancroft as pioneers of the realistic box-set, but they deserve our full respect for writing and producing in the 1860's a series of plays of contemporary life that were far more credible than anything turned out by earlier Englishmen. Well directed by Robertson in settings that seemed almost as real as the rooms from which the audience had come, his plays with monosyllabic titles—*Society*, of 1865, *Ours*, *Caste*, *Play*, and *School*—were dubbed "cup and saucer dramas" by the hostile, but won success for him as well as the Bancrofts.

Robertson might have found a rival in Dion Boucicault. Boucicault was not yet twenty when he wrote the very successful *London Assurance*, and for fifty years he was a famous playwright, actor, manager, director, and technician. How much of the wit and polish of *London Assurance* was contributed by Mme. Vestris, Mathews, and others, we shall never learn, but we do know that his enormous output—listed at anywhere from 140 to 400 pieces—included very few original plays and nothing of the quality of *London Assurance*. As a man of business, Boucicault can hardly be blamed for adapting novels and French plays. Managers paid as much for these as for original work, and they were far easier to write. Before he left for the United States in 1852, he had little to his credit except adaptations like *The Corsican Brothers*, written while he was literary adviser to Charles Kean. His work in America culminated in his only fresh contribution to the drama, *The Colleen Bawn*, the first of a series of plays about Irish life, in which he proved a particularly brilliant actor. Except for these plays and his first comedy, he contributed little through his writings.

From Robertson in the '60's to Pinero and Jones in the '80's, English playwrights showed so little talent that Matthew Arnold was justified in saying in 1879: "In England we have no modern drama at all."

NATURALISM VERSUS *REALISM*

Before we return to the Continent and the progress in playwriting through about three-quarters of the nineteenth century, we must pause for some definitions. These will carry us beyond the "romanticism" of Victor Hugo, Goethe, and Schiller and beyond the classicism of Corneille and Racine. (The comedies of Molière and Sheridan are a law unto themselves.) We must try to define "naturalism" and "realism," and to distinguish between them. We must also set apart the "well-made play" of Scribe and Sardou from the "well-made play" of Ibsen and his followers.

"Realism" should be simple enough. A realistic play is written in colloquial prose. It may be laid in the time of Hannibal, like Sherwood's *The Road to Rome*, but its characters speak naturally, and their psychology is the psychology of men and women as we understand them today. In the realistic play, things seem to happen to people on the stage as naturally, plausibly, and inevitably as they might in real life. Realism has two difficult tasks. One is to reach an elevation of spirit and expression, and the other to achieve an exciting dramatic effect without violating a feeling of naturalness.

Yes, "realism" should be easy enough to recognize and define, if the problem were not complicated by another name for a play that is neither romantic nor classic. Obviously, the essence of realism is that its plays must seem natural; but the word "naturalism" was invented almost a hundred years ago to apply to a very special kind of naturalness. From 1868 onward, the great Émile Zola applied the term to his novels and the novels of Edmond and Jules de Goncourt. Zola also applied it—hopefully—to the drama. His naturalism was a product of the scientific theories of heredity and evolution that we associate with Charles Darwin and his *On the Origin of Species,* but that Zola adopted from French writers as well. On a philosophical plane, this meant that all men were controlled by the so-called "laws" of heredity and by the influence of environment, with environment itself a product of heredity. Thus, deprived of free will, most men were doomed to misery. Along with this pessimistic view of society—heightened by the vice and squalor of so much of Paris under the Second Empire of Louis Napoleon— went a theory of writing. To Zola, writing a play or writing a novel was simply a business of observing and recording facts. Imagination and invention were unnecessary. A play was a scientific document, "a slice of life." People and their actions were to be reported as truth, not organized as art. Zola and his followers could not recognize that, in terms of the theater, this was a sheer impossibility. Besides observation, there has to be selectivity and organization, imagination and inventiveness. Otherwise there can be no satisfactory impact on the audience in the theater.

Oddly enough, the plays of Zola and the Goncourt brothers, though they were theatrical failures, were never truly naturalistic. Yet the work of the three men—mainly through their novels and Zola's polemics—had a considerable effect on the French drama. Unfortunately, so far as definitions go, the school of Zola sowed confusion. Today critics and laymen are all too apt to use "naturalism" and "realism" as if they were interchangeable terms for the same real, or natural, quality in most modern plays.

THE "WELL-MADE PLAY"

The expression "well-made play" involves less confusion than "naturalism." When Bernard Shaw was a critic in the 1890's, he used those words as a term of opprobrium for the plays of Scribe and Sardou. Shaw was curiously mistaken. Those French plays lacked practically all values except those of theatrical effect, and they were not nearly so well-made as Ibsen's were to be. The shoddy carpentry of Scribe and Sardou provided no more than a false façade. Ibsen built his characters, plots, and themes into a solid structure. He was the master architect of the truly well-made play.

Eugène Scribe—the man who invented the term *pièce bien faite* for the well-made play—turned out more than 400 pieces of ingenuity. They ranged from a musical sketch of 1816, through comedies, farces, librettos, and melodramas, to one celebrated tragedy. (This tragedy, *Adrienne Lecouvreur,* the story of a long-dead star, Scribe wrote in 1849 with the aid of a minor playwright.) The same ingenuity in comedy, melodrama, and tragedy—and the same lack of substance—appeared in Victorien Sardou, the man who followed Scribe as the most popular playwright of the second half of the century,

From the success of *Les Pattes de mouche* (*A Scrap of Paper*) in 1860, he went triumphantly onward through his frisky farce *Divorçons!* (*Let's Get Divorced!*), the historical comedy *Madame Sans-Gêne*, and *Fédora, La Tosca*, and other tragedies for Sarah Bernhardt in the '80's, to *Robespierre* for Henry Irving in 1902. Together, Scribe and Sardou worked for more than eighty years at the profitable trade of theatrical carpentry.

REALISM IN GERMANY AND RUSSIA

Before 1850, there was more realism to be found outside France than within it. Germany and Russia made notable contributions.

In the first half of the '30's, Georg Büchner, a young German, turned away from revolutionary propaganda and spent his last three years—he died at twenty-four—in writing plays. His *Leonce and Lena* is a whimsical satire on the aristocracy. *Danton's Death*, produced successfully in 1916 by Max Reinhardt, is a strong, tersely-written tragedy, free of the cheap romantic taint of his time. In *Woyzeck*, an almost psychotic tragedy, we find a hint of the expressionism that we will discuss later. In this play—perhaps because Büchner left it in an unfinished and chaotic state—realism comes close to the ideal of naturalism as well as expressionism.

Also in Germany, Friedrich Hebbel turned away momentarily from historical plays in verse, and wrote the first realistic tragedy that anticipated the social pessimism of the coming naturalists. This was his *Maria Magdalena* of 1844. The outstanding German playwright between Schiller and Hauptmann, Hebbel won distinction with dramas on biblical subjects, such as *Judith* and *Herodes und Mariamne*, as well as with his *Die Nibelungen*, but he may be remembered longest as the pioneer of realistic tragedy.

Despotism and censorship turned a number of Russian playwrights toward satire and comedy, where realism unites with the fantastic and the grotesque. In this field lie Alexander Griboyedov's *Woe from Wit*, written in the '20's, and Nikolai Gogol's *The Inspector General* and *The Gamblers*, from the '30's and '40's. In 1846 Alexander Ostrovsky began the writing of his many realistic comedies of middle-class life, including *Enough Stupidity in Every Wise Man* and *The Bankrupt*. Ten years before his tragedy *The Thunderstorm* appeared in 1859 or 1860, Turgeniev had written his fine comedy-drama *A Month in the Country*. These last two plays are true pieces of realism, but they are not well-made plays in the Ibsen sense. They are written in the vein and pattern of a later Russian, Anton Chekhov.

BALZAC, DUMAS, AND AUGIER

Honoré de Balzac might have been the first great realist among French playwrights. Indeed, Zola called him the first naturalist. But Balzac was too wrapped up in his long series of novels, *La Comédie humaine*, to write many plays or to give them the care they deserved. The best that can be said for his play of 1848, *La Marâtre* (*The Stepmother*), is that it may have given Turgeniev the stimulus to write *A Month in the Country*. By the time Balzac's *Mercadet, le faiseur* (*Mercadet, the Jobber*) appeared in 1851, the younger Dumas was turning his novel *La Dame aux camélias* into a tragedy to which we have given the illogical title of *Camille*. Émile Augier was trying to use verse in plays with middle-class characters before he turned to realism.

Dumas *fils*—as the French call him to distinguish him from his great father—and Augier wrote for the stage through some thirty-five years. They competed in realistic observation and sometimes even in their themes. Two years after Dumas' romantic eulogy of a reformed "daughter of joy" in *Camille*, Augier replied with a portrait of an unscrupulous courtesan in *Le Mariage d'Olympe* (*The Marriage of Olympia*). By this time, Dumas had joined Augier as a writer of "thesis plays" designed to attack or correct social

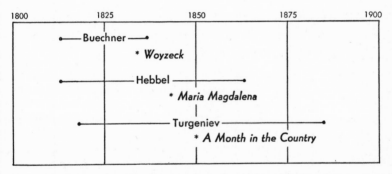

Forerunners of realism. *Here in three playwrights and three plays we have the first examples of the realistic—almost the naturalistic—approach to the drama. This was well ahead of Zola and Ibsen.*

abuses. In the same year as Augier's exposure of sexual depravity, Dumas attacked the Bohemian society in which his father had moved, fastening on it the title of his play, *Le Demi-monde*. From his own experience as a child born out of wedlock, he drew the materials for *Le Fils naturel* (*The Illegitimate Son*). The evils that Dumas and Augier exposed went beyond the sexual. Between them, they dealt with the cupidity of the self-made man, anti-clericalism, religious bigotry, the unscrupulous press, corruption in politics. Augier's best work was his comedy of 1854, *Le Gendre de M. Poirier* (*The Son-in-Law of M. Poirier*), a satire on the relations between an ambitious middle-class father and the lazy aristocrat who has married his daughter.

Augier and Dumas *fils* turned their backs on the dying drama of romanticism. They despised the trivialities of Scribe and the speciousness of Sardou, and they earnestly exposed the ills of middle- and upper-class society. Their plays competed successfully with the "boulevard" (read "Broadway" or

"West End") farces of men like Eugène Labiche and the collaborators Meilhac and Halévy. Yet Augier and Dumas never brought to their plays complete reality and never achieved the penetrating power of Ibsen and the dramatists that followed him.

NATURALISM BECOMES REALISM IN FRANCE

Before Ibsen took to realism, there were Frenchmen who tried to give drama the sense of contemporary truth that had been lacking. The Goncourts turned from their naturalistic novels in 1865 to write a play called

French realism before Antoine. *With the exceptions of the meretricious Scribe and Sardou, this chart shows writers who contributed to the growth of the serious realistic play before Antoine opened his Théâtre-libre in 1887. Zola's battle for what he called "naturalism" began in the middle sixties, as the dotted line indicates. Ibsen's consummate realism, which began to develop only in the late seventies, had little effect in France before Antoine produced* Ghosts *in 1890.*

Henriette Maréchal. This mingling of naturalism and realism, and of the morbid and poetic, failed at the Comédie-Française. Five years later, from another and far less noted writer, came a drama of solid power. A one-act play, *La Révolte,* anticipated by ten years the theme and the technical approach of Ibsen's *A Doll's House,* but its author, Count Villiers de L'Isle-Adam, never tried to follow his own lead.

In 1873 Zola followed his polemics for naturalism by dramatizing his novel *Thérèse Raquin.* This was a failure in spite—or perhaps because—of its sensational story of a wife and her lover who murder her husband and, haunted by the eyes of the dumb and paralyzed mother of the dead man, commit suicide. Zola's purpose, as he put it, was to seek "the beast" in this woman and her lover, "to see nothing but the beast, to throw them into a violent drama, and note scrupulously the sensations and acts of these creatures." His only success on the stage came when other writers dramatized his novel *L'Assommoir*.

Other French novelists tried to conquer the stage and failed. Alphonse Daudet wrote only one play of significance, *L'Arlésienne* (*The Woman of Arles*); produced in 1872, it won success later, but only as the libretto for Bizet's opera. Gustave Flaubert, author of the novel *Madame Bovary*, had no better luck with his play *Le Candidat*.

The one outstanding dramatist of this period, Henri Becque, began writing as early as 1867, but had no financial success until the '90's. He wrote his bitter masterpiece *Les Corbeaux* (*The Vultures*) in 1877, but it was not produced for five years, and then had only three performances. In 1885, his brilliant and ironic comedy *La Parisienne* (*The Woman of Paris*) won respect, but, like *Les Corbeaux*, had to wait another decade to win a place in the national repertory of France.

AUSTRIA'S PLAYWRIGHTS

Except for Hebbel with his realistic *Maria Magdalena* and his historical dramas, Germany had no playwrights of note between the 1830's and the 1890's. Austria did a little better through three actors who turned writers. Before Ferdinand Raimund killed himself in 1836, he wrote folk-comedies and allegorical fairy tales. His rival and successor, Johann Nestroy, turned out dialect farces and witty parodies. In the '70's and the '80's, Ludwig Anzengruber wrote folk-plays on serious themes. One attacked conservatism in the church, another exposed the depravity of the middle-class. He wrote a rustic farce based on *Romeo and Juliet*, which he called *The Double Suicide*.

ACTORS WITHOUT AN ENSEMBLE

Until the triumph of realism in the last decade of the nineteenth century, acting was essentially and almost everywhere a bravura display of individual talent. Today we still clap a player when he has made an exit after a particularly fine effort, but audiences used to interrupt an actor to applaud the delivery of an emotional speech. Like an operatic aria, the scene was sometimes repeated if the applause was loud enough. Consequently, there was a lack of ensemble in most theaters, and of both an inner and an outer resemblance to life. This was changed, in varying degrees, by three men. The work of Richard Wagner, the creator of "music drama," lies outside our field, but his idea of fusing all the factors of production into an expressive whole (*Gesantkunstwerk*) had its effect on the theater. The Duke of Saxe-Meiningen and his court company demonstrated the virtues of ensemble to all Europe. André Antoine's amateurs at the Théâtre-libre in Paris found worldwide imitators of its realistic treatment of realistic plays.

The stars were many and bright in the theatrical firmament of the nineteenth century. In Paris there were, first, the powerful Frédérick-Lemaître and the eternal Pierrot called Deburau. In the '40's and '50's, the actress Rachel re-established the classic tragedies of Corneille and Racine, toured the world from Russia to the United States, and died at thirty-eight. In the last half of the century came the great comedienne Gabrielle Réjane, the equally great tragedienne Sarah Bernhardt, the elder Coquelin, who played both comedy and tragedy, the fiery Mounet-Sully, and Lucien Guitry, who left his talent as an actor and much more than his talent as a playwright to his son Sacha Guitry. Italian, Czech, and Polish stars found the same international audience as Réjane and Bernhardt. Adelaide Ristori rivaled Rachel when the Italian played in Paris, and, like Tommaso Salvini, she toured and co-starred abroad. Fanny Janauschek began in her native Bohemia, then toured Europe, and spent the latter part of her life mainly on the American stage.

ENSEMBLE FIRST IN VIENNA

During a good part of the nineteenth century, the Vienna Burgtheater—then the greatest playhouse of the German-speaking world—rose to distinction through its directors Schreyvogel and Laube and their productions, rather than through its stars. Here there was a considerable measure of ensemble. Visiting stars from Germany—Ludwig Devrient in the early part of the century and, later, Ernst von Possart, Rudolph Schildkraut, and Friedrich Haase—fitted as readily into the company as did permanent members like Adolph Sonnenthal and Friedrich Mitterwurzer.

The example of the Burgtheater did not spread to all the companies of the German court and the municipal theaters. The self-display of stars and a sloppiness in production called for a reform. It came from the tiny duchy of Saxe-Meiningen.

THE MEININGEN PLAYERS

The "Theater Duke," as the duchy's ruler was called through most of his life, saw the work of Charles Kean in London and, surely, the Burgtheater. When, in 1866, he assumed the direction of what we call the Meiningen players he went beyond the historical accuracy and ensemble of both. His company was not a distinguished one. The actors we know best were Joseph Kainz and Albert Bassermann, but they joined the ensemble late, and they won their fame still later in other institutions.

A gifted artist and scene designer, the Duke recognized the value of various playing levels on the stage. He saw to it that his settings, costumes, and properties were illusive as well as accurate. His great distinction, however, lay in long and careful rehearsals. In this, he anticipated Stanislavsky and the Moscow Art Theater. His chief players acted small parts as well as big ones. In plays that called for mob scenes he paid equal attention to the super-

Two examples of nineteenth century stage design. *Above, a design by the Duke of Meiningen: a scene from Ibsen's* The Pretenders. *Below, the Duke's sketch and plan for a box-set production of the banquet scene from* Macbeth. (*From Grube,* Geschichte der Meininger.)

As Gogol saw *The Inspector General*. *The Russian playwright sketched the last scene of his farce, when he wanted the characters to stand for three minutes frozen in terror at the entrance of the officer who is to end their thievery.* (From Gorelik, New Theaters for Old.)

Antoine's *The Wild Duck*. *A contemporary sketch of a scene from* The Wild Duck *at the Théâtre-libre in 1891.* (Drawing by Lucien Metivet from Darzens, *L Théâtre-libre illustré*.)

numeraries. Like Kean, he divided his mobs into small groups, each headed by a competent actor. The Duke's repertory consisted mainly of Shakespeare and Schiller, but he resurrected Kleist and Grillparzer, revived Lessing and Molière, and made the first Continental production of Ibsen's *Ghosts*. The tremendous effect that the Meiningen ensemble had on the European theater from Moscow to London came through the tours from 1874 to 1890 that took the Duke's players to thirty-eight cities in forty-one plays. Stanislavsky acknowledged how much their example influenced his work. Henry Irving was obviously very greatly affected. Before he saw the Meiningen company in London in 1881, he had already proved himself a distinguished actor in *Hamlet*—which he played 200 times in London in 1874-75 and 108 times in 1878-79—as well as in claptrap like *The Bells*. When, in 1895, he became the first actor to be knighted by a British monarch, no one could say how far this distinction was due to his employment of noted historians, painters, and musicians, to his personal genius and the high quality of his company, which included the brilliant Ellen Terry from 1878 to 1902, or to Irving's intelligent and effective use of the Duke of Meiningen's methods.

STAGES FOR SHAKESPEARE IN GERMANY

If the productions of the Duke of Meiningen had a serious fault it lay in too lengthy intermissions while settings were being changed, which happened often in the plays of Shakespeare, Schiller, and Kleist. The old wing sets, with or without grooves, had made scene shifting easy. But the Duke liked to vary the level of different parts of the stage, to use large set pieces such as rocks, and even to build box-sets. If he had not been so "modern," he might have turned back profitably to three or four early attempts to create a stage almost as well suited to Shakespeare's plays as the poet's own Globe.

There were Germans who did this. Shortly after 1800, the architect Karl Friederich Schinkel put permanent and molded columns and dark draperies in the place of wings, depending on his backdrop for changes of scene. In the '20's and '30's, a poet and playwright named Ludwig Tieck saw the proscenium doors and the fore-stages then used in Covent Garden and Drury Lane, and he read a builder's contract for an Elizabethan theater. With the aid of an architect named Gottfried Semper, he reconstructed—on paper only—the old Fortune playhouse. Unfortunately, when Tieck staged *A Midsummer Night's Dream* in 1843, he complicated his set with many stairs and platforms. Three years earlier, Karl Immermann, a director at Düsseldorf, built on his stage a structure that included many of the elements of the Elizabethan playhouse. His failure to find a profitable audience for a theater without the support of duke or king unfortunately obscured the value of his Shakespearean stage. At about the time when the Duke of Meiningen was ending his tours, experiments began at the Munich Court Theater that led to an effective solution early in the twentieth century. This scheme used portals and an inner proscenium within the ordinary picture frame opening.

WILLIAM POEL'S ELIZABETHAN REVIVALS

The first English attempt to play Shakespeare without awkward changes of sets came in 1844, when the elder Ben Webster produced *The Taming of the Shrew* against various curtains between two screens. Not until the last two decades of the century were there any other attempts in England to give Shakespeare's plays in full and with their scenes in the proper order. The most notable pioneer was William Poel. He began in 1881 by staging the First Quarto of *Hamlet* with only curtains for a background. In 1893, when he produced *Measure for Measure* in a London theater, he came as close as he could to an Elizabethan stage within a conventional one. He built an inner proscenium and a raised gallery in the back that could be hidden by transverse curtains for changes of set or properties. This production led to the formation of the Elizabethan Stage Society in 1895. During the next ten years—once in Gray's Inn and usually in other halls such as Shakespeare might have used—Poel gave a few performances of some twenty tragedies and comedies by Shakespeare and his contemporaries, as well as later works by Molière, Calderón, Schiller, and others. Poel's costumes and music were almost always good, and Shaw once said that these performances of Shakespeare were the only ones by which he "had been really moved." Poel made a notable success with the revival, after 400 years, of the medieval morality play *Everyman* with Edith Wynne Matthison in the title role. Miss Matthison and other players repeated the old drama in Great Britain and America.

REALISM WAITING FOR ITS THEATER

Except for the production of Shakespeare in England, we are ending the story of the nineteenth-century theater of Europe roughly in the middle '80's. By 1885, the stage had learned how to give romantic and historical drama in accurate and often over-elaborate productions. In the face of a general emphasis on stars and star parts, the directors of the Vienna Burgtheater and the Duke of Meiningen had established the value of a rounded ensemble. In the repertories of the state-endowed theaters of Germany and France their directors were presenting a library of new and standard plays in opposition to the growth of long runs. But there was not yet a truly realistic theater with an appropriate technique of acting.

seven

The COMING Of REALISM

THERE WERE REALISTIC PLAYWRIGHTS BEFORE THERE WAS A REALISTIC THE-
ater, before there was acting that could give the plays their full life, and
before there was an audience ready to receive them. The first experimenters,
from the Goncourts and Zola to Ibsen and Strindberg, were few, and they
faced bitter discouragement. Only the most stubborn and courageous of new
playwrights were likely to embrace realism without the encouragement of a
director who wanted to produce their plays and knew how to do it properly.
The writers needed an interested audience that wanted to see such plays. It
might be a small audience, but it had to be a sympathetic one.

ANTOINE'S THÉÂTRE-LIBRE—SHOWCASE
FOR REALISM

André Antoine supplied all this through the Théâtre-libre. His Free
Theater was a unique venture. It set a pattern that many more have followed
in Germany, Russia, England, and America. With the propaganda of Zola
and the Goncourts behind him, he opened the way for a new drama and a new
style of acting.

Antoine was an amateur actor who kept himself alive through a clerk's
job with the Paris Gas Company. In the spring of 1887 he gathered together
a company of fellow-amateurs, and gave a bill of one-act plays in a hall in
Montmartre that seated 342 people. The Théâtre-libre moved twice, first to
an 800-seat house in the Latin Quarter, then to the Théâtre Menus-Plaisirs

in the center of the city; but, until Antoine's venture closed in 1894, it was an institution doggedly devoted to certain unique ideas and policies.

The Théâtre-libre was a private playhouse open only to subscribers. For a season and a half, there was a single performance of each bill; then at the Menus-Plaisirs there were two. Very rarely indeed Antoine offered a public performance to non-members. His theater was a showcase for playwrights who could get no production anywhere else. Many of the one-act plays were taken over as curtain-raisers in the regular playhouses. The playwrights who won success with full-length plays were free to offer their new work elsewhere. Antoine's job, as he saw it, was priming the pump, and he primed it well. The Théâtre-libre produced plays by fifty-one authors, forty-two of them under forty; among them were men who won notable success by the turn of the century. But, of the 111 plays that Antoine produced, almost two-thirds were short plays, for the one-act was a new and easier field for experiment.

Antoine wanted to make the Théâtre-libre a playhouse known for its broad and catholic repertory. In this he failed. He gave more than a dozen one-act plays in verse. He produced Hauptmann's *Hannele,* which mixed realism and poetry. Yet the Théâtre-libre was stamped in the public mind as a house of "naturalism." This was partly due to the fact that most of the new playwrights wrote in the realistic vein, and partly to the fact that the opening bill of the Théâtre-libre was carried to success by a short dramatization of one of Zola's stories. Furthermore, Ibsen's *Ghosts* and *The Wild Duck,* Strindberg's *Miss Julia,* and Hauptmann's *The Weavers* fitted best the acting and producing methods of Antoine.

REALISTIC TRIUMPH—FINANCIAL FAILURE

Though Antoine himself had a weak voice, he was unquestionably a fine actor. At the end of his first spring season, the state-endowed Odéon—which he was to direct twenty years later—tried to add him to its company. Antoine saw the Meiningen players in 1888, and adopted their way of handling crowds, but he had already developed an ensemble, and had gone far beyond the Meiningen troupe or any other company in naturalness on the stage. He made his actors speak and move about as if the characters they played were actual human beings; greatly daring, he often had them speak lines with their backs to the audience. Antoine built his ensemble and achieved his reforms with a company that included at various times a traveling salesman, a bookbinder, a chemist, a wine merchant, an architect, a dressmaker, a manufacturer, and, of course, clerks. At the Menus-Plaisirs, he began to build realistic settings. He had never used "wood wings" and backdrops with stairs painted on them, but now he called for solid moldings, and doors and panels of wood instead of canvas. He borrowed or rented everyday furniture, and in one play he used as props real legs of lamb and carcasses of beef.

At the end of the season of 1889-90—when over 12,000 articles had been written about the Théâtre-libre, and Antoine was in debt for the same number of francs—he drew up the first concrete, detailed plan and program for a truly modern playhouse and a repertory company; but no one came forward with the money to make it a reality. Without such a house and a paid company that could give many performances of a successful play, the Théâtre-libre was doomed to financial failure. Short tours to Belgium, Germany, England, and Italy brought no substantial profit. Other theaters lured away some of Antoine's best actors. Discouraged and owing 100,000 francs, in 1894 he turned over the Théâtre-libre to another director, who kept it going only through 1895 and 1896.

THE INFLUENCE OF ANTOINE

Besides giving distinguished foreign playwrights like Ibsen, Tolstoy, Strindberg, Björnson, and Hauptmann their first hearings in Paris, Antoine's theater did the same for Eugène Brieux and François de Curel. Brieux is known best as the writer of thesis-plays, dramas exposing social evils. In *Blanchette* he attacked discrimination against women in education, in *The Red Robe* he exposed legal chicanery, and in *Damaged Goods* he dealt with the menace of venereal disease. Today these plays seem a bit labored and doctrinaire, but he wrote two mordant comedies, *The Three Daughters of M. Dupont* and *Les Hannetons*. The same bill that introduced a second play by Brieux, the son of a carpenter, included the first production of a play by the son of a nobleman, François de Curel. A writer of uncompromising integrity, he submitted his first three plays to Antoine under pseudonyms. His second play at the Théâtre-libre, *Les Fossiles* (*The Fossils*), was a study of decadent aristocracy.

Another dramatist of distinction, Georges de Porto-Riche, turned definitely away from romantic historical drama when he saw his realistic one-act play, *La Chance de Françoise,* produced at the Théâtre-libre in 1888. Three years later, he found himself completely in his comedy of married love *L'Amoureuse.*

Though Antoine's venture was a financial failure, it set a pattern of realistic drama that later playwrights followed even into the twentieth century. Among these were Henri Lavedan, who contributed only a short collaboration to the Théâtre-libre, but went on to a series of sound dramas like *Le Prince d'Aurec;* Maurice Donnay with his *Amants* (*Lovers*) and *L'Age difficile* (*The Difficult Age*); two moralizers, Paul Hervieu and Octave Mirbeau, the first best known in America for *Connais-toi* (*Know Thyself*), and the second for *Les Affaires sont les affaires* (*Business is Business*); and the sensitive Henri Bataille, author of *La Tendresse* and a dramatization of Tolstoy's *Resurrection.*

The Théâtre-libre accomplished four important things. It demonstrated how to produce realistic plays realistically, and it humanized the acting of poetic or romantic drama. It stimulated new playwrights; some wrote first for Antoine's venture, some only for the commercial theaters. Antoine himself went on to a distinguished career as the leading French director prior to World War I; in 1897, backed at last by stock-holders, he made the Menus-Plaisirs into the Théâtre Antoine, and then was called to head the Odéon from 1906 to 1914. More important still, the example of the Théâtre-libre created imitators in Paris itself and in Berlin and London. Even the "little

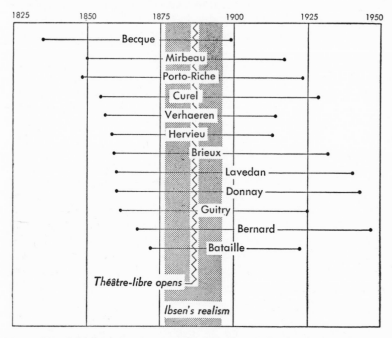

French realism after Antoine. *The first plays of Curel and Brieux were acted at the Théâtre-libre. There Porto-Riche turned away from historical drama and wrote a realistic one-acter, while Lavedan collaborated on a short play. All, including the Belgian Verhaeren, found other theaters receptive after Antoine had shown the way.*

theaters" of the United States with their amateur companies and their sub-scription memberships, as well as the Moscow Art Theater, owe something to Antoine.

A "FREE THEATER" FOR GERMANY

The effect of Antoine was greater, perhaps, on the German stage than on the French, for the German was in a far worse state. Though Prussia crushed France in 1871 and created the German Empire, French playwrights of the most conventional type dominated the Teutonic stage well into the '90's. To be sure, the Meiningen company, which was formed before the Prussian victory, produced no French trash, but the "Theater Duke" staged only one of Ibsen's plays besides *Ghosts* (his historical tragedy *The Pretenders*) while the other court theaters and the playhouses under commercial management did nothing to open the way for realism.

Adolf L'Arronge, who made a fortune writing German farces, founded—in Berlin—the new Deutsches Theater in 1883, and attempted a few reforms. He boldly opposed the growing policy of long runs, and kept to a changing repertory. He aimed at a high acting standard through a company headed by Ernst von Possart, Joseph Kainz, and Agnes Sorma. But the acting was not realistic, and the stars could not be molded into an ensemble. As for L'Arronge's repertory, he stuck largely to the Meiningen policy, *sans* Ibsen, of classic and historical drama.

The break came in 1889. In Berlin, the great journalist Maximilian Harden and eight friends chose a critic named Otto Brahm to direct a German version of the Théâtre-libre and to meet a serious and peculiar problem. Though theater monopoly had gradually disappeared in Germany between 1848 and 1870, police censorship as well as the mediocre taste of most playgoers barred the production of plays that dealt too frankly with sexual problems or the miseries of the common people. Following Antoine's policy, Brahm gave only private performances, which the police could not stop, and he drew upon a superior audience by selling tickets only to annual subscribers. Like Antoine, Brahm got his actors gratis, but he used professionals rather than amateurs. Instead of renting a small hall, he gave his performances at noon on Sundays in theaters that sympathetic managements let him have without charge. Again like Antoine, Brahm hoped that, when he had shown the merit of new plays, commercial managements would take them over or accept the later work of his writers.

THE FREIE BÜHNE'S SUCCESS ENDS ITS CAREER

Brahm began with *Ghosts*, which had been banned by the Berlin censor. Much more important, Brahm followed this in just a month with *Vor Sonnenaufgang* (*Before Sunrise*), the first play of a new writer, Gerhart Hauptmann, who was to lead the playwrights of Germany, and excel most of them for more than a generation. In the spring of 1890, Brahm produced another new German drama, the naturalistic *Die Familie Selicke*, by Arno Holz and Johannes Schlaf. Brahm also revived Anzengruber's *The Double Suicide*, and staged translations of Tolstoy's *The Power of Darkness*, which Antoine had already produced, Zola's *Thérèse Raquin*, the Goncourts' *Henriette Maréchal*, Becque's *The Vultures*, and Strindberg's *The Father* and *Miss Julia*.

Just as Brahm had hoped, the example of the Freie Bühne improved the level of the commercial theater. It improved the level so much that within a couple of years there seemed to be no reason for Brahm to continue production. Occasionally, however, the Freie Bühne had to be reanimated. For instance, after L'Arronge had taken over *Lonely Lives* he refused Hauptmann's next play, *The Weavers;* so Brahm gathered his forces together again to produce it.

The rapid improvement of the Berlin stage is shown by two offshoots of Brahm's institution. During its second season, Bruno Wille organized in Berlin the Freie Volksbühne (Free People's Stage). This institution anticipated the Book-of-the-Month Club in another field. By paying for special performances of various plays by various commercial managements, it was able to sell tickets to its subscribers at lower than regular prices. Occasionally it made productions of its own, for example Ibsen's *The Pillars of Society.* As the level of the Berlin theater continued to rise, a new institution appeared called the New Free People's Stage. By 1914 it had 50,000 subscribers, and could build its own playhouse, the magnificent Volksbühne. During the 1920's the subscription list ran as high as 120,000.

BRAHM AN OUTSTANDING DIRECTOR

For the plays of the Freie Bühne, Brahm enlisted fine actors such as Joseph Kainz, Emanuel Reicher, and Agnes Sorma, and he fused them into a brilliant ensemble. In 1894, when L'Arronge retired from active management of the Deutsches Theater, and entrusted the theater to Brahm, he had, besides these three, Else Lehmann, Max Reinhardt, Rudolf Rittner, and other excellent players. In 1905 Brahm moved to the Lessing Theater, and enjoyed for a time the services of the distinguished Albert Bassermann, who had had his training with the Meiningen company.

As a critic, Brahm had been brilliant, incisive, and often bitter. As a director, he was as uncompromising, but he was patient and selfless, calm and considerate. He excelled Antoine as a director of realistic plays, but unfortunately his range was not so wide. As his first production after he took over the Deutsches Theater, he tried to stage in the modern manner the classic *Kabale und Liebe,* by Schiller. The result was a disaster. Though he once used or tried to use Gordon Craig, Brahm was never a contributor, like Reinhardt, to the fresh and imaginative ways of the twentieth-century theater. But Brahm made over the German theater, and he remained for twenty years a dominant figure on the realistic stage of Europe.

FROM HAUPTMANN TO WEDEKIND

Hauptmann turned from sculpture to playwrighting, and from 1889 almost until his death in 1946, his output was varied in kind and quality, but it always had some measure of distinction. He dealt with the personal tragedy of working class people in *Before Sunrise,* and with their mass miseries in *The Weavers.* Of his peasant dramas, the best was *Rose Bernd.* He wrote plays in the vein of Ibsen, such as *Lonely Lives* and *Michael Kramer,* comedies such as *Der Biberpelz* (*The Beaver Coat*), and historic dramas such as *Florian Geyer,* dealing with the Peasant's War, and *Der Weisse Heiland*

(*The White Redeemer*), about Cortes and the conquest of Mexico. He also tried the poetic in *Hannele* and the symbolic in *Die Versunkene Glocke* (*The Sunken Bell*).

Other new German playwrights appeared in the early 1890's. Hermann Sudermann, best known for *Heimat*, which we call *Magda*, might have been a French practitioner of the well-made play. There was more stature to the comedies and dramas of Ludwig Fulda and Otto Erich Hartleben, and to the tragedies of Max Halbe. The satirist Carl Sternheim introduced into his comedies the crisply "telegraphic" style that expressionistic writers later adopted.

Next to Hauptmann, the outstanding German who began to write for the stage in the last decade of the nineteenth century was Frank Wedekind. He was as obsessed as Strindberg with sexual tragedy. In 1890, with *Die junge Welt* (*The World of Youth*), and the next year with *Frühlings Erwachen* (*The Awakening of Spring*), Wedekind brought the "slice of life" technique to the problem of adolescents who are given no guidance as to sex. *Erdgeist* (*Earth Spirit*), of 1895, and *Die Büchse der Pandora* (*Pandora's Box*), of 1902, showed the same character, Lulu, instinctively and ruthlessly preying on men and meeting a horrible end. Wedekind's plays were both moral and morbid. They were naturalistic-realistic, and they also introduced some aspects of twentieth-century expressionism. The tragedy in *The Awakening of Spring* is as real as it is affecting, yet it ends bizarrely with one of the two boy-heroes returning from the grave to urge suicide on the other, while "A Masked Man," symbolizing life, comes to persuade him not to kill himself.

German playwrights born in the nineteenth century. *The work of Anzengruber is almost unknown outside the Teutonic stage. Sudermann now seems passé. Wedekind has not yet been successful in English.*

SCHNITZLER AND THE AUSTRIANS

The tragedy and even morbidity that stamped the awakening drama in Germany is less apparent in the plays that came out of Austria at the same time. The greatest of her playwrights, Arthur Schnitzler, wrote comedies as well as dramas and tragedies. His first work for the theater, in 1893, was the group of gay, amatory one-act plays called *Anatol*. One of his finest tragedies, *Liebelei* (*Light o' Love*), came two years later, and another, *Der Einsame Weg* (*The Lonely Way*) in 1904. Schnitzler had a fondness for the one-act play, wrote many, and often related them skilfully together—as with *Anatol*, *Reigen* (*Hands Around*), and *Lebendige Stunden* (*Living Hours*). He wrote one of his best, *Der grüne Kakadu* (*The Green Cockatoo*) in 1899. His strong attack on anti-Semitism, *Professor Bernhardi*, appeared in 1912.

After a fling at morbid drama in 1891, another Viennese, Hermann Bahr, turned toward comedy, and won success in 1898 with *Josephine*, written around the young Napoleon. He is best known in America for the Belasco-Ditrichstein version of his amusing play, *The Concert*.

Though Hugo von Hofmannsthal wrote and adapted comedies, this Viennese poet was at his best in his tragedies in verse. He began these in the early '90's, but his finest is perhaps *Oedipus and the Sphinx* of 1906. From then onward he adapted many plays for Reinhardt—including *Jedermann*, from the medieval morality *Everyman*, and three from Calderón, *Dame Kobold*, *Der Turm*, and *Das grosse Welttheater*—and he wrote librettos for six of Richard Strauss's operas, including *Elektra* and *Der Rosenkavalier*.

LONDON'S "INDEPENDENT THEATER"

A Dutchman brought the "Free Theater" idea to London. Like Brahm, J. T. Grein had been a dramatic critic. At twenty he wrote the introduction to a Dutch translation of Ibsen's *An Enemy of the People*. Two years later, he was the reviewer of an Amsterdam daily paper. When he was not yet thirty and had made London his home, he launched the Independent Theater Society in the spring of 1891. Grein himself and men like William Archer, translator of Ibsen, and George Moore, the novelist, hoped to discover and develop English playwrights. Grein began, of course, with *Ghosts*. Not content with hundreds of violent reviews and letters to the editor, he followed it up with Zola's *Thérèse Raquin*. Then he put on bills of short and full-length English plays that caused no great stir. At last, toward the end of 1892, the Independent Theater produced George Bernard Shaw's first play, *Widowers' Houses*, thus doing the same service for the man who was to become England's leading playwright that the Freie Bühne had done for Hauptmann. Among Grein's later productions was Ibsen's *The Wild Duck*.

Though the plays of the Independent Theater Society—produced at matinees with volunteer actors—were a heavy drain on Grein's income, this venture that ended in financial failure had a very considerable effect on the English stage. In 1899 came the Incorporated Stage Society, which for forty years gave outstanding Continental and English plays on Sunday nights with casts that included some of the best of London's actors. From the work of this society, the stimulus of Grein, and the great repute of Brahm and Antoine may be traced more successful undertakings of the greatest importance: the work of Granville-Barker, the Abbey Players, the Manchester Repertory Theater, and other ventures that we shall describe in due course.

IBSEN AND BJÖRNSON—GIANTS OF THE NORTH

As we have said, there were realistic playwrights—sound and effective ones—before there were theaters or audiences to welcome them. Only two, however, were writing steadily and abundantly before Antoine opened his Théâtre-libre. These were Henrik Ibsen and Björnstjerne Björnson, and they were born in remote and sparsely populated Norway.

Both Scandinavians began by writing historical and poetic plays that suited the taste of Norwegian audiences. Both men held posts, at various times during the 1860's and '70's, in Norwegian theaters. Such modest success must have heartened them while they began to write a type of play not so readily accepted as the historical and romantic. Björnson—poet, novelist, and newspaper editor—turned to realism about five years before Ibsen wrote *The League of Youth,* and a decade before his next play in that genre, *The Pillars of Society.* Politically, both men were rebels; Björnson was a leader in the liberal party, while Ibsen was for a time a socialist. They both attacked the social evils of their day, but in different moods. For *A Bankruptcy,* built around a dishonest business man, and *A Gauntlet,* an attack on the "double standard" in sex morals, Björnson found happy endings that Ibsen could never have conceived. While Ibsen placed a greater emphasis on psychological analysis and depth of character, his friend and rival wrote more superficially, though with a theatrical skill that won him a greater success at home than Ibsen enjoyed. The different outlook of the two men may have been somewhat due to the different circumstances of their youth. The happily optimistic Björnson was brought up by wealthy parents, and lived in a lovely section of Norway. Ibsen's parents lost their fortune when he was eight; when he was fifteen, they apprenticed him to an apothecary in a grim provincial town.

Between 1855 and 1865 Björnson wrote a number of historical plays in verse, few of which were popular outside Scandinavia. During the same period Ibsen used the ballads and the sagas of old Norway as the material for a number of poetic plays such as *The Vikings at Helgeland* and *The Pretenders.* Toward the end of their work, both men emphasized spiritual rather than social values in their realistic plays. Björnson's *Beyond Human Power,* of 1881, is the outstanding play of his later period. From Ibsen's *The Master Builder,* in 1892, through *Little Eyolf* and his last drama, *When We Dead Awaken,* he injected more and more symbolism into his work.

FROM VERSE TO REALISM WITH IBSEN

When Ibsen first wrote of the contemporary scene in 1862, the poet in him forced the characters of *Love's Comedy* to speak in verse. Before he committed himself definitely to realistic prose in *The League of Youth,* he used poetic rhythms in two long plays dealing with his own times. (Like his later dramas, he wrote them in voluntary exile abroad.) *Brand,* of the middle '60's, is a somber "all or nothing" attack on compromise; it won no lasting popularity outside Scandinavia. *Peer Gynt,* which followed shortly after, is a colorful but rambling play which tells with considerable satire the story of a rascally country boy who becomes a millionaire and returns to face a peculiar and bizarre end. Between *The League of Youth,* which followed in 1869, and *The Pillars of Society,* the first of the realistic plays that occupied him for fifteen years, Ibsen wrote another historical drama in verse. This gigantic script, *Emperor and Galilean,* deals with the struggle between Christianity and paganism in the fourth century.

There is a dual greatness about Ibsen. One lies in his technique. The other is his ability to understand human beings and present them on the stage. Technically, he far outdistanced the men like Scribe and Sardou who had manufactured "well-made" plays. He threw away all their devious devices, their coincidences and startling denouements. He began his realistic plays just before the crisis in their stories, skilfully exposed the past, and used it to provide complications with ever-mounting suspense. His understanding of human character and his ability to make it come to life must be clear to anyone who has read *Ghosts, A Doll's House, The Wild Duck, Rosmersholm,* or *Hedda Gabler.* His gravest fault was to accept too literally at first the half-baked theories on heredity that had infected Zola and the naturalists, a fault shared by Hauptmann in his early plays. But Ibsen compensated for this by never clinging to the doctrinaire in other respects. His themes and his ideas grew from play to play. Even in his historical dramas there was character analysis. Philosophically as well as psychologically, his plays have a depth found in very few dramas before 1890.

STRINDBERG—GREATER THAN IBSEN?

Scandinavia contributed another giant to the modern theater. This was a Swede, August Strindberg. Like Ibsen and Björnson—though born a generation later—Strindberg began by writing historical plays, then took up realism, and finally turned to a form that might be called a symbolic interpretation of actuality, and that was a forerunner of expressionism. He was even more versatile than Ibsen and Björnson; besides directing productions, managing two theaters, writing fifty plays, long and short, and theorizing radically on stage technique, he wrote novels, short stories, histories, and autobiographies that laid bare his inner life as if he were lying on a psychiatrist's couch.

In other respects Strindberg and the two Norwegians were worlds apart. Even in his realistic period, and much more so toward the end, he wrote with a far greater intensity and violence, and he analyzed and sublimated the materials of life as neither of his rivals ever did. His genius was tinged with madness. Some of the psychoses that are now familiar to so many laymen—

from overcompensating arrogance, through mother-fixation, to persecution mania—are evident enough in the years that preceded and followed his nervous breakdown from 1895 to 1897.

Superficially, Strindberg is best known for his violent misogyny. From *The Father*—his first realistic play, written in 1887—through *Comrades, Creditors, The Stronger,* and parts or all of many more dramas, Strindberg pictured woman as preying on man and destroying him, usually in marriage and sometimes out of it. Into this theme he poured all the violence of his nature, and all the vigor of his great art. After his mental illness and until his death from cancer in 1912, his plays ranged from a historical drama, *Gustavus Vasa,* through another sex-struggle, *The Dance of Death,* and a symbolic religious drama, *Easter,* to a group of plays including *Toward Damascus, The Spook Sonata,* and *The Dream Play,* in which life is presented with a strange distortion that seems to be the basis and the root—even more than Wedekind's work—of German expressionism. This we will discuss in the next essay.

The work of this man who said he searched for God and found the devil won the warmest of praise from two later playwrights of outstanding position, and a most significant comment from Ibsen. Sean O'Casey, author of *Juno and the Paycock,* wrote: "Strindberg, Strindberg, Strindberg, the greatest of them all! . . . Strindberg shakes flame from the living planets and the fixed stars. Ibsen can sit serenely in his Doll's House, while Strindberg is battling with heaven and hell." O'Neill called him "the precursor of all modernity in our present theater." And, commenting on Strindberg, Ibsen said to a visitor, "There is one who will be greater than I."

THE MOSCOW ART THEATER

Russia gave three great realists to the theater—Tolstoy, Chekhov, and Gorky. The work of all three is tied in closely with one of the finest institutions of modern theatrical history, the Moscow Art Theater. In 1891, when one of its two directors, Constantin Stanislavsky, was still an amateur, he produced Tolstoy's satirical comedy *The Fruits of Enlightenment.* Tolstoy's first outstanding play, the powerful peasant tragedy *The Power of Darkness,* was written just before Antoine opened the Théâtre-libre, and it had its world première there in 1888, but this drama was first staged in Russia by Stanislavsky only after the Moscow Art Theater was on its feet. By successfully reviving Chekhov's *The Sea Gull,* after its failure at another house, the Moscow Art Theater dissuaded him from giving up playwriting. The success of Chekhov turned Gorky toward the stage, and the playhouse was able to present his powerful tragedy *The Lower Depths.*

More has probably been written about the Moscow Art Theater than about any modern playhouse. Constantin Stanislavsky was the son of rich parents who built him a log cabin theater on their country estate and another in their Moscow town house, where he acted with relatives and friends. In 1888 he helped to found the Society of Literature and Art, and in a few years—when he was hardly twenty-five—he began directing plays. We have heard how a man of similar interests, Vladimir Nemirovich-Danchenko, had been teaching acting at the Moscow Philharmonic Society, and how Stanislavsky and Danchenko met at a famous artists' restaurant, and in fifteen hours of talk outlined the policy and the organization of the Moscow Art Theater. We know that the best of their student-actors and amateurs, together with certain professionals, were fused through long study and rehearsal—by what came to be called "the Stanislavsky method"—into a matchless ensemble. The purpose, as we have been so frequently told, was not to achieve the surface aspects of naturalism, but to capture and convey what Stanislavsky described as "the inner truth, the truth of feeling and experience."

The actors through whom the Moscow Art Theater created what might best be called a profound psychological realism came partly from the amateurs of Stanislavsky and Danchenko, and partly from the profession. The best known and most adept—many of whom New York saw in 1922-23—were Olga Knipper, Ivan Moskvin, Vasili Kachalov, Maria Germanova, Leonid Leonidov, Alla Nazimova, Richard Boleslavsky, Leo Bulgakov, Akim Tamiroff, and Olga Baclanova. Among distinguished Russian actors who did not play in the Moscow Art Theater was Paul Orlenev; America saw him in *Ghosts* with Nazimova about 1905.

OTHERS BESIDES STANISLAVSKY

When any institution is so striking and so rich in detail as the Moscow Art Theater—and has lived in triumph for more than half a century—many aspects are underestimated or almost ignored. For instance, hardly a writer mentions the fact that the wealth of the upper bourgeoisie made the theater possible, while Antoine, in Paris, pleaded vainly for money to build his ideal theater. Not only was Stanislavsky's family well supplied with worldly goods, but his pupils and Danchenko's, who were the nucleus of the company, came from the wealthier classes. More than that, a fabulous patron named Savva Morozov provided the funds for rebuilding a playhouse and carrying the company and its repertory through the lean times before the plays of Chekhov brought fame and fortune.

There has never been enough credit given the predecessors of the Moscow Art Theater. The Maly Theater, the smaller of the two imperial playhouses, was the first to produce Gogol, Ostrovsky, and Ibsen in Russia. As far back as 1853, it threw away the French soubrette costume and coiffure of the maidservant, and gave her a plain cotton frock and smooth hair. When the imperial monopoly of the theater ended in 1882, there appeared what were called "people's theaters." The manager of one of these—a man named Lentovsky—encouraged Tolstoy to write *The Power of Darkness*, though censorship balked its production till the theater of Stanislavsky and Danchenko waxed powerful. Lentovsky was the first Russian producer to take the direction of a play out of the haphazard hands of his cast; in addition, he introduced electric light to the Russian stage.

Because Danchenko was no actor—and perhaps because Stanislavsky centered attention upon himself with his fine book *My Life in Art*—Danchenko's share in the making of the Moscow Art Theater has been overshadowed by Stanislavsky's. It was Danchenko who called the meeting with Stanislavsky. By the initial agreement, Stanislavsky had absolute control of production—while, incidentally, he managed the business that his father had left him—and Danchenko was in charge of financial and "literary" matters. Literary matters, however, meant the choice of plays, and Danchenko was the one who lured Chekhov back to playwriting, and made the fortune of

INFLUENCES ON MODERN PRODUCTION

Meininger Tour of European Capitals	1874-1890
Théâtre-libre, Paris (Antoine)	1887-1894
Freie Buehene, Berlin (Brahm)	1889-1891
Neue Freie Volksbuehne, Berlin	1890-
Independent Theater, London (Grein)	1891-1892
Elizabethan Stage Society (Poel)	1893-1905
Moscow Art Theater	1898-
Incorporated Stage Society, London	1899-1939

the playhouse by reviving *The Sea Gull*. More than that, Danchenko—as novelist and playwright as well as teacher of acting—had the right to determine how each play was to be approached in order to bring out its meaning. Stanislavsky himself tells how his partner "hammered all the beauties of Chekhov into my head. He could talk of a play so well that one had to like it before he was through." Though under the basic agreement, Danchenko was not supposed to be concerned with the staging of plays, "two stage directors," wrote Stanislavsky, "sat at the director's table, Nemirovich-Danchenko and I." Later Danchenko had his own table, and created the Music Studio of the Moscow Art Theater, where *Lysistrata* became lyric, and *Carmen* took on the true qualities of drama.

CHEKHOV, GORKY, AND TOLSTOY

There was a curious paradox about the Moscow Art Theater. The founders said that, unlike the institutions springing up in France and Germany and England, it was to be an actor's theater, not a director's theater or a theater for playwrights. Yet, though Stanislavsky and his associates made over the art of acting in Russia, the theater also spawned directors of distinction —Stanislavsky himself, Danchenko, Meyerhold, Vakhtangov, Michael Chekhov, the playwright's nephew, even Balieff of the satiric Chauve-Souris. And just as definitely this was the playwright's theater.

The progress of Russian realism. *Though Pushkin wrote poetic and historical drama, his work was a commentary on his times. Gogol's comedies, bitterly observant, were swiftly followed by realistic dramas. Tolstoy finished no plays until 1886, when he wrote* The Power of Darkness. *Gorky, too, began late; his first play,* The Lower Depths, *came in 1902.*

After revivifying *The Sea Gull* in 1898, it drew from Chekhov three more fine plays before his early death in 1904. Thus we owe to the Moscow Art Theater *Uncle Vanya, The Three Sisters,* and, above all, *The Cherry Orchard.* His last play is the finest demonstration of Chekhov's ability to build quietly into a simple plot—almost a formless structure—characters that are believable, poignant, touching, utterly human.

Gorky wrote plays from about 1902 to 1934. But only the second, *The Lower Depths,* and the next to last, *Yegor Bulychov,* are truly memorable. He drew the material for the first from the years he had had to spend in the flop houses of Russia with "creatures that had once been men." In *Yegor Bulichov* he saw tragedy from the other side; he showed us a rich merchant dying of cancer, surrounded by cruel, ignorant, corrupt, and contemptible friends, and dying disillusioned as the sound of the Bolshevik Revolution comes to his ears—"the burial service, singing me out of the world." When Gorky chose his nom de plume ("gorky" means "bitter") he chose well.

With or without Antoine or Brahm or Stanislavsky and Danchenko, Leo

Tolstoy would have been a dramatist. And he would probably have written no fewer than the four plays that added stage repute to the author of the novel *War and Peace*. *The Power of Darkness* is a grim and horrifying tragedy of a debased peasantry. *The Fruits of Enlightenment* satirizes the country gentry. *Redemption*—as Arthur Hopkins called *The Living Corpse* when he produced it with John Barrymore—is a powerful and pitiful drama of a man who is forced by social circumstances to kill himself so that his wife may be happy with another man. In his last play, *The Light That Shines in Darkness*, Tolstoy left, with its last act unfinished, an attempt to contrast the uselessness and the tragedy of a wealthy family and poverty-ridden peasants.

THE IRISH NATIONAL THEATER

Two women played a very important part in the creation of theater companies as well as in the promotion of the realistic drama in England and Ireland. To Lady Gregory and Miss A. E. F. Horniman the stage owes the so-called Irish Players at the Abbey Theater, Dublin, and to Miss Horniman the Manchester Repertory Company, whose pioneering led to other ventures in a number of British cities. Out of these theaters came playwrights of unusual quality.

The Dublin venture began as the Irish Literary Theater of 1899. It sprang partly from the Nationalist political movement, and partly from the enthusiasm of the poet William Butler Yeats. He and Lady Gregory saw it, at first, as a vehicle for poetic drama. In the beginning, the players were English, and there were all too few Irish people who wanted to see their plays. Then, in 1901, some amateur actors of Dublin, the Fay brothers, joined Yeats, Lady Gregory, and their associates to form the Irish National Theater Company. The result was a performance of genuine native flavor. In 1903 the company appeared triumphantly in London. Miss Horniman—who had financed the first London production of Shaw's *Arms and the Man* almost ten years before—was so aroused by the Irish performances that she rebuilt the Abbey Theater for them, and supported the venture until 1910, when it was on its feet.

Under the direction of the Fays, the actors followed the realistic style that Antoine had set, and played with simplicity and yet with both humor and power. New Irish writers turned to the stage because the Abbey was there to welcome them. Their work, from the plays of Synge to the plays of O'Casey, was rooted in the actualities of Irish life. Yeats continued loyal and indefatigable in the management of the company, but his poetic plays were few and they did not set the pattern. Paradoxically, the theater that was to be poetic turned to realism. Again paradoxically, this realism at its best rose to high beauty of expression because that was the nature of peasant speech. The theater had indeed, as Lady Gregory put it at the beginning, "a

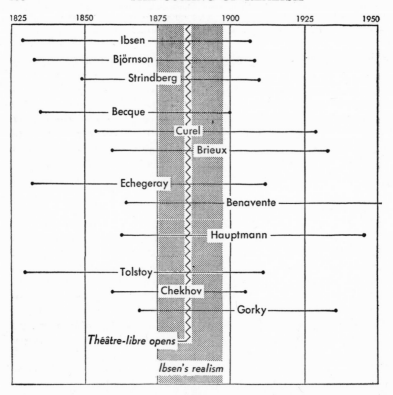

The rise of realism on the continent. *Omitting England, Ireland, and the United States, this chart shows the Norwegians Ibsen and Björnson as the forerunners of realism. The rest, including Tolstoy, turned to realism after Ibsen and Björnson had begun to write in that vein. The gray band indicates the years during which Ibsen concentrated all his power on the realistic medium.*

base of realism and an apex of beauty." America could recognize this even as early as 1911 when George C. Tyler brought over the company as the Irish Players.

IRELAND'S RICH DRAMA

Out of Dublin and also Belfast in Northern Ireland came a surprising number of native dramatists, some writing one-act plays and some writing long ones. Among the earliest, John Millington Synge, was easily the best. Yeats brought him from a Paris lodging to live with the Irish peasants and learn their tongue. The result, between 1903 and Synge's too-early death in 1909, were six plays that combined truth of character with the beauty of Irish speech—and usually great humor. His second, *Riders to the Sea*, is still one of the finest one-act tragedies ever written in the speech of either Ireland or

England. The peak of his work was the highly original and brilliant comedy *The Playboy of the Western World*.

Besides these and Yeats' fine *Cathleen ni Houlihan*, Ireland has given us —to name only a few plays—Lady Gregory's one-act comedies of folk-life, such as *Spreading the News* and *The Workhouse Ward*, as well as her patriotic drama, *The Rising of the Moon*, and her tragedy *The Gaol Gate*, Lennox Robinson's delightful comedy *The White-Headed Boy*, St. John Ervine's *John Ferguson* and *Mixed Marriage*, Paul Vincent Carroll's subtle and significant *Shadow and Substance* and *The White Steed*, and Sean O'Casey's satirically bitter *Juno and the Paycock* and *The Plough and the Stars*. It is an output unequalled by modern English playwrights unless we include among them two Dublin-born men, Oscar Wilde and Bernard Shaw.

MISS HORNIMAN AND GRANVILLE-BARKER

With the Abbey Theater safely launched, Miss Horniman gave her native city, between 1908 and 1921, the Manchester Repertory Theater. It was distinguished by fine performances from new players, many of whom went on to success in London, and also by local plays. Half of the 200 productions were of new material. Among these were Stanley Houghton's *Hindle Wakes*, Harold Brighouse's *Hobson's Choice*, and plays by St. John Hankin. Here Ervine's *Jane Clegg* had its first production, as well as John Masefield's fine play *The Tragedy of Nan*. Miss Horniman's pioneering work had its effect in London as well as in other British cities.

While Miss Horniman was supporting the Abbey Theater, H. Granville Barker—hyphenating himself later as Harley Granville-Barker—joined the manager John E. Vedrenne in repertory seasons in London from 1904 to 1907. A fine actor himself—as he had demonstrated in other performances besides Marchbanks in Shaw's *Candida* for the Incorporated Stage Society —he proved an able director and playwright. Besides Barker's dramas *The Voysey Inheritance*, *Waste*, and *The Madras House*, Vedrenne and he presented plays by Euripides, Maeterlinck, Schnitzler, and Hauptmann. They produced eleven plays by Shaw, five for the first time, and they brought out the first work of a new dramatist of distinction, John Galsworthy, who had made his reputation as a novelist. The Vedrenne-Barker seasons, through their high standards of plays and acting, had a greater influence on the British stage than Herbert Beerbohm Tree, George Alexander, Cyril Maude, and all the other actor-managers combined.

OSCAR WILDE AND BERNARD SHAW

Realism of a kind came to the British drama in the 1880's with Henry Arthur Jones and Arthur Wing Pinero. Both may have gained something from Ibsen, but more from the "well-made plays" of France. Jones, the more conscientious writer, came close to something good in the middle '90's with his *Michael and His Lost Angel* and *The Liars*. Pinero waited until 1909 and 1910 to desert theatrical trash for *Mid-Channel* and *The Thunderbolt*. J. M. Barrie began successfully with comedy romance in the '90's, and produced some pleasant comedies ten years later in *The Admirable Crichton* and *What Every Woman Knows*. His fantasy *Peter Pan*, of 1904, was a foretaste of the somewhat more serious unreality of *A Kiss for Cinderella* and *Mary Rose*

The 1890's offered to the English stage the first plays of Bernard Shaw—which it would not accept—and the four comedies that Oscar Wilde wrote before his disgrace and death. London adored the smartly cynical dialog of Wilde that reached its height in *The Importance of Being Earnest*. The fact that theatergoers of the '90s could also enjoy the artificial plotting of his *Lady Windermere's Fan*, *A Woman of No Importance*, and *An Ideal Hus-*

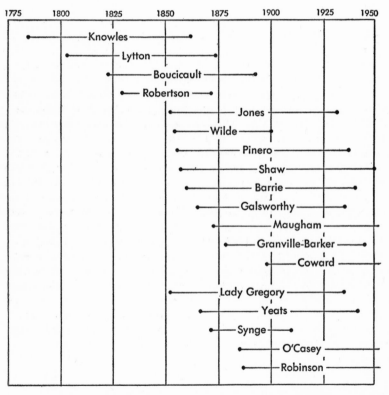

150 years of British drama. *Reality did not invade the plays of London until Tom Robertson began to write comedies six years before his death. Nothing else of merit appeared before 1895. The Irish playwrights, grouped at the bottom of the chart, wrote mainly of and for their own people, but wrote with outstanding distinction.*

band should account for the fact that the London stage had no use for Shaw's *Widowers' Houses* or even *Arms and the Man*. It was Barker, with 701 performances of Shaw's plays in the years before the First World War, who saw Shaw through to victory in England. The comic genius that rose through *Candida, The Devil's Disciple, Caesar and Cleopatra, Man and Superman, Major Barbara, The Doctor's Dilemma, Androcles and the Lion,* and *Pygmalion,* fell away pitiably after *St. Joan* of 1923. Yet—despite Galsworthy's fine social dramas such as *The Silver Box, Justice, The Skin Game, Loyalties,* and *Escape*—Shaw remained the greatest of modern English playwrights.

Somerset Maugham's best plays, *The Constant Wife* and *The Circle,* suffer by comparison with his own novel *Of Human Bondage,* let alone Shaw's work. From *The Vortex* to *Cavalcade* and *Design for Living,* Noel Coward is smart, witty, and at times moving, but he will be forgotten sooner than J. B. Priestley, Emlyn Williams, and Terence Rattigan with their few but deeply sincere plays.

REALISM LAGGARD IN AMERICAN DRAMA

The realistic playwright developed far later in the United States than in the Old World. Examples from the work of the better Europeans were scantily imported until after 1915. Pinero and Jones were popular because they were obvious, but Ibsen languished, and Shaw won meager attention only through three stars: Richard Mansfield in the '90's, and Robert Loraine and Arnold Daly around 1905. Of Americans who began to write in the nineteenth century, Clyde Fitch was, except for a couple of plays, a maker of facile but shallow comedies, while Augustus Thomas turned from melodramas to turgid dramas about telepathy or the "double standard," such as *The Witching Hour* and *As a Man Thinks*. Only four writers of any merit appeared in America before 1915. Langdon Mitchell dramatized a few novels, but wrote only one original play, a brilliant comedy of divorce, *The New York Idea,* which Mrs. Fiske produced with some success in 1906. In the same year came a rather powerful play by the poet William Vaughn Moody, *The Great Divide,* but his only other drama, *The Faith Healer,* proved less effective in the theater. Edward Sheldon wrote *Salvation Nell,* in which Mrs. Fiske starred, and *Romance,* which occupied Doris Keane for some five years. Elmer Rice—now known for his later plays *Street Scene* and *Counsellor-at-Law*—wrote his *On Trial* only a couple of seasons before that crucial year of 1915 when the Provincetown Players began to develop the talent of Eugene O'Neill.

DAVID BELASCO AND ARTHUR HOPKINS

Realism in production came to the American stage through David Belasco. He had always been a pioneer of illusion through lighting, but it was not until after the turn of the century that he began to use solidly built box-sets. In 1909, for *The Easiest Way,* he literally transferred to his stage wallpaper, doors, and furniture from a dilapidated rooming house. A few years later he reached the climax of his realism by copying a corner of one of the Childs restaurants for *The Governor's Lady.* His actors—good as were David Warfield, Blanche Bates, Leo Ditrichstein, Holbrook Blinn, and George Arliss—never matched the realism of the plays of Otto Brahm or the Moscow Art Theater. Belasco had a theatrical instinct that forced his actors beyond the realism of his sets.

A later director came nearer the ideal of Brahm. This was Arthur Hopkins. In dramas by Ibsen, Tolstoy, Gorky, and O'Neill, as in comedies by Philip Barry and in other plays, he used simplified and suggestive backgrounds by America's best scene designer, Robert Edmond Jones. In Hopkins' handling of his actors, he followed quite unconsciously Brahm's method. Movement and business could be largely laid out by a stage manager; Hopkins concentrated on content. To the actors he explained their parts, the quality of the characters, the relation of one to the other. He never coached and seldom interrupted a scene. He corrected an actor's performance only after the rehearsal was over, and in a quiet, intimate talk. Perhaps he never brought out in his productions the ingenious intensities that another outstanding director, Elia Kazan, achieved in *Death of a Salesman* or *A Streetcar Named Desire.* Hopkins was content to seek and find inner truth.

A number of the excellent directors that developed in the '20's, and almost all the actors that might have become legitimate players of distinction, turned to Hollywood film production. The New York stage was left to such fine players of the '20's as Helen Hayes, Katharine Cornell, Alfred Lunt, and Lynn Fontanne while the screen employed the magnetic personalities of John Barrymore, Charles Boyer, Katharine Hepburn, Edward G. Robinson, Leslie Howard, James Cagney, and Fredric March, as well as many vivid character actors.

THE PLAYWRIGHT'S THEATER

Until 1915, there was no theater so receptive to the new playwright as Antoine's and Brahm's had been. Then came two. Both were amateur, both were small, and both were started by the kind of authors, painters, and actors who would have lived on the Left Bank in Paris if they had not been living in the Greenwich Village of New York City.

The first, by about six months, was the Washington Square Players. Though it presented new plays by Zoë Akins and a few minor writers, the bulk of its bills were from established Europeans. A war casualty of 1917, it was resurrected two years later as the Theatre Guild. Again the emphasis was almost entirely on foreign playwrights until, in its fourth season, it found Arthur Richman's *Ambush,* in its fifth, Elmer Rice's *The Adding Machine,* and in its seventh, Sidney Howard's *They Knew What They Wanted* and John Howard Lawson's *Processional.*

The Provincetown Players was much more important to the development of American drama. It called itself the Playwright's Theater, and in its seven years it produced nothing but native plays. It began humbly enough in an artists' colony at the tip of Cape Cod, Massachusetts, during the

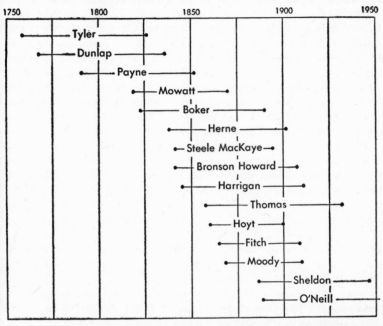

From the first American playwright to O'Neill. *After more than a century of slow development, the advent of William Vaughn Moody with* The Great Divide *in 1906, and Edward Sheldon with* Salvation Nell *in 1908, prepared the American stage for the significant drama that Eugene O'Neill and others were to provide from 1920 onward.*

summer of 1915. Its theater was still humble when the Provincetown Players moved to a stable in Greenwich Village. All of its new plays were not of lasting importance, though they included work by the novelists Theodore Dreiser and Susan Glaspell, and the poetess Edna St. Vincent Millay. The Provincetown's chief distinction was that it produced the first plays of Eugene O'Neill. If *Beyond the Horizon* and *Anna Christie* had not found Broadway sponsors, the Provincetown would have been ready to produce them. The spirit of the workers and the audience at the Provincetown gave O'Neill the stimulation and the confidence that he needed when he was beginning to write. Without the Playwright's Theater, his genius might never have found itself.

UNIVERSITY PLAYWRIGHTS

Even earlier than 1915, another force was beginning to create American playwrights, but the results were to be seen mainly in the '20's. This force was Professor George Pierce Baker. First at Radcliffe College and then at Harvard in 1906, Baker began to teach playwriting. He was not only an inspiring teacher, but among his early students he was lucky enough to have Edward Sheldon, whose *Salvation Nell* was successfully produced while he was still a student. Such publicity, plus Baker's own talents, brought to his classes unproduced playwrights like O'Neill, S. N. Behrman, Sidney Howard, Philip Barry, George Abbott, and Robert Sherwood. After studying with Baker, Frederick Koch began to cultivate the writing of folk-drama in North Dakota and North Carolina; out of Koch's classes came another playwright, Paul Green.

The fame of Baker's work at Harvard caused other universities to develop theater studies much more extensive than Harvard permitted. Beginning with the Carnegie Institute of Technology in 1914 under Thomas Wood Stevens, more than 300 curriculums had developed by 1958, as well as some sixty or seventy courses in playwriting. The results have not been so startling as Baker's, but Arthur Miller of *Death of a Salesman,* Tennessee Williams of *A Streetcar Named Desire,* and William Inge of *Come Back, Little Sheba* studied playwriting or took part in workshop productions.

THE NEW DRAMA OF THE 1920'S

The effect of the Provincetown Players, the Washington Square Players-cum-Theatre Guild, and Professor Baker began to be felt sharply in the 1920's. Following O'Neill's *Beyond the Horizon* and *The Emperor Jones* of 1920 and 1921, there came a flood of new writers. Owen Davis turned from popular melodramas like *Nellie the Beautiful Cloak Model* to write the serious and mature plays *The Detour* and *Icebound.* During the '20's came more good drama of a realistic kind: Gilbert Emery's *The Hero;* Arthur Richman's *Ambush; Dulcy,* the first of George S. Kaufman's collaborations; George Kelly's *The Torchbearers* and *Craig's Wife;* Sidney Howard's *They Knew What They Wanted* and *The Silver Cord;* Philip Barry's *Holiday* and *Paris Bound;* Maxwell Anderson's and Laurence Stallings' *What Price Glory?,* Anderson's *Saturday's Children;* Lillian Hellman's *The Children's Hour;* Robert Sherwood's *Waterloo Bridge* and *The Road to Rome;* S. N. Behrman's *The Second Man;* John van Druten's *Young Woodley;* and Dorothy and Du Bose Heyward's *Porgy.*

To the later plays of importance by these writers—and to non-realistic dramas like O'Neill's many experiments, Anderson's poetic *Elizabeth the Queen* and *Winterset,* Marc Connelly's *The Green Pastures,* Howard's *Yellow Jack,* Rice's *The Adding Machine,* Clifford Odets' *Waiting for Lefty,* and Thornton Wilder's *Our Town* and *The Skin of Our Teeth,* as well as most of Miller's and Williams' plays—must be added Sidney Kingsley's *Men in White,* John Patrick's *The Hasty Heart,* Emmet Lavery's *The Magnificent Yankee,* Steinbeck's *Of Mice and Men,* and William Saroyan's *The Time of Your Life.*

REALISM IN SPAIN AND HUNGARY

As we have seen, sound realism came to France and Germany in the last decade of the nineteenth century. It won its place in England and Ireland around 1910, and in America only after 1920. On the Continent, twentieth-century drama ran different courses in various countries.

Spain clung to realism from the early days of Echegaray till the destruction of the Loyalist republic—and the playwright García Lorca—in 1936. It was a realism touched at times with fantasy and lyricism. Jacinto Benavente ranged from his peasant tragedy *The Passion Flower* to his cynical comedy *The Bonds of Interest* with its use of *commedia dell'arte* characters. The Quintero brothers usually wrote lightly in the spirit of their one-act comedy *A Sunny Morning*, yet they touched a deeper note in the drama *Malvaloca*. In Gregorio Martinez Sierra's two plays *The Kingdom of God* and *Cradle Song*, he presented the life of a convent with delicate sympathy and deep feeling. In the few short years that the poet Federico García Lorca could give to the theater before he was shot by one of Franco's firing squads, he wrote with great and poetic power in *Blood Wedding* and *The House of Bernarda Alba*, and with humor and fantastic imagination in lesser plays.

Hungary's playwrights, some of them remarkably successful in America, were varied in interests and styles. Alexander Brody handled social problems somewhat in the spirit of Brieux. Melchior Lengyel and Ernö Vajda were shallower, perhaps, but theatrically effective, as Broadway found in Lengyel's *Typhoon* and Vajda's *Fata Morgana*. Sigmund Moritz wrote mainly of small-town life, while Ferenc Molnár clung to the sophistication of his beloved Budapest. The most popular and brilliant of the Hungarians, Molnár ranged from the intricate comedy of *The Guardsman* and *The Play's the Thing* and the subtle drama of *The Swan* to the fantastic symbolism of *The Red Mill*. In between lay the fantasy of *The Phantom Rival* and the mingling of reality and other-worldliness in the deeply touching play *Liliom*.

Spain's modern playwrights. *Echegaray was rather a slow starter. He wrote his first plays in his forties. Within twenty years, Benavente was close upon the much older man.*

IN FRANCE AND ITALY: POETIC DRAMA

In the early years of this century, poetic drama, romantic tragedy, and the subtle play of symbolic moods absorbed three outstanding playwrights: Edmond Rostand, Maurice Maeterlinck, and Gabriele d'Annunzio. Rostand's vastly popular *Cyrano de Bergerac,* Maeterlinck's fantasy *The Blue Bird* and his tenuous *Pelléas et Mélisande,* and d'Annunzio's *Francesca da Rimini* and *The Daughter of Jorio* are a few of the many plays that these poets wrote in rebellion against the rising power of the theater typified by Antoine.

Italy produced no realists of any merit after Guiseppe Giacosa with his *Falling Leaves* of 1900. France could point to little more than a few plays like Edouard Bourdet's *The Captive,* Sacha Guitry's *Pasteur* and Charles Vildrac's *S. S. Tenacity.* Realism faded out in Germany before the onslaught of expressionism toward the end of World War I. France found in Lenormand and Cocteau men to follow the German fashion, and in Giraudoux, Anouilh, and Sartre nonrealistic playwrights of a subtler and a more powerful kind.

The plays of Rostand, Maeterlinck, and d'Annunzio cried for a type of scenery and lighting that was to serve the expressionists and men like Sartre. It was also to serve, ironically enough, the Englishmen and Americans who still wrote in the realistic vein.

eight

The THEATRE

Of TODAY

And TOMORROW

THE NINETEENTH CENTURY GAVE TO THE STAGE THE REALISTIC PLAY AND its fourth wall. The twentieth century provided settings and lights that were far more beautiful and expressive than anything the theater had known before. The new stagecraft—as this movement came to be called—made over the production methods of the theater of the civilized world. Also, it enabled plays to be written in new ways. It made the realistic drama more illusive, but it also helped the writer to develop a very different technique.

ATTACKS ON PERSPECTIVE AND FOOTLIGHTS

Before 1905 in Europe and 1915 in America, the stage still made exteriors out of wings, borders, and painted drops; they were an unillusive sham compared with the solid and convincing box-sets that might be seen in the same production. The glare of footlights and border lights spoiled both kinds of settings. Zola, Antoine, and Strindberg criticized the production methods of their day, but to little avail. Between 1895 and 1905 the writings and the sketches of two men—the Swiss Adolphe Appia and the Englishman Edward Gordon Craig—and six English productions by Craig set the basis for a complete revolution in the designing and lighting of scenery. The first battles of the revolution were won in Berlin by the Austrian-born director Max Reinhardt.

ADOLPHE APPIA—PROPHET OF THE NEW STAGECRAFT

Critics had pointed out that the nineteenth-century type of scenery had been invented, some two hundred years earlier, for the production of opera. And it was for opera that Appia theorized and designed when he published *The Staging of Wagnerian Drama* in 1895 and *Music and Stage Production* four years later. Craig's first production, made in London in 1900, was also for an opera, Purcell's *Dido and Aeneas,* but his first book, *The Art of the Theatre,* published in 1905, and those that followed showed by their titles as well as their text and illustrations that his concern was with the drama. Appia too, turned away from opera and designed scenery for the works of Shakespeare, Goethe, Ibsen, and other playwrights.

Appia did not approach production as a painter. Indeed, in his first book there were no illustrations. Though he later drew and published brilliant designs, his value lay in the *theory* he put forth. His basic aim was to "strengthen the dramatic action." This was to be done not only through a three-dimensional setting with various levels for the actor to work upon, but quite as much through the lighting. Appia asked for "living light." He wanted the lighting on the stage to change with the passage of time; or to change in a way that threw the action of the play into sharper relief. "The mise-en-scène," he wrote, "is a picture composed in time."

In his writings Appia analyzed scene after scene from Wagner's music-dramas, and showed how the effect of the setting, the moving actor, and the changing lights would follow and heighten the course of the action. For instance, in dealing with the third act of Wagner's *Die Walküre* Appia did not provide merely one design, as most scenic artists do; he made seven drawings that traced the changing lights and the positions of the singers through the whole scene.

GORDON CRAIG'S CONTRIBUTION

By training, Craig was more a man of the theater than Appia. He practiced the art of acting before he practiced the art of design. If talents are inheritable, he drew the player's skill from his mother, Ellen Terry, and the designer's from his father, Edward Godwin, who was a painter and an architect, and did some scenery for the theater. Craig left the stage to think about the scenic problems of production. He returned in 1900 to mount *Dido and Aeneas,* and in the next few years he made almost a dozen productions. They caused no such stir, however, as his vividly written and richly illustrated book, *The Art of the Theatre,* and other volumes that followed.

Craig never exalted the artist above the theater. To him the stage was not a place that offered its backdrop as the hugest canvas any painter ever had. "The theater," he wrote, "should not be a place in which to exhibit scenery . . . it should be a place in which the entire beauty of life can be unfolded . . . the inner beauty and the meaning of life." If that is vague and even mystical, much of his theory and practice was intensely practical— as well as stimulating. Though most of his published designs were bigger than any proscenium arch could hold, they always had simplicity as well as grandeur. He knew the power of suggestion. He recognized, as Appia had done, that the stage must be three-dimensional. He forswore perspective unless at a great distance. He put into his designs no place "which could *not* be traveled into actually by the actors," unless so far away that no one could see figures, and "our imagination alone could people it."

TOWARD A NEW THEATER

Craig recognized that the theater is a synthesis of many arts and many skills. It is not merely the play or acting, scenery, lights, music, movement, or dance. The theater, he felt, was all or many of these things. From this thought, he moved on to the ideal conception that one man and one man alone must create all these things. Though this led him to ideas not so sound, we must recognize the immense effect which the man's brilliant writings and even more brilliant designs had on the new generation. We must turn to the passages in which he analyzed plays—*Macbeth,* for example—and drew forth, as Appia had done, the basis for imaginative and inspiring treatments.

Let us summarize the chief elements of the new stagecraft as established by Appia and Craig, and see what changes they led to in the physical side of production.

First comes simplification of means and effect: *A simple setting emphasizes the actor and therefore the play*. The complement to simplification is sugges-tion: *A single Gothic pillar can create in the imagination of the audience the physical reality and the spiritual force of the church that looms above Marguerite in* Faust. Finally, there is synthesis: *The production must be a clean and clear fusion of settings, costumes, movement, and perhaps music, so that the acting may present the play in its fullest effect.*

NEW EQUIPMENT FOR THE NEW STAGECRAFT

Giving up wings and drops in favor of three-dimensional structures meant that, whether the play was realistic or not, the settings were heavier than before. Quick changes of scene required new mechanisms in place of wings, grooves, chariots, or stage braces, and devices to supplement or supersede the lines and pulleys of flies and gridiron. There were three possibilities, and the burgeoning theater of Germany tried them all before the First World War. One was the revolving stage that Lautenschläger brought to Munich from Japan in 1896. Wheeled wagons carrying a whole set or a part of a set were invented by an American, Steele MacKaye, but were first employed effectively by Fritz Brand of Berlin about 1900. A third device was the elevator stage, which MacKaye had used in 1880. Between 1904 and 1913, the two court theaters in Dresden combined wagons and elevators.

MAX REINHARDT, THE PERFECT REVOLUTIONARY

If Steele MacKaye had lived in the time of Craig, the American playwright, director, manager, actor, designer, and inventor might have come close to Craig's ideal master of the theater. Instead we have Max Reinhardt. This revolutionary not only freed the world-theater from nineteenth-century thraldom, and made it over in the image—and, indeed, beyond the image—of Appia, but he also met the challenge of Craig as far as it could be met. He combined the widest possible range of theater talents.

For nine years Reinhardt was an actor in Brahm's company at the Deutsches Theater. Toward the end, he had permission to make experimental productions of his own at the Kleines Theater, and there he produced Strindberg's *There Are Crimes and Crimes*, Oscar Wilde's *Salome*, Wedekind's *Erdgeist*, and Gorky's *The Lower Depths*. On New Year's Day, 1903, he left Brahm, and within two months he opened the Neues Theater. There, early in 1905, Reinhardt made his first great directorial success with *A Midsummer Night's Dream*. It is not important that he placed his scenery on a revolving stage, and chased his fairies and yokels through a moving and changing wood. In this production, and in every one that was not of necessity realistic, he threw out the dry conventions of the theatrical past, and he used one of a number of vivid and imaginative styles entirely fresh to the stage. Reinhardt's success was so electric that in 1905 L'Arronge selected him to direct the Deutsches Theater, which his old master Brahm had once managed.

REINHARDT'S WIDE-RANGING CAREER

Next to the Deutsches Theater, Reinhardt built a luxurious and intimate little theater called the Kammerspiele. There he made yet another new and very different success with Wedekind's *The Awakening of Spring*. From the opening of the Kammerspiele in 1906 until Reinhardt settled in America in 1938, his career was a fantastic one. It included directing in Munich, Vienna, Salzburg, Paris, Venice, Stockholm, New York, Hollywood, and London. From the intimacy of the Kammerspiele, he plunged into a mass production of Sophocles' *Oedipus Rex* in the huge Circus Schumann; then he converted the building into the Grosses Schauspielhaus, with a sky-dome, a revolver, a deep forestage, and room for 3500 spectators. He produced the pantomime *The Miracle* on a similar scale in London, Vienna, Berlin, and New York. In Salzburg, Austria, as the heart of the summer festival, he staged *Everyman* in front of the cathedral, Calderón's *The Great World Theater* inside another church, and *Faust* in the old Imperial Riding School. He gave *The Merchant of Venice* across a canal in Venice, and *A Midsummer Night's Dream* out of

Craig's *Macbeth. Craig's drawings are as impossible to render completely in line sketches as are Appia's. The sleepwalking scene from* Macbeth *conveys, however, the grandeur of his conceptions and the effectiveness with which he organized forms, levels, and details to aid the dramatist. As Lady Macbeth moves down the steps towards the audience she passes a sculptured row of kings who have pursued their ambitions and gone down to death.* (Drawing by Gerda Becker With, after Craig, *Towards a New Theatre.*)

From Danchenko's Musical Studio. *Through the designer J. V. Rabinovitch, Danchenko provided a graceful kind of constructivism for Aristophanes'* Lysistrata. *The central part of the setting revolved into different positions during the action.* (Sketch by Fouquet from *Theatre Arts Monthly*, 1927.)

Continental post-war designs. *A design by Tobias Schiess for a projected Swiss production of Molière's* Tartuffe. *Conditions since the war have compelled most artists in Germany to use the simplest of construction and materials.* (*From* Das Kunstwerk, *1953.*)

doors at Berkeley, California, and in the Hollywood Bowl. Opera came under his hand: Strauss's *Der Rosenkavalier* in Dresden; Mozart in the Redouten-saal, the reconstructed ballroom of Maria Theresa's Viennese palace. He managed two more playhouses, the restored Theater in der Josefstadt in Vienna, and a new house, the Komödie, in Berlin, both for light comedy in the main. Meantime he toured his companies to Russia, Sweden, Switzerland, and America. Reinhardt built up an international repertory, a repertory that spread through all the German and Austrian theaters of his time. It was as varied as his styles of production, for it included, besides the dozen play-wrights we have mentioned, Schiller, Shaw, Gozzi, Goldoni, Grillparzer, O'Neill, Büchner, Werfel, Kleist, Hasenclever, and Euripides. What he did to reanimate Shakespeare on the German stage is remarkable. Between 1905 and 1930, Reinhardt personally directed 136 plays for a total of 8393 per-formances. Of this total, 2531, or almost a third, were of plays by Shake-speare.

EXPRESSIONISM IN GERMANY

A new kind of play and a new kind of production followed or, in some cases, grew up side by side with Brahm and Reinhardt in Germany, the Moscow Art Theater in Russia, Antoine and the Théâtre-libre in France, and Grein and Barker in England. On the whole, the plays and the produc-tions of Europe after the First World War veered away from the realistic concept. They followed paths that led to a greater and freer expressiveness, yet sometimes ended in a blind alley of chaotic and ineffective theatricalism.

Expressionism came to the fore in the years of 1917 and 1918 when a disillusioned Germany realized that it was losing the war. Expressionism continued to feed, until about 1925, on the spiritual chaos of a broken na-tion. Yet the roots of expressionism lie farther back; there are strong hints of it in some of Wedekind's plays, and it is obvious in the later plays of Strindberg. Expressionism made its first important entry on the stage in 1916 with a private performance of *Der Sohn* (*The Son*), which Walter Hasenclever had written in 1912, but which was banned from public per-formance until 1918. Reinhardt, not too sympathetic to expressionism, pro-duced one example privately, Reinhard Sorge's *Der Bettler* (*The Beggar*) in 1917.

EXPRESSIONISM IN PLAY AND PRODUCTION

In its materials, the expressionist play was a curious mixture of the ab-stract and the concrete. It tried to present subjective values, to see beyond and above reality to emotional truth. Yet it was also a drama of immediate revolt that often attacked war, the business world, or parental authority. Its construction was apt to be episodic, while the dialog ranged from the lyric to the telegraphic. Its characters were usually types instead of rounded human beings.

In production, expressionism went in for symbols rather than scenery. A Gothic arch made a cathedral. A snow-covered tree symbolized death. Stage design was flat, angular, distorted. Signs or numbers were projected on a setting to express a subjective idea. The stage became a phantasmagoria of startling and often incomprehensible effects.

Besides Sorge and Hasenclever, the most important writers in the new dramatic medium were: Georg Kaiser, with *From Morn to Midnight* and *Gas;* Ernst Toller, with *Masse-Mensch* (*Man and the Masses*), *Die Wandlung,* and *Die Machinenstürmer* (*The Machine Wreckers*); and Fritz von Unruh, with *Ein Geschlecht* (*A Clan*). Two Czech writers of the '20's provided plays that were partly expressionist and partly more conventional. Karel Čapek, writing sometimes with his brother Josef, is remembered for his fantastic drama *R.U.R.* and his allegory *The Insect Comedy,* known in America as *The World We Live In.* Franz Werfel ranged from complete expressionism in *Spiegelmensch* (*The Mirror Man*) through his symbolic play *Bocksgesang* (*The Goat Song*) to his realistic drama of Mexican history *Juarez and Maximilian.* The German Bertolt Brecht, whose writing has lyric vitality, began in 1923 with his rather realistic *Trommeln in der Nacht* (*Drums in the Night*), and continued into the '30's, with *Die Dreigroschenoper,* adapted from *The Beggar's Opera,* and polemic pieces reminiscent of expressionism like the group of one-act plays called *The Private Life of the Master Race,* and his best drama *Mother Courage.* Brecht himself called his work "epic drama," stressing the narrative nature of it. Though much of German expressionism now seems an ineffective gesture rather than an artistic accomplishment, some plays and productions left powerful impressions behind them.

NEW RUSSIAN DIRECTORS AND DESIGNERS

It took no revolution to make the Russian theater more radical in production methods than any other in Europe. For a time the Soviet encouraged the wildest of experiments, then condemned them as "formalistic." In the 1920's the communist government encouraged—perhaps we should say, forced—playwrights to write propaganda plays.

Fine artists came into the Russian theater earlier than elsewhere, painters of the quality of Golovin, Roerich, Anisfeld, Benois, and Bakst. Most of them worked in opera—some before 1900—and for the ballet, painting brilliantly on huge backdrops and great wings. Very different kinds of artists, however, gave the Russian theater its particular flavor. There was the cubist Alexandra Exter, for example, employed by Alexander Taïrov in the intimate but very radical Kamerny Theater that he opened in 1914. In his *Salome,* on the brink of the Revolution, you could see a stage floor broken up into a maze of slanting levels, and actors in stiffly formalized costumes like nothing in the history of man's clothing. Add cubist settings that anticipated German expressionism, and you were in a world of angular and splintered shapes and movements.

The Moscow Art Theater provided two of the most startling directors in Vsevolod Meyerhold and Eugene Vakhtangov. As early as 1905, Stanislavsky and Danchenko began to set up "studios" in which experiments could be carried on in methods far removed from the realism of their theater. Both Vakhtangov and Meyerhold worked in such studios. Michael Chekhov, nephew of the playwright, succeeded Vakhtangov when he died, but left in 1927 to teach acting in America. Danchenko, as we have said, opened the Musical Studio about 1920.

Vakhtangov proved a director with both original ideas and a capacity for solid accomplishment. His *Macbeth* and *The Dybbuk*, which he directed for the Jewish group called the Habima, as well as *Turandot*, which he did not live to see, all showed his devoted attempts to find new concepts of production, often grotesque, that fitted the plays he produced.

MEYERHOLD AND "THE THEATER THEATRICAL"

Meyerhold, the dominant director outside the Moscow Art Theater, began as one of its actors. He ended as a tragic sacrifice to communist policy toward the stage. His basic ideas were far removed from anything remotely approaching realism. Even more than Taïrov, Meyerhold stood for "the theater theatrical." He would have no "fourth wall." He wanted the audience to be eternally conscious that they were in a theater. To that end, he abolished the curtain, left auditorium lights blazing, let the playgoers see the naked brick walls of the stage. He dressed his actors in overalls, and trained them to run and leap over skeleton settings of wood, glass, and metal. In such a fashion—it was usually called constructivist because of his sets— Meyerhold produced plays like Belgium-born Fernand Crommelynck's *The Magnificent Cuckold*, and in another radical style, Gogol's *The Inspector General*. For a time, Meyerhold rode the wave of success. In 1937 the government began the building of a special kind of theater for him, a theater without a proscenium and with various new ways of relating audience to actors. Before it could be completed, Meyerhold fell under disfavor for what was called his "formalism"—a familiar charge during the time of the purges. He denied this publicly in a speech, and called the state of the Russian theater "pitiful and terrifying." Meyerhold was arrested the next day, and was never heard from again.

There is one more director to consider, Nikolai Okhlopkov. Younger than the rest and innocent of any contacts with the Moscow Art Theater, he distinguished himself by creating the first professional "theater in the round," really a flexible playhouse. From 1932 to 1938—its success was not too great—he staged Gorky's *Mother* and other plays with the actors in unexpected and intimate relations with their audiences. "On my stage," he said, "when the mother cries, a dozen people in the audience must want to leap up and wipe away her tears." Independently of the Russian, the theater in the round and a more flexible form developed in America after 1940.

THE FATE OF THE RUSSIAN PLAYWRIGHTS

Between the abortive rebellion of 1905 and the revolution of 1917, the baffled intelligentsia of Russia produced playwrights who were more extreme in expression than those of other European countries. Their work was far from satisfying or lasting. Michael Artsybashev dwelt hopelessly on sexual tragedy. Alexander Blok was extravagantly symbolic. Leonid Andreyev began with realism in *To the Stars* and satire in *The Sabine Women,* and went over to allegory in *The Life of Man* and *King Hunger.* The one play from this period that has interested the audiences of other nations was his dramatic but perplexing tragedy *He Who Gets Slapped.* Nikolai Evreinov, director as well as playwright, dedicated himself to an eccentric vision of the theater. In his short "monodrama" of 1906, *The Theater of the Soul,* he divided his hero into three characters M1, M2, and M3, and presented his heroine as the different kind of woman each would see. After the materialistic revolution, he wrote in *The Chief Thing* a play that exalted the life of illusion.

The effect of the revolution on production and playwrights was profound. At first the government encouraged the theatrical "formalism" of Taïrov and Meyerhold largely because the regime of the Czar had been against it. Then communism turned thumbs down. The state, which looked on the theater as a weapon in its fight against capitalism, increased enormously the number of playhouses. In Moscow alone they grew from sixteen in 1914 to sixty in 1934. The new audiences may not have supported the aesthetically radical productions, but they thronged to the older plays that censorship had banned, and to a wide range of drama from the rest of Europe and from America. They certainly delighted in the "socialist realism" of propaganda plays about the struggles and triumphs of revolutionaries and partisans, whether out of past history or from their own times. The Moscow Art Theater was preserved as an "academic" institution, a kind of museum of the best of the past. In time it began to produce some of the better propaganda plays. Among them should be mentioned *Days of the Turbins* and *Armored Train 14-69. Roar China!* and *Counterattack* were produced in New York, the first by the Theatre Guild.

JEWISH THEATERS IN RUSSIA

Facing the problem of the many racial elements of Russia, the Soviet encouraged two notable Jewish groups in Moscow. The first and the greatest was the Habima (a word meaning "stage") founded in 1917 by the brilliant Nahum Zemach with the help of the Moscow Art Theater. The Habima's outstanding production was Salomon Ansky's peasant play of demoniac possession *The Dybbuk*. Magnificently directed by Vakhtangov, it was the chief play in a repertory seen in New York in 1926-27. The Habima's permanent home is now in Tel Aviv. The State Jewish Theater, playing in Yiddish instead of the Hebrew of the Habima, had a fine director in Alexander Granovsky, and produced in cleverly distorted settings a series of plays including Shakespeare's as well as works by Jewish writers like Sholem Aleichem and Isaac Peretz.

ROSTAND, MAETERLINCK, AND LUGNÉ-POË

Antoine and his realists were not the only significant figures on the Paris stage of the '90's. There was a romantic who turned to symbolism, and a symbolist who became romantic. These were Edmond Rostand and Maurice Maeterlinck. Each wrote a play of world-wide popularity.

Rostand had no ability new to the theater except the ability to write poetic drama that could be popular when the stage of Europe lay under the growing shadow of Ibsen. Rostand's first play, a short one called *Les Romanesques* (*The Romancers*), was an immediate success when the Comédie-Française produced it in 1894. Three years later came his *Cyrano de Bergerac*. The great actor Coquelin triumphed in this swashbuckling romance with a pleasantly tragic ending, and it was played by many other stars, including America's Richard Mansfield and Walter Hampden. After the sentimental *L'Aiglon*, which neither Sarah Bernhardt nor Maude Adams could save from failure, Rostand's lyric vigor returned in *Chantecler*, a play that made the birds of the barnyard symbols of man. He gave us both irony and tenderness in the play that he wrote just before he died at forty-nine, *The Last Night of Don Juan*.

Antoine, who tried vainly to make the Théâtre-libre a theater of poetry as well as realism, might have mounted *Les Romanesques* if Rostand's play had been offered to him. Antoine had no taste for Maeterlinck, however, and neither had the managers of the state and the commercial theaters. So the Belgian poet who wrote in rhythmed prose had to turn to another rebel theater. This was the Théâtre d'Art, founded in 1890 by the seventeen-year-old symbolist poet Paul Fort as an opening for plays by men called "symbolists" or "imagists." Here Maeterlinck's short plays *The Intruder* and *The Blind* were produced. Fort retired shortly to write poetry, and his collaborator, Lugné-Poë—who had worked under Antoine—turned the venture into the more celebrated Théâtre de l'Oeuvre, which he managed until 1929. He began with Maeterlinck's *Pelléas et Mélisande*, but he followed the eclectic pattern that Antoine had hoped to achieve. Among the plays he produced were Ibsen's *Rosmersholm* and *The Master Builder*, and Tolstoy's *The Living Corpse*, as well as Hauptmann's *Hannele* and his symbolic drama *The Sunken Bell*, Wilde's *Salome*, a number of d'Annunzio's dramas, Crommelynck's *The Magnificent Cuckold*, *Shakuntala*, and *The Little Clay Cart*, *Peer Gynt*, and many poetic plays that are now forgotten. He staged Maeterlinck's romantic drama *Monna Vanna* in 1902, but he had to wait for the Moscow Art Theater to give the first performance of the playwright's symbolic fairy tale *The Blue Bird* in 1908. Lugné-Poë enjoyed the distinction of staging Paul Claudel's religious drama *L'Announce faite à Marie* (*The Tidings Brought to Mary*), and thus launching on his theatrical career the man who in the '50's was the leading poetic playwright of France.

The neo-romanticists. *In the face of the realism of Ibsen and a score of other acclaimed playwrights, the men of this chart wrote almost nothing but poetic or imaginative drama. The first to attract attention was Maeterlinck with* Pelléas et Mélisande *in 1892. Rostand began with* Les Romanesques *in 1894.*

COPEAU, REMAKER OF THE PARIS STAGE

The greatest force in the French theater of the twentieth century was Jacques Copeau. His remarkable playhouse, the Théâtre du Vieux-Colombier, was the first to throw out the "fourth wall." His repertory was a fine mingling of the realistic and the poetic, of the classic and the modern drama. And from his company came three of France's leading directors and actors.

In 1913 Copeau turned from a brilliant career as a critic to create his Théâtre du Vieux-Colombier. During the First World War New York's wealthy patron of the stage Otto Kahn enabled Copeau to remake the Garrick Theater to suit his purposes. In 1922, Copeau was able to reopen the Vieux-Colombier in Paris, and add some refinements to his stage. Whether in Paris or New York, Copeau and his company were dedicated to producing a wide range of drama with the greatest fidelity, simplicity, and clarity, and also to developing an ensemble of acting that departed from strict realism without indulging in theatrical display. Their artistic success was notable.

The theater that Copeau made over from a small hall had no obvious division between audience and actors, except that he did use a draw curtain during changes of setting or properties. Stage and auditorium were an organic whole, the walls of one merging with those of the other. There were no footlights between the spectators and a low forestage that led by three steps, at the sides and in the center, to the main platform. On and above this platform was a permanent structure that included an arch at the back and a stair at one side that led up to the arch and over it. On this stage of many levels Copeau placed screens or suggestions of realistic props and backings, and in the arch he set doors or windows. The lighting came from above and the sides; some sources were openly but gracefully displayed in the auditorium. The Vieux-Colombier was the first of many later attempts to break away from the theater of illusion dominated by the proscenium arch. It presented frankly to its audience the first "formal" stage.

NEW DIRECTORS, NEW PLAYHOUSES

When Copeau closed his theater he took with him to the countryside—as he had done before 1913—a group of young actors to study and practice their art. Under one of their number, Michel Saint-Denis, they later became the distinguished Compagnie des Quinze, which he took on tour before he began to work in England. In the early '20's two of Copeau's finest players, Louis Jouvet and Charles Dullin, left the Vieux-Colombier to act and direct with distinction elsewhere. Besides these men and Lugné-Poë, there were others who succeeded in bringing out new French playwrights: Jean-Louis Barrault, a brilliant actor and the producer of Claudel's *Le Livre de Christophe Colomb;* and Jean Vilar, who made a notable success of the management of the new Théâtre National Populaire.

Among the new playwrights whose plays these directors produced were: Jean Giraudoux, with *Siegfried, Amphitryon 38, The Mad Woman of Chaillot,* and *Ondine;* Romain Rolland, with his *The Game of Love and Death;* Jules Romains, with his satiric *Dr. Knock* and his *Donogoo* employing film effects; Jean Cocteau, with his *bizarreries* such as *Les Mariés de la Tour Eiffel, The Infernal Machine,* and *Orphée;* expressionistic Henri-René Lenormand, with *The Failures, Time Is a Dream,* and *Man and His Phantoms;* Jean-Paul Sartre, with *No Exit, The Flies,* and *The Respectful Prostitute;* and Jean Anouilh, with *The Waltz of the Toreadors, Time Remembered,* and *Ring Around the Moon.*

The total effect of the directors who came out of the theaters of Antoine and Copeau and of those who had their beginnings elsewhere was the making over of the Paris theater. Even the hide-bound Comédie-Française capitulated to the new playwrights; in 1936, it invited Copeau, Jouvet, Dullin, and Baty to direct plays, and in 1941 Copeau became its administrator. Beginning in 1945, the French government organized four "centers" for the production and touring of plays in the provinces, while it maintained in Paris the Opéra, the Opéra-Comique, the Comédie-Française, and the Odéon, and added the Théâtre National Populaire.

ITALY ESCAPES FROM REALISM

Italy, like France, began the century with poetic drama. D'Annunzio's infatuation for the greatest of modern actresses, Eleonora Duse, may have increased his interest in the theater, but it did not lift his poetic dramas much above the easy ideal of theatrical effectiveness. Duse played in *The Dead City* for many years, and also in *La Gioconda,* which he wrote to exalt her beautiful hands. His best drama, however, *The Daughter of Jorio,* was played by another actress, Emma Gramatica.

The theater, even more than painting or the novel, is apt to lag behind life. In Italy we may have an exception. The end of World War I, in which she lost a half million men, left her in disillusioned chaos, a ready prey to the violence and corruption of Fascism. At such a time, writers might ques-

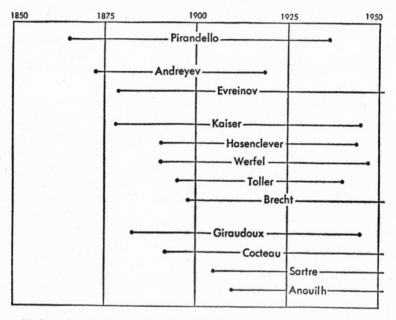

Modern playwrights against realism. *The plays of these men are more "intellectual" than the work of neo-romantic writers such as Maeterlinck and Rostand. All labored for a theater that abjured realism.*

tion the value of existence. Italy's outstanding dramatist, Pirandello, went further. He questioned its reality, and most playwrights followed him. The results were plays in which the values of life, as we have conceived them, are completely reversed. Nothing is objective; all is relative. Experience is useless. The sense of individual existence disappears, and psychic bewilderment and frustration take its place. To parody W. S. Gilbert, "Things are seldom what they seem; cream masquerades as skimmed milk," and usually it's sour.

Before the war, Pirandello wrote in *Sicilian Limes* a straight-forward drama of unhappy reality. After the war, came *Six Characters in Search of an Author,* in which the inability of people to communicate with one another is complicated by a pretense that they are creatures in a play; *Right You*

Are If You Think You Are, in which the psychic identities of a man's two wives and a mother-in-law are perversely confused; and *Henry IV,* which deals with the relativity of madness. At best, Pirandello anticipates in a minor way the French existentialists with faith in deeds as the only reality.

In *Madmen on the Mountain,* Alessandro de Stefani shows that only madmen are sane. Luigi Antonelli's *What You Don't Expect* shows a man mistaking a motion picture for reality and reality for a motion picture. The title of his *The Man Who Met Himself* is key enough to the play, and so is the title of Rosso di San Secondo's *What Passion, Ye Marionettes!* In Alberto Casella's *Death Takes a Holiday,* in which the Grim Reaper takes human shape, and no one dies while he is on earth, the heroine falls in love with him, knowing psychically who he is, and Death falls in love with life. In *The Mask and the Face* and other plays Luigi Chiarelli followed the pattern of disillusionment with reality, but treated the matter with comic cynicism.

FROM BELGIUM, SPAIN, AND ENGLAND

Besides Maeterlinck and Crommelynck, Belgium supplied a minor figure in Émile Verhaeren with his *Les Aubes* (*The Dawn*). In Spain, García Lorca tinged his realism with a lyric quality, and he wrote a few plays, such as *The Butterfly's Crime,* which anticipated *The Insect Comedy* of Karel Čapek, some puppet plays, and a surrealist tragedy, *El Publico* (*The Public*).

The poetic dramas that Swinburne, Tennyson, and Matthew Arnold wrote in the nineteenth century were merely "closet dramas," better when read than when produced. The work of Stephen Phillips came nearer true theater. Oscar Wilde's *Salome* reached some success with Reinhardt, but his *The Duchess of Padua* never touched an audience. With the twentieth century came Lord Dunsany's precious plays; of ten effective short ones in rhythmed prose, the best was *A Night at an Inn.* The novelist J. B. Priestley added to his realism a mystical concept of time in his *Time and the Conways* as well as in other plays, and he experimented with expressionism in *Johnson Over Jordan.* The poets W. H. Auden and Christopher Isherwood linked the poetic and the polemic not too successfully in their *The Dog Beneath the Skin* and *The Ascent of F.6.* In 1949, a true and effective poetic drama by an Englishman appeared in Christopher Fry's *The Lady's Not for Burning,* preceded by some trial runs such as *A Phoenix Too Frequent,* and followed by *Venus Observed.* T. S. Eliot began well with *Murder in the Cathedral,* a poetic tragedy on Thomas à Becket, and with *Family Reunion,* but it is hard to see more than literate and sometimes elevated prose in his later plays, *The Cocktail Party* and *The Confidential Clerk.*

POETIC DRAMA IN AMERICA

Poetic plays of the conventional sort came from Percy MacKaye early in the century. *The Canterbury Pilgrims,* of 1903, and *Jeanne d'Arc,* three years later, were produced by E. H. Sothern and Julia Marlowe. His New England fantasy *The Scarecrow* followed a highly original attempt to link past and present in *Sappho and Phaon*. The only American dramatist who has written plays in verse with both power and considerable success is Maxwell Anderson. Between 1930 and 1935, he reached the peak of his career with *Elizabeth the Queen, Mary of Scotland,* and *Winterset.* In the '20's Eugene O'Neill tried rhythmed prose in *The Fountain, Marco Millions,* and *Lazarus Laughed,* but the only memorable passage was the speech of Kubla-Khan over the body of his dead daughter in the second of these plays.

EUGENE O'NEILL—DRAMATIC PIONEER

The escape of the American playwright from the bonds of strict realism has been through a greater freedom in construction and new experiments in production methods, rather than through poetry. O'Neill broke the way in 1920 with *The Emperor Jones,* in which a series of short scenes showed the Negro dictator regressing in a kind of panic delirium through the story of his race. The next year, in *The Hairy Ape,* O'Neill tried the pattern of German expressionism, as did Elmer Rice, a season later, in *The Adding Machine.* During the next ten years O'Neill experimented in a number of ways, besides the expressionistic, as he strove to drive drama up and beyond simple realism. In one of his finest plays, *Desire Under the Elms,* he used a composite setting of the exterior and four rooms of a farmhouse. In *The Great God Brown* and *Days Without End,* he dramatized the dual nature of personalities, using for most characters a mask as well as the normal face in the first, and having two actors play the same character in the second. All the cast wore masks in his symbolic play *Lazarus Laughed.* In *Strange Interlude,* much more constantly than in *The Great God Brown,* he used soliloquies to convey the inner thoughts that his men and women could not otherwise express. For *Mourning Becomes Electra*—like *Strange Interlude,* almost a trilogy in length—he met with remarkable success the severest problem he had ever set himself. Going frankly to Aeschylus for his plot, he combined Clytemnestra's murder of her husband, plus the son's murder of his mother and her lover, with the atmosphere of Civil War days, and with certain Freudian concepts of O'Neill's own time. Some playgoers felt that at the end, when O'Neill added an incestuous impulse of brother toward sister, *Mourning Becomes Electra* went somewhat astray. For others in the theater it replaced *Desire Under the Elms* as the writer's finest play.

During the last ten years of O'Neill's life—when palsy halted his work— the theater somewhat forgot his stature. As a realist he may have been no match for Lillian Hellman, author of the strong play *The Little Foxes.* He had shortcomings as a master of words, which may explain why he experimented with so many devices for breaking the realistic pattern. Nevertheless, he went further than any American dramatist in seeking and realizing deep and bitter psychological truths. O'Neill, more than anyone else, made over the drama of the New World.

OTHER REBELLIONS AGAINST REALISM

After *The Hairy Ape,* expressionism appeared again in John Howard Lawson's *Processional* and Francis Faragoh's *Pinwheel.* A freer form—freer than expressionism as well as realism—appeared in Irving Shaw's anti-war play *Bury the Dead,* and in Thornton Wilder's *The Skin of Our Teeth.* Without benefit of any scenery except black curtains and shifting lights, Clifford Odets presented his short but powerful play *Waiting for Lefty,* and in *Our Town* Wilder told a moving story against the bare walls of the stage, with only the aid of a folksy narrator and suggestive props. Humor and imagination served Marc Connelly well in *The Green Pastures,* his dramatization of Roark Bradford's account of Negro interpretations of the Bible. After the work of O'Neill, the most effective evasions of a cramping realism have been Tennessee Williams' *A Streetcar Named Desire,* and, above all, Arthur Miller's *Death of a Salesman.*

THE UNIVERSITY THEATER

The most original contribution of America to the theater has been the development of dramatic studies and production in the colleges and universities. Since Professor Baker's days at Harvard, the writing of new plays, the performance of new and old ones, and the teaching and practicing of the many arts of production have grown to the point where, in 1955, there were 320 institutions with curriculums in which students could concentrate on the theater arts as a chief study. The instruction staffs were large enough to form the American Educational Theatre Association with 2000 members. The Association's *Educational Theatre Journal* estimated in 1953 that there were over 1800 colleges and universities giving annually 5500 to 6500 plays in some 60,000 performances. A few universities sent their actors on tour.

Beyond building up a new audience of critical playgoers and training theater workers, the universities have done much to fill the void left when the touring system shrank from thousands of road houses to hardly fifty. Most university theaters supply their communities with the only good performances they can regularly see. The lack of professional touring companies has tended to turn the community theaters away from the classics and the finer European and American plays of the past, and to concentrate too much on reproducing Broadway successes. The universities have escaped this danger to some extent, but if the future of the American stage is to be a bright one, these institutions must produce more new plays and far, far more of the finest drama of past and present, of the Old World as well as the New. These are our only endowed theaters, the only playhouses that receive large and dependable public and private funds.

THE FUTURE OF THE AMERICAN THEATER

War halted playwriting in Europe, but it did not cripple the theater perma nently. Even in hard-hit Germany, where there were 250 theaters before the last war, over 175 were operating in West Germany by 1955. Europe suffered less than America from the competition of the silver screen of the film and its little brother in the television set—not to mention the radio. Fire laws prevented most of London's fifty theaters from being leased for motion pictures; tradition saved from such a fate most of the commercial as well as all of the state and municipal theaters of Germany and France. But, at the same time, New York's 85 theaters of the middle '20's shrank to 25 thirty years later, while the touring system suffered even more. The American National Theater and Academy, charted by Congress but without public funds, and the National Theatre Council, supported for a time by foundations, have not succeeded in doing for the American stage what the Arts Council has done for the English. In the burgeoning of the university theaters and, perhaps to a lesser extent, in the community theaters, we may see a hopeful portent. We still have a living theater. It is a theater that has grown while Broadway has declined. Perhaps in this spread of producing institutions across the three and a half million square miles of the United States may lie the roots of a national theater of the future.

Through a hundred centuries, theater has never died. *The* theater—the theater that includes good plays and good performances—comes and goes, expires and is reanimated once more. Like its special god, it may be destroyed and the parts of its body scattered abroad. But, because there is a kind of divinity about the theater, it is always born again. The history of the living stage proves the eternal vitality of the "fabulous invalid."

bibliography

The select list of "Paperbacks" is mainly compiled from R. R. Bowker Company's *Paperbound Books in Print* (Vol. 4, No. 1) which should be consulted for additional titles. A more inclusive bibliography pertinent to the essays in this volume is appended to *The Living Stage*.

I. *GREECE AND ROME.*

1. Hamilton, Edith. *The Greek Way to Western Civilization,* Mentor (M 32), New American Library of World Literature, Inc., New York.
2. Kitto, H. D. F. *Greek Tragedy.* Anchor (A 38), Anchor Books, Doubleday and Inc., New York.
3. Lind, L. R., ed. *Ten Greek Plays in Contemporary Translations* (C 19), Riverside Editions, Houghton Mifflin Company, Boston, Mass.
4. Copley, Frank O., transl. *Terence: The Woman of Andros.* The Library of Liberal Arts (LLA 18), Liberal Arts Press, Inc., New York.
5. Hamilton, Edith. *The Roman Way to Western Civilization.* Mentor (M 213), New American Library of World Literature, Inc., New York.

II. *RENAISSANCE ITALY.*

1. Burckhardt, Jacob. *The Civilization of the Renaissance in Italy.* 2 vols., Harper Torchbooks (40, 41), Harper & Brothers, New York.
2. Burroughs, Betty. *Vasari's Lives of the Artists.* Simon and Schuster, New York.
3. Paolucci, Anne and Henry, trans. *Machiavelli, Niccolà. Mandragola.* The Library of Liberal Arts (LLA 58), Liberal Arts Press, Inc., New York.

164   BIBLIOGRAPHY

4. Sypher, Wylie. *Four Stages of Renaissance Style: Transformations in Art and Literature, 1400-1700.* Anchor (A 45), Anchor Books, Doubleday & Co., Inc., New York.

III. *SPAIN'S GOLDEN AGE.*

1. Bentley, Eric, ed. *The Classic Theater,* Vol. III: *Six Spanish Plays.* Anchor (A 155c), Anchor Books, Doubleday & Co., Inc., New York.

IV. *ELIZABETHAN ENGLAND.*

1. Chute, Marchette. *Shakespeare of London.* Dutton Everyman Paperbacks (D 1), E. P. Dutton & Co., Inc., New York.
2. Dunn, Esther C., ed. *Eight Famous Elizabethan Plays.* Modern Library College Editions (T 13), Modern Library, Inc., New York.
*3. Nagler, A. M. *Shakespeare's Stage.* Yale University Press, New Haven, Conn.
4. Parrot, Thomas Marc and Robert Hamilton Ball. *A Short View of Elizabethan Drama.* Charles Scribner's Sons, New York.
5. Wilson, John Dover. *Life in Shakespeare's England.* Penguin Books, Inc., Baltimore, Maryland.

V. *BAROQUE FRANCE.*

1. Gilbert, Stuart, trans. *Alexis de Tocqueville. The Old Regime and the French Revolution.* Anchor (A 60), Anchor Books, Doubleday & Co., Inc., New York.
2. Lapp, John, trans. & ed. *Corneille. Le Cid.* Crofts Classics. Appleton-Century-Crofts, Inc., New York.
3. Lewis, W. H. *The Splendid Century. Life in the France of Louis XIV.* Anchor (A 122) Anchor Books, Doubleday & Co., Inc., New York.
4. Molière, Jean Baptiste. *Eight Plays.* Modern Library College Editions (T 29), Random House, Inc., New York.
5. Racine, Jean Baptiste. *Andromache.* Barron's Educational Series, Inc., Great Neck, New York.
6. ————. *Phaedra.* Barron's Educational Series, Inc., Great Neck, New York.

VI. *NINETEENTH CENTURY EUROPE AND THE COMING OF REALISM.*
England

1. Chesterton, G. K. *George Bernard Shaw.* Dramabooks (D 3), Hill and Wang, Inc., New York.
2. Pearson, Hesketh. *Oscar Wilde: His Life and Wit.* Grosset's Universal Library, Grosset & Dunlap, New York.
3. Shaw, George Bernard. *Four Plays (Candida; The Devil's Disciple; Caesar and Cleopatra; Captain Brassbound's Conversion).* Dell Publishing Co., Inc., New York.
4. Wilde, Oscar. *Plays.* Penguin Books, Inc., Baltimore, Maryland.

*Not paperbound but low priced.

France

5. Stanton, Stephen S., ed. *Camille and Other Plays*. Dramabooks (MD 6), Hill and Wang, Inc., New York.

Germany

6. Bentley, Eric, ed. *The Classic Theatre, Volume II: Five German Plays*. Anchor (A 155b), Anchor Books, Doubleday & Co., Inc., New York.

Russia

7. Chekhov, Anton. *Four Great Plays*. Bantam Books, Inc., New York.

Scandinavia

8. Le Gallienne, Eva, trans. *Henrik Ibsen. Six Plays: A Doll's House, Ghosts, An Enemy of the People, Rosmersholm, Hedda Gabler, The Master Builder*. Modern Library College Editions (T 24), Modern Library, Inc., New York.
9. Shaw, George Bernard. *The Quintessence of Ibsenism*. Dramabooks (D 9), Hill and Wang, Inc., New York.

Sweden

10. Sprigge, Elizabeth, trans. *August Strindberg, Six Plays*. Anchor (A 54), Anchor Books, Doubleday & Co., New York.

VII. *THE CONTEMPORARY THEATER.*

1. Bentley, Eric. *The Dramatic Event,* Beacon Press, Boston, Mass.
2. ————. *The Playwright as Thinker*. Meridian Books, Inc., New York.
3. Clark, Barrett H. *Eugene O'Neill: The Man and His Plays*. Dover Publications, Inc., New York.
4. Clurman, Harold. *The Fervent Years*. Dramabooks (D 8), Hill and Wang, Inc., New York.
5. Fergusson, Francis. *The Idea of a Theater: The Art of Drama in Changing Perspective*. Anchor (A 4), Anchor Books, Doubleday & Co., Inc., New York.
6. Young, Stark. *Immortal Shadows*. Dramabooks (D 13), Hill and Wang, Inc., New York.
7. ————. *The Theatre*. Dramabooks (D 12), Hill and Wang, Inc., New York.

Plays.

8. Anouilh, Jean. *Five Plays (I)*. Dramabooks (MD 10), Hill and Wang, Inc., New York.
9. ————. *Five Plays (II)*. Dramabooks (MD 13), Hill and Wang, Inc., New York.
10. Betti, Ugo. *Three Plays*. Dutton Everyman Paperbacks, E. P. Dutton & Co., Inc., New York.
11. Brecht, Bertolt. *Parables for the Theater. The Good Woman of Setzuan and The Caucasian Chalk Circle*. Dutton Everyman Paperbacks, E. P. Dutton & Co., Inc., New York.
12. Giraudoux, Jean. *Four Plays*. Dramabooks (MD 12), Hill and Wang, Inc., New York.

13. Hauptmann, Gerhart. *The Weavers, Hannele, The Beaver Coat*. Rinehart & Co., Inc., New York.
14. Lorca, Federico Garcia. *Three Tragedies (The House of Bernada Alba, Blood Wedding, Yerma)*. New Directions, New York.
15. Miller, Arthur. *Death of a Salesman*. Compass Books (C 32), The Viking Press, Inc., New York.
16. O'Neill, Eugene. *The Iceman Cometh*. Modern Library Paperbacks, Random House, Inc., New York.
17. Pirandello, Luigi. *Naked Masks*. Five Plays. Dutton Everyman Paperbacks, E. P. Dutton & Co., Inc., New York.
18. Sartre, Jean-Paul. *No Exit and Three Other Plays*. Vintage Books (K 16), Alfred A. Knopf, Inc., New York.
19. Wilder, Thornton. *Three Plays (Skin of Our Teeth, Our Town, Matchmaker)*, Dell Publishing Co., New York.
20. Williams, Tennessee. *A Streetcar Named Desire*. New American Library of World Literature, Inc., New York.

SPECTRUM PAPERBACKS

A selected list of other SPECTRUM Books . . . quality paperbacks that meet the highest standards of scholarship and integrity.

For complete Spectrum Book Catalogue
write to the publisher.